From the Pulpit to the Palm-Branch

COPYRIGHT.

The above Portrait of Mr. Spurgeon has been produced from *the last Photograph* taken at Menton, January 8, 1892. (*See page* 32.)

From the Pulpit
to the
Palm-Branch

A Memorial of

Charles H. Spurgeon

Sequel to the Sketch of His Life, Entitled

From the Usher's Desk to the Tabernacle Pulpit

Including

The Official Report of the Services
in Connection with His Funeral

Also Including

The Complete Text of the Final Four Sermons Preached by Charles H. Spurgeon at the Metropolitan Tabernacle.

Solid Ground Christian Books
Birmingham, Alabama USA
2006

Solid Ground Christian Books
2090 Columbiana Rd, Suite 2000
Birmingham, AL 35216
205-443-0311
sgcb@charter.net
http://solid-ground-books.com

FROM THE PULPIT TO THE PALM-BRANCH
A Memorial of Charles H. Spurgeon

Edited by Arthur T. Pierson (1837-1911)

Solid Ground Classic Reprints

First printing of new edition January 2006

Special thanks to Mark and Ann Solan who gave this book to the publisher as a Christmas gift on December 15, 1993.

Cover work by Borgo Design, Tuscaloosa, AL
Contact them at nelbrown@comcast.net

ISBN: 1-59925-036-5

Table of Contents

Table of Illustrations	1
Introduction to New Edition: *The Last Lap*	3
Preface	7
Adieu to the Tabernacle	13
Breaking the Long Silence	20
The Last Month – January 1892	32
Home in February	40
Two Characteristic Illustrations	46
Memorial Service at Mentone, France	50
The Bereaved Church	55
The Blessedness of the Holy Dead – A Sermon	61
A Door Opened in Heaven – A Sermon	76
The First Day of the Second Week	90
Tributes of Affection	95
Memorial Meeting for Members of the Church	99
Memorial Meeting for Ministers and Students	125
Memorial Service for Christian Workers	153
Memorial Meeting for the General Public	176
The Funeral Service	191
From the Tabernacle to the Tomb	205
Memorial Service for Children	212
An Example of Service – A Sermon	219
Remember Your Leader – A Sermon	231
A Thoroughly Furnished Life – A Sermon	247
List of Deputations FROM Various Societies	267
List of Churches, Societies, and Public Bodies sending Letters of Sympathy and Condolence	268
Lo, I Come – Doctrinal Sermon by CHS	285
Lo, I Come – Applicatory Sermon by CHS	301
My Times are in Thy Hand – Sermon by CHS	317
The Statute of David – Final Sermon by CHS	333

Table of Illustrations

Final Photograph of Charles H. Spurgeon	Frontispiece
CHS and J.C. Houchin	15
Facsimile of Actual Letter from CHS	18
Photograph of Mrs. C.H. Spurgeon	33
Drawing of Hotel Beau Rivage, Mentone	35
Photo of Mr. J.W. Harrald	37
Photo of Mr. Spurgeon's "cosy corner"	42
Photo of Mr. Spurgeon's bedroom	45
View of Mentone from Boulevard Victoria	47
Funeral Cortege at Menton Station	53
Drawing of Pastor James A. Spurgeon	57
Drawing of Dr. Arthur T. Pierson	59
Olive Casket under the Palm-Branches	97
Funeral Cortege entering Norwood Cemetery	207
Pastor Brown's Address at the Grave	209

Introduction to New Edition

"The Last Lap"

Holy Scripture depicts the Christian life as a race that must be run with perseverance. In Hebrews 12:1-3 the picture is widened to the likeness of an Olympic stadium full of athletes who have previously and successfully run the marathon and who now watch with fascination as other runners come into the stadium to complete that last lap. Charles Haddon Spurgeon was the outstanding spiritual athlete of the 19th Century. This book describes the last weeks, days and hours of his phenomenal life as well as the funeral services and sermons which followed.

In a sermon titled 'Sermons from Saintly Death-beds' [no. 783, preached on 1st December 1867] on the text, "And when Jacob had made an end of commanding his sons, he gathered up his feet into his bed, and yielded up the ghost, and was gathered unto his people" (Genesis 49:33), Spurgeon makes the observation that 'God permits the Jordan to overflow its banks when some of his best children are passing through, for he designs to magnify his grace in the last trial of their faith, and thus to show to men, and angels, and devils, who are looking on, how he can triumph in his servants when flesh and heart are failing.'

Thus we would expect a choice instrument like Martin Luther who was used massively to destroy the dominions of Satan on earth to be put to the test in his last hours. In his life Luther experienced colossal spiritual trials and agonies some of which were referred to in German as *anfechtung* which means a mixture of intense spiritual horror, doubt, terror and anxiety, bordering on despair. Luther was taken suddenly ill at the end of three weeks spent at Eisleben the town of his birth. The journey to Eisleben during January 1546 was freezingly cold and exhausting. The mission was for Luther was to settle a dispute. This was exacting and tiring but was achieved at the end of three weeks. Then suddenly Luther fell ill. The end came in a couple of days. There were no violent conflicts. His disciples, friends and sons who were with him were acutely aware that those loyal to the Pope would dearly like to be able to spread the rumour that at the end of his life Martin turned back to Rome. On the last day of his life as he became weaker he kept repeating the words of John 3:16. In the last moments close friend and companion Professor Jonas said to Martin, "Do you want to die standing firmly in Christ and the doctrines you have taught?" Very clearly for all round his bedside to hear Martin replied, "Yes!" His testimony to the teaching of justification by faith alone was kept to his last breath.

In the exposition, 'Sermons from Saintly Death-beds' Spurgeon refers to the deaths of many who were weak. 'To many saints departure has been a peaceful entrance into the fair haven of repose. The very weakest of God's servants have frequently been happiest in their departing moments. John Bunyan, who had observed this fact, in the description of Mr Feeble-mind's passage across the river, "Here also I took notice of what was very remarkable; the water of that river was lower at this time than ever I saw in my life. So he went over at last not much above wetshod." Heaven's mercy tempers the wind to the shorn lamb, and gives to babes no battle, because they have no strength for it: the lambs calmly rest on the bosom of Jesus, and breathe out their lives in the Shepherd's arms. What an encouragement this ought to be to you who are the tender ones among us! What cheering tidings for you who are weak in faith! Like Mr-Ready-to-halt, you shall cry, "Now, I shall have no more need of these crutches, since yonder are chariots and crutches, since yonder are chariots and horses for me to ride on."'

Biblical support for interest in the manner in which we end the race is provided in 2 Kings 2:1-18. Elisha having requested of the LORD a double portion of Elijah's spiritual endowment Elisha followed Elijah determined to be at his side when he was taken up to heaven. When that moment came Elijah was taken up to heaven in a whirlwind. Elisha cried out "My father! My father! The chariots and horsemen of Israel!" or in the words of Krummacher, "thou wast Israel's artillery and cavalry – its glittering legion, and its invincible host". In some ways Spurgeon's departure was like that for it marked the end of a ministry of extraordinary effective gospel preaching combined with a life of practical good works. These works resulted in innumerable gospel ministries emanating from the Metropolitan Tabernacle. As this book shows Spurgeon's industrious life was industrious to the very end. He died as he had lived in the Lord's glad service. His work of defending the faith in controversy was just as vital as the other works foreordained by our Father for him to achieve. His was the most effective voice for the truth (Jude 3) in the downgrade controversy.

Spurgeon always lived with eternity in view. Preaching from the text "The time is short" (1 Corinthians 7:29) he urged his hearers as follows: 'Do you believe that these eyes shall see the King in that day when he comes in his glory, and that these bones shall rise again from the grave, and your bodies shall be endowed with an incorruptible existence? "Yes," say you, "we do believe it, and believe it intensely, too." Well, then, I would that you realized it as so very near that you were expectant of its fulfillment. Who would cry and fret about the passing troubles of a day when he saw the heavens open, beheld the beckoning hand, and heard the voice that called him hence? Oh, that the glory might come streaming into your soul till you forget the darkness of the way! Oh, that the breeze from these goodly mountains would fan you! Oh, that the spray from that mighty ocean would refresh you! Oh, that the music of those bells of heaven in yonder turrets would enliven you! Then would you speed your way towards the rest that remaineth for the people of God, inspired with sacred ardor and dauntless courage." '

This whole volume will help to inspire the reader with that 'sacred ardour and dauntless courage' necessary to complete the race of faith.

Erroll Hulse

PREFACE.

THIS volume, which was at first intended merely to be a report of the Memorial Services held in the Metropolitan Tabernacle, while the mortal body of its late beloved Pastor lay asleep in the Olive Wood, under the Palm Branches, has, during its preparation, been enlarged to make a place for a brief history of the last chapter in Mr. Spurgeon's faithful and fruitful earthly life. Beginning with his last appearances in his pulpit, the course of the final months, so fraught with interest, is traced through their varying events. A short account is given of the terrible illness which caused such widespread anxiety, and evoked such world-wide sympathy; of the gracious recovery granted in answer to the continued prayers of God's people; of the journey to the sunny South, and the happy months at Menton; of the entrance of the Pastor into the presence of the King; and of the memorable days thereafter.

Since this good gift, which the Giver of all good bestowed upon the Church, and upon the world, was to be taken from us, we are constrained to say that he could have gone from our midst in no better way. This is not only a matter of faith, but, having tried to imagine other methods of departure, we are compelled to fall back on God's way as the wisest and the best.

Had Mr. Spurgeon been called suddenly, we should have been so stunned by the blow as to have been scarcely able to stand upright beneath it : a waiting time was, therefore, in mercy, granted to us, during which the forces at command were organized in such a way that, with the exactness of a machine, all worked smoothly when the terrible tidings at last came.

Had Mr. Spurgeon been taken before such marvellous solicitude was shown around his sick bed, the enemies of the truth would have blasphemed; now they are fain to be silent, seeing that, even in this life, fidelity to the truth, and faithfulness to conviction have been so greatly honoured.

Had Mr. Spurgeon passed away amid the fogs of London, we should have imagined that, had he only been permitted to live beneath bluer skies, his life would have been prolonged; now we thank God that those three bright months were added to it, and that he was able, with his beloved wife, to have such uninterrupted joy on earth, ere he passed to his reward in heaven.

Had Mr. Spurgeon ended his course in England, for a few days only would people have paused to have asked the secret of his marvellous influence; whereas, under the actual circumstances, *for twelve days* the attention of the civilized world was centred in the testimony borne, not only to the servant of God, but to the Gospel he preached, in column after column of almost every newspaper. Truly, the Lord hath done all things well!

Many years ago, in one of his sermons, published at the time, he attempted to picture the scene at his own funeral, and expressed his own desire concerning it.

"In a little while," he said, "there will be a concourse of persons in the streets. Methinks I hear some one enquiring:—"

"What are all these people waiting for?"

"Do you not know? He is to be buried to-day."
"And who is that?"
"It is Spurgeon."
"What! the man that preached at the Tabernacle?"
"Yes; he is to be buried to-day."
"That will happen very soon. And when you see my coffin carried to the silent grave, I should like every one of you, whether converted or not, to be constrained to say, 'He did earnestly urge us, in plain and simple language, not to put off the consideration of eternal things; he did entreat us to look to Christ. Now he is gone, our blood is not at his door if we perish.'"

Far more abundantly than he dared to hope have his wishes been fulfilled, and only in the day when all things shall be revealed, shall it be known how many have been turned to the Lord by the death of the man who was so greatly honoured to lead people to the feet of Jesus during his life.

Now he has left the Tabernacle pulpit for ever, and he stands amongst the great multitude who are before the throne and before the Lamb, "clothed with white robes, and palms in their hands." He is not in strange company there, for the song of those who wave the palm-branch was ever his theme as he stood in the pulpit: "Salvation to our God who sitteth upon the throne, and unto the Lamb." *From the Pulpit to the Palm-Branch* has been for him a very natural transition. He preached Christ here; he praises Him yonder. Long ago, when the lowly Saviour was going up to Jerusalem, they "took branches of palm-trees, and went forth to meet Him, and cried 'Hosanna.'" When Charles Haddon Spurgeon, the humble servant of his glorious Lord, was going up to the New Jerusalem, did not some of the white-robed worshippers meet him also with palm-branches? If they did, he would be the first to lay them at his Master's feet, bowing low in grateful adoration, and giving Him all the praise.

None on earth can estimate his worth. He was *the Evangelical Prophet* of his age; our modern Isaiah. Like Isaiah, he early saw "the Lord sitting upon a throne, high and lifted up;" he had his lips purged with the live coal; and when he heard the call, "Whom shall I send, and who will go for Us?" he gladly answered, "Here I am, send me." Beholding the Lord in His temple, he laid himself upon the altar, and like Isaiah, he was "very bold" to declare the Word of God. Filled with the thought of the glory of God, he lived for the good of the people; he delighted to speak of Him who "was wounded for our transgressions, and bruised for our iniquites;" and to invite thirsty souls to come and buy the grace of God, "without money and without price." Like Isaiah, too, he has been sawn asunder by some critics who would sever his philanthropy from his faith, not recognizing that the one was the outcome of the other, and that the same clear head and the same warm heart belonged to both.

Of this man of God, who passed away after almost fifty-eight years on earth, the fifty-eighth chapter of Isaiah is a full-length portrait. In the midst of the surface religion of his day, he obeyed the word, "Cry aloud, spare not, lift up thy voice like a trumpet, and shew My people their transgression, and the house of Jacob their sins." Who more than he dealt his bread to the hungry, and brought the poor that are cast out to his house? Let the Orphanage and Almshouses answer. Did not he truly realize that the secret of strength lay in not doing his own ways, nor finding his own pleasure, nor speaking his own words? He called the Sabbath a delight, the holy of the Lord, honourable; and God gave him a sevenfold blessing, even according to His word.

His light rose in obscurity, and broke forth as the morning. He deliberately set his heart against seeking great things for himself, yet fair and clear he shone undimmed before the world for forty years; shining more and more until the perfect day.

He had many answers to prayer; his communion with God became intensely real. The promise was fulfilled to him, "Then shalt thou call, and the Lord shall answer; thou shalt cry, and He shall say, Here I am." The record of his answered prayers would, of itself, fill a volume.

The Lord guided him continually; like a little child he was willing to be led. His whole life was a series of steps, taken at the bidding of his Master, and never was this more so than towards the end. It seemed as if God said to him, "Thy righteousness shall go before thee; the glory of the Lord shall be thy rereward."

Fruitfulness was the result. In every good word or work he abounded, and this other promise of the Lord was realized abundantly,—"Thou shalt be like a watered garden, and like a spring of water, whose waters fail not."

The twelfth verse of the chapter is startling in the correctness of its application to him. In vain men speak of Spurgeon as "the last of the Puritans." The leader of them he may have been, and the greatest of them, but not the last of them; as long as the age continues, God will raise up for himself a godly seed. "They that shall be of thee" we read, and we can apply the words to both Mr. Spurgeon's sons and to his students,—"They that shall be of thee shall build the old waste places : thou shalt raise up the foundations of many generations." Multiplication follows on fruitfulness.

Joy is the sixth blessing promised. "Then shalt thou delight thyself in the Lord,"—a word which surely was fulfilled in his experience. To him living for God was luxury, not drudgery. He could say, with a wonderful emphasis of heart,—

> "How glorious is my King !
> 'Tis joy, not duty,
> To speak His beauty !
> My soul mounts on the wing,
> At the mere thought,
> How Christ my life has bought."

Last of all comes honour. "I will cause thee to ride upon the high places of the earth." No stronger comment on this is necessary than the record of the following pages. "The mouth of the Lord hath spoken it," and the hand of the Lord hath performed it. Honour came to him who sought it not, who even counted it a light thing. Truly it is no vain thing to serve the Lord !

Added to this sevenfold promise of blessing, a name is given in the twelfth verse to him who lives such a life. No more suitable title could be selected for the sainted man, of whom this volume is a very inadequate memorial.

"Thou shalt be called,
'The Restorer of Paths to dwell in.'"

From the Pulpit to the Palm-Branch.

Adieu to the Tabernacle.

Standing in the Metropolitan Tabernacle, the scene for so many years of his marvellous ministry, Mr. Spurgeon, on *Lord's-day morning, May 3rd,* 1891, commenced his sermon upon Ps. xl. 7: "Then said I, Lo, I come" (No. 2,203), with the following memorable statement:—

"To my great sorrow, last Sunday night I was unable to preach. I had prepared a sermon upon this text, with much hope of its usefulness; for I intended it to be a supplement to the morning sermon, which was a doctrinal exposition. The evening sermon was intended to be practical, and to commend the whole subject to the attention of enquiring sinners. I came here feeling quite fit to preach, when an overpowering nervousness oppressed me, and I lost all self-control, and left the pulpit in anguish. I come hither this morning with the same subject. I have been turning it over, and wondering why it was so. Peradventure, this sermon was not to be preached on that occasion, because God would teach the preacher more of his own feebleness, and cast him more fully upon the divine strength. That has certainly been the effect upon my own heart. Perhaps, also, there are some here this morning who were not here last Lord's-day evening, whom God intends to bless by the sermon. The people were not here, peradventure, for whom the eternal decree of God had designed the message, and they may be here now. You that are fresh to this place, should consider the strange circumstance, which never happened to me before in the forty years of my ministry; and you may be led to enquire whether my bow was then unstrung that the arrow might find its ordained target in your heart. The two sermons will now go forth together from the press; and perhaps, going together, they may prove like two hands of love wherewith to embrace lost souls, and draw them to the Saviour, who herein saith, 'Lo, I come.' God grant it may be so!"

Although probably no one suspected it at the time, this was "the beginning of the end" of that noble life that closed at Menton on January 31st, 1892. The preacher was at the time terribly overworked, and applications for additional services were continually coming. He struggled on bravely, however, and on *May* 17th, preached a sermon on the text: "My times are in Thy hand" (No. 2,205), which many people regarded as almost prophetic of the great illness he was about to suffer. He was even then attacked by that terrible scourge, misnamed "influenza"; and on the following day, Dr. R. M. Miller, of Upper Norwood, who was called in to attend him, forbade his venturing to the Tabernacle. He was, indeed, closely confined to the house for nearly three weeks; but at the end of that time, on *Lord's-day morning, June 7th*, he preached from 1 Samuel xxx. 21-25, the sermon afterwards published under the title of "The Statute of David for the Sharing of the Spoil" (No. 2,208). This will ever be a most memorable discourse, for it was practically *the Pastor's farewell to the Tabernacle*. He was never inside the building again, until all that remained of him was brought from Menton, in the olive-wood casket, amid universal mourning.

C. H. SPURGEON AND J. C. HOUCHIN.

On *Monday morning, June 8th*, Mr. Spurgeon went into what he called, in his preface to *Memories of Stambourne*,* " my grandfather's country." One object he had in going was that he might obtain photographs to illustrate that little work. In that he succeeded. We have reproduced, on page 15, one of the views taken by Mr. Nash, representing C. H. Spurgeon and J. C. Houchin, the present pastor at Stambourne, as they appeared on June 10th, 1891.

In the preface already mentioned, Mr. Spurgeon wrote :— " On the *Thursday* of the week, an overpowering headache came on, and I had to hurry home on *Friday*, to go up to that chamber wherein, for three months, I suffered beyond measure, and was often between the jaws of death."

From that time Dr. Miller was again in constant attendance; and on *June 24th*, Dr. Joseph Kidd was called in for consultation. For a time, all that medical skill, patient watching, and careful nursing could do, appeared of no avail for the beloved sufferer's recovery. Meanwhile, prayer without ceasing was made to God for him, the world over, in ordinary meetings and in special gatherings. As soon as the critical condition of the Pastor was made known, the Church at the Tabernacle constituted itself into one great protracted prayer-meeting. Not only did thousands gather together for a day of prayer; but for weeks special prayer-meetings were continued two or three times daily. Also, in many other places, meetings for earnest supplication on Mr. Spurgeon's behalf were held, showing, in a remarkable manner, the real unity of the One Church of Christ.

Besides numerous callers at "Westwood", letters and telegrams of sympathy came in great numbers from all sorts and conditions of men, and from all parts of the world.

Memories of Stambourne. By C. H. Spurgeon and B. Beddow. Passmore and Alabaster. 1s. and 2s.

The archbishops, bishops, and clergy of the Church of England were largely represented; while Nonconformist ministers, of all denominations, were most hearty in their sympathetic utterances; and cablegrams, telegrams, letters, and resolutions came from almost endless Associations, Assemblies, Colleges, Committees, Conferences, Congresses, Conventions, Institutions, Missions, Societies, Synods, Unions, &c., including almost all the great religious and philanthropic agencies of the Metropolis, the United Kingdom, and many parts of the Continent and the English Colonies throughout the world.

(We have not given here any list of the thousands of friends who thus expressed their sympathy with Mr. and Mrs. Spurgeon during the trying months that the Pastor was lying in such a critical condition at "Westwood"; nor of those who united in the hearty congratulations that greeted his partial recovery. They were duly recorded at the time in *The Sword and the Trowel;* but at the end of this volume we have printed a list of the Churches and Societies from which resolutions of sympathy have come to Mrs. Spurgeon or the Tabernacle since the "promotion to glory" of the beloved Pastor. It was quite impossible to make any record of the telegrams and letters from individuals; that would have expanded the list into a Memorial Volume by itself. The present list, lengthy as it is, must necessarily be incomplete, for the letters from distant parts will, doubtless, continue to arrive for a long time to come; but it is as correct as it can be made up to the date of publication.)

The letter to the congregation at the Tabernacle, dated *August 9th*, of which, a reduced *fac-simile* appears on the next page, was the first Mr. Spurgeon was able to write with his own hand after his long illness:—

Westwood
Beulah Hill
Upper Norwood
1891 Aug 9

Dear Brethren

The Lord's name be praised for first giving & then hearing the loving prayers of his people Through these prayers my life is prolonged. I feel greatly humbled & very grateful at being the object of so great a love & so wonderful an outburst of prayer.

I have not strength to say more. Let the name of the Lord be glorified

Yours most heartily
C H Spurgeon

In *The Sword and the Trowel* for October appeared a long note from Mr. Spurgeon, thanking "the thousands of friends, of all ranks and religions", who had expressed their sympathy with him in his long and trying affliction. On *October 3rd*, Mr. Spurgeon and his private secretary, Mr. Harrald, went to Eastbourne, in the hope that a short stay at the seaside might bring to him sufficient strength to enable him to take the journey to Menton. Mrs. Spurgeon also went for a few days; and the experiment appeared quite satisfactory, so that, when the Pastor returned to "Westwood", on *October 16th*, he was so much stronger that the arrangements for starting for Menton were completed.

On *Monday, October 26th*, Pastor and Mrs. C. H. Spurgeon, Pastor and Mrs. J. A. Spurgeon, and Mr. Harrald started on their thousand miles' journey to the sunny South. They were accompanied as far as Calais by two of the Tabernacle deacons, Messrs. Allison and Higgs. It has been very widely published that Baron Rothschild placed his saloon carriage at Mr. Spurgeon's disposal; but the fact is, that Messrs. Alabaster, Passmore, & Sons, and Mr. John M. Cook most generously defrayed the cost of the saloon carriage from Calais to Menton, and so enabled the whole party to travel in ease and comfort, and to arrive at their destination on *Thursday, October 29th*. Dr. FitzHenry at once took charge of his illustrious patient, and aided him greatly by his wise and kindly advice. The appearance of Mr. Spurgeon, from this time until a few days before he was called home, led many beside himself to hope that a long rest by the sunny shore of the Mediterranean would complete his restoration. He gradually gained strength, and his weekly letters to the church at home continued to be an unfailing source of interest to thousands. Not, however, until the last day of the old year, was he able to conduct a service. Then, to a little group of delighted friends, he gave the following memorable address:—

Breaking the Long Silence.

Two Brief Addresses delivered by C. H. Spurgeon at Menton.

On the Last Evening of 1891.

DEAR FRIENDS,—I am not able to say much to you at present. I should have gladly invited you to prayer every morning if I had been able to meet you; but I had not sufficient strength. I cannot refrain from saying a little to you, on this the last evening of the year, by way of *Retrospect*, and perhaps on New Year's morning I may add a word by way of *Prospect*.

We have come so far on the journey of life; and, standing at the boundary of another year, we look back. Let each one gaze upon his own trodden pathway. You will not need me to attempt fine words or phrases: each one, with his own eyes, will now survey his own road.

Among the striking things to be noted are *the dangers we have escaped*. After Bunyan's pilgrim had safely traversed the Valley of the Shadow of Death, the morning light dawned upon him, and sitting down, he looked back upon the terrible road which he had passed. It had once seemed an awful thing to him that he had marched through that valley by night; but when he looked back, and saw the horrors he had escaped, he must have felt glad that darkness had concealed much of its peril when he was actually in the midst of it. Much the same has it been with us: thank God, now that we clearly see the perils, we have passed them in safety.

During the year which closes this night, certain of us have been very near to the jaws of death, and some of us may also have skirted the abyss of despair; and yet we live and hope. Our path has been full of trials and temptations, and yet we have not been permitted to fall. Our heart has been torn with inward conflicts, and yet faith has proved victorious. No one of us knows how near he has been to some great sin, or some false step. A single act might have changed the whole aspect of life to us; but from that act we have been preserved. Others have stumbled, and sadly fallen; and we are of like passions with them: blessed be the hand which has held us up! The Greek liturgy speaks of the Saviour's "unknown sufferings." Doubtless they were the greatest of all his woes. We may with equal accuracy speak of our "unknown dangers," for probably they have been the greatest of our perils. The Lord saw what we could not see, and kept us where we could not have kept ourselves.

I would remind you that to have evils averted is a choice favour. A Puritan father met his son by arrangement. They had each travelled several miles to reach the appointed spot, and when they came together, the son thankfully observed, "Father, I have experienced a most remarkable providence on the road; for my horse stumbled three times, and even threw me, and yet I am unhurt." His father answered, "It is well; but I also have enjoyed a remarkable providence on the road, for my horse came all the way without stumbling once." Truly, to be kept *from* danger is as great a privilege as to be kept *in* danger; but we forget this. Let us thank God for preserved lives, continued comforts, and unspotted characters; for these wares are marked

"*Fragile*," and that they are not broken is a marvel of grace. Since last we met, how many have died! Plagues and deaths have been flying around us, like shots in the heat of an action; and only he who, of old, covered David's head in the day of battle, could have kept us from death. Our spiritual life still survives, and only he who holds the stars in their courses could have maintained us in our integrity. It ought to bring tears of gratitude to our eyes while, to quote the language of the Song of Solomon, we "look from the top of Hermon; from the lions' dens, from the mountains of the leopards."

For my own part, I dare not omit from my retrospect *the sins of the past year*, of which I would unfeignedly repent. He who does not know himself to be sinful does not know himself at all. He who does not feel his own unworthiness must surely have grown callous or conceited. Sins of omission are those which trouble me most. I look back, and remember what I might have done, and have not done; what opportunities of usefulness I have not seized; what sins I have allowed to pass unrebuked; what struggling beginners in grace I have failed to help. I cannot but grieve that what I have done was not done better, or attended with a humbler dependence upon God. I now perceive, in my holy things, faults in their beginning, faults in their carrying on, and faults in their ending. Delay to commence, slackness in the act, and pride after it, defile our best service. What an endless list our faults and failings would make! Oh, friends, when we examine one year of life carefully, looking into the thoughts and motives and secret imaginings of the soul, how humbled we ought to be! As I rode through the streets of Menton this day, I felt bowed down with a sense of sin; and on a sudden it flashed into my mind, "Yes, and therefore I have my part and lot in the work of the Lord Jesus, for he said expressly, 'I came not to call the righteous, but sinners.'" Note that the words "to repentance" are most properly omitted from the Revised Version (Mark ii. 17).

Why did Jesus die? He died for our sins: he would not have needed to die for men if men had not sinned. Where there is no sin, there is no share in the sin-offering. If we have no sin, we have no connection with that Saviour who came to save his people from their sins. For whom does Jesus plead? He makes intercession for the transgressors: if I am not a transgressor, I have no assurance that he pleads for me. The whole mediatorial system is for sinful men; and as I am conscious of guilt, so am I assured, by faith, that I am within the circle of divine grace. My faith places her hand upon the head of him who was our Substitute and Scapegoat, and I see all my sins and all the sins of all believers for ever put away by him who stood in the sinner's place. Let your tears fall because of sin; but, at the same time, let the eye of faith steadily behold the Son of man lifted up, as Moses lifted up the serpent in the wilderness, that those who are bitten by the old serpent may look unto him and live. Our sinnership is that emptiness into which the Lord pours his mercy. "This is a faithful saying, and worthy of all acceptation, that Christ Jesus came into the world to save sinners." On that blessed fact I rest my soul. Though I have preached Christ crucified for more than forty years, and have led many to my Master's feet, I have at this moment no ray of hope but that which comes from what my Lord Jesus has done for guilty men.

> "Behold him there! the bleeding Lamb!
> My perfect, spotless Righteousness,
> The great unchangeable, 'I AM,'
> The King of glory and of grace."

A flood of light breaks over the scene if we look back upon *our mercies!* Now for your arithmetic! Now begin to make your calculations! Think of major mercies and minor mercies; fleeting mercies and eternal mercies; mercies by day, and mercies by night; mercies averting evil, and mercies securing good; mercies at home, and mercies abroad; mercies of bed and board, of city and field, of society and seclusion. Mercy affects every faculty of the mind, and every portion of the body. There are mercies for conscience, and fear, and hope; mercies for the understanding and the heart; and, at the same time, there are mercies of eye, and ear, and head, and hand. The whole landscape of life is golden with the light of mercy. In the love of God we have lived, and moved, and had our being. We see mercies new every morning, mercies old as the eternal hills; streams of mercy; oceans of mercy; mercy all, and all mercy.

God has been specially good to me. I think I hear each heart whisper, "That is just what I was going to say." Dear friends, I will not monopolize the expression; it is most true from me; I doubt not that it is also true of each one of you. Can we conceive how God could have been more gracious than he has been? If you are familiar with the Lord of love, so that you dwell in him, and his Spirit dwells in you, you will join me in abundantly uttering the memory of his great goodness. How wonderful is his lovingkindness! How free! How tender! How faithful! How lasting! How everlasting! No, I cannot even attempt an outline of the Lord's goodness to us during the year which is now waning: we must each one review the record for himself. "How much owest thou unto my Lord?" is an enquiry which must be personally answered by each one as an individual.

One thing more before I close. What are *the lessons which our gracious God has intended us to learn* by all that has happened during the year? Each one of us has had his own order of discipline and line of learning; but all have not had the same. It is written, "All thy children shall be taught of the Lord," but all the children are not reading from the same page, at the same moment.

Have we not learned to expect more of God, and less of men? To make fewer resolutions, but to carry out those which were wisely and devoutly formed? Have we not seen more of the instability of earthly joys? Have we not learned more fully the need of using time present, and ability possessed? Are we not now aware that we are neither so good, so wise, so strong, nor so constant as we thought we were? Have we been taught to go down that Jesus may rise, after the manner of John the Baptist, who cried, "He must increase, but I must decrease"? These are truths worth learning. I have neither time nor strength to suggest more of those lessons which experience teaches us when our hearts are made ready for the divine schooling. We ought to have learned much in 365 days. I hope we have. Permit me only to hint at a truth which has come home to me.

During the past year I have been made to see that there is more love and unity among God's people than is generally believed. I speak not egotistically, but gratefully. I had no idea that Christian people, of every church, would spontaneously and importunately plead for the prolonging of my life. I feel myself a debtor to all God's people on this earth. Each section of the church seemed to vie with all the rest in sending words of comfort to my wife, and in presenting intercession to God on my behalf. If anyone had prophesied, twenty years ago, that a dissenting minister, and a very outspoken one, too, would be prayed for in many parish churches, and in Westminster Abbey and St. Paul's Cathedral, it would not have been believed; but it was so. There is more love in the hearts of Christian people than they know of themselves. We mistake our divergencies of judgment for differences of heart; but they are far from being the same thing. In these days of infidel criticism, believers of all sorts will be driven into sincere unity. For my part, I believe that all spiritual persons are already one. When our Lord prayed that his church might be one, his prayer was answered, and his true people are even now, in spirit and in truth, one in him. Their different modes of external worship are as the furrows of a field; the field is none the less one because of the marks of the plough. Between rationalism and faith there is an abyss immeasurable; but where there is faith in the Everlasting Father, faith in the Great Sacrifice, and faith in the Indwelling Spirit, there is a living, loving, lasting union.

I have learned, also, that when the one church pleads with hearty entreaties, she must and will be heard. No case is hopeless when many pray. The deadliest diseases relax their hold before the power of unanimous intercession. As long as I live, I am a visible embodiment of the fact that, to the prayer of faith, presented by the Church of God, nothing is impossible. It is worth while to have been sore sick to have learned this truth, and to have proved it in one's own person.

In this little circle, probably one and another may say, "These are not exactly the lessons that we have learned this year." Perhaps not. But if you have learned more of Jesus, and of his love, which passes knowledge, it suffices. Be thankful if you have learned even a little of Jesus. Do not judge yourself by the attainments of others who are older or more experienced; but rejoice in the Lord. Bless God for starlight, and he will give you moonlight; praise him for moonlight, and he will give you sunlight; thank him for sunlight, and you shall yet come to that land where they need not the light of the sun, for the Lord God giveth them light for ever and ever. May this year close with blessing! Amen.

On the First Morning of 1892.

In the morning the friends came together again, and Mr. Spurgeon sat as before, and spoke with them; this time more briefly.

Passing at this hour over the threshold of the New Year, we look forward, and what do we see? Could we procure a telescope which would enable us to see to the end of the year, should we be wise to use it? I think not. We know nothing of the events which lie before us: of life or death to ourselves or to our friends, or of changes of position, or of sickness or health. What a mercy that these things are hidden from us! If we foresaw our best blessings, they would lose their freshness and sweetness while we impatiently waited for them. Anticipation would sour into weariness, and familiarity would breed contempt. If we could foresee our troubles, we should worry ourselves about them long before they came, and in that fretfulness we should miss the joy of our present blessings. Great mercy has hung up a veil between us and the future; and there let it hang.

Still, all is not concealed. Some things we clearly see. I say, "*we*"; but I mean those whose eyes have been opened, for it is not everyone who can *see* in the truest sense. A lady said to Mr. Turner, "I have often looked upon that prospect, but I have never seen what you have put into your picture." The great artist simply replied, "Don't you wish you could see it?" Looking into the future with the eye of faith, believers can see much that is hidden from those who have no faith. Let me tell you, in a few words, what I see as I look into the new year.

I see *a pathway made* from this first of January, 1892, to the first of January, 1893. I see a highway cast up by the foreknowledge and predestination of God. Nothing of the future is left to chance; nay, not the falling of a sparrow, nor the losing of a hair is left to hap-hazard; but all the events of life are arranged and appointed. Not only is every turn in the road marked in the divine map, but every stone on the road, and every drop of morning dew or evening mist that falls upon the grass which grows at the roadside. We are not to cross a trackless desert; the Lord has ordained our path in his infallible wisdom and infinite love. "The steps of a good man are ordered by the Lord; and he delighteth in his way."

I see, next, *a Guide provided*, as our companion along the way. To him we gladly say, "Thou shalt guide me with thy counsel." He is waiting to go with us through every portion of the road. "The Lord, he it is that doth go before thee; he will be with thee, he will not fail thee." We are not left to pass through life as though it were a lone wilderness, a place of dragons and owls; for Jesus says, "I will not leave you comfortless; I will come to you."

Though we should lose father, and mother, and the dearest friends, there is One who wears our nature, who will never quit our side. One like unto the Son of man is still treading the life-ways of believing hearts, and each true believer cometh up from the wilderness, leaning upon the Beloved. We feel the presence of the Lord Jesus even now, in this room, where two or three are gathered in his name; and I trust we shall feel it through all the months of the year, whether it be the time of the singing of birds, or the season of ripe fruits, or the dark months when the clods are frozen into iron. In this Riviera, we ought the more readily to realize our Lord's presence, because the country is so like "thy land, O Immanuel!" Here is the land of oil olive, and of figs, and of the clusters of Eshcol. By such a blue sea he walked, and up such rocky hills he climbed. But whether here, or elsewhere, let us look for HIM to abide with us, to make this year truly to be "a year of our Lord."

Beside the way and the Guide, I perceive very clearly, by

the eye of faith, *strength for the journey provided.* Throughout the whole distance of the year, we shall find halting-places, where we may rest and take refreshment, and then go on our way singing, "He restoreth my soul." We shall have strength enough, but none to spare; and that strength will come when it is needed, and not before. When saints imagine that they have strength to spare, they turn sinners, and are apt to have their locks shorn by the Philistines. The Lord of the way will find the pilgrims with sufficient spending-money for the road; but he may not think it wise to burden them with superfluous funds.

God all-sufficient will not fail those who trust him. When we come to the place for shouldering the burden, we shall reach the place for receiving the strength. If it pleases the Lord to multiply our troubles from one to ten, he will increase our strength in the same proportion. To each believer the Lord still says, "As thy days, so shall thy strength be." You do not yet feel that you have grace to die with: what of that? You are not yet dying. While you have yet to deal with the business and duty of life, look to God for the grace which these require; and when life is ebbing out, and your only thought is about landing on the eternal shore, then look to God your Saviour for dying grace in dying moments. We may expect an inrush of divine strength when human strength is failing, and a daily impartation of energy as daily need requires. Our lamps shall be trimmed as long as they shall need to burn. Let not our present weakness tempt us to limit the Holy One of Israel. There is a hospice on every pass over the Alps of life, and a bridge across every river of trial which crosses our way to the Celestial City. Holy angels are as numerous to guard us as fallen ones to tempt us. We shall never have a need for which our gracious Father has furnished no supply.

I see, most plainly, a *power overruling* all things which

occur in the way we tread. I see an alembic in which all things are transformed. "All things work together for good to them that love God, to them that are the called according to his purpose." I see a wonder-working hand which turns for us the swords of disease into the ploughshares of correction, and the spears of trial into the pruning-hooks of discipline. By this divine skill, bitters are made sweet, and poisons turned to medicines. "Nothing shall by any means harm you," is a promise too strong for feeble faith; but full assurance finds it true. Since God is for us, who can be against us? What a joy to see Jehovah himself as our banner, and God himself with us as our Captain! Forward then into the New Year, "for there shall no evil befal you."

One thing more, and this is brightness itself: this year we trust we shall see *God glorified* by us and in us. If we realize our chief end, we reach our highest enjoyment. It is the delight of the renewed heart to think that God can get glory out of such poor creatures as we are. "God is light." We cannot add to his brightness; but we may act as reflectors, which, though they have no light of their own, yet, when the sun shines upon them, reflect his beams, and send them where, without such reflection, they might not have come. When the Lord shines upon us, we will cast that light upon dark places, and make those who sit in the shadow of death to rejoice in Jesus our Lord. We hope that God has been in some measure glorified in some of us during the past year, but we trust he will be glorified by us far more in the year which now begins. We will be content to glorify God either actively or passively. We would have it so happen that, when our life's history is written, whoever reads it will not think of us as "self-made men," but as the handiwork of God, in whom his grace is magnified. Not in us may men see the clay, but the Potter's hand. They said of one, "He is a fine preacher"; but of another they said,

"We never notice how he preaches, *but we feel that God is great.*" We wish our whole life to be a sacrifice; an altar of incense continually smoking with sweet perfume unto the Most High. Oh, to be borne through the year on the wings of praise to God; to mount from year to year, and raise at each ascent a loftier and yet lowlier song unto the God of our life! The vista of a praiseful life will never close, but continue throughout eternity. From psalm to psalm, from hallelujah to hallelujah, we will ascend the hill of the Lord; until we come into the Holiest of all, where, with veiled faces, we will bow before the Divine Majesty in the bliss of endless adoration. Throughout this year may the Lord be with you! Amen.

The Last Month.

On the first morning of January, 1892, Mr. Spurgeon gave the delightful address which occupies the preceding pages. "Great mercy," he said, "has hung up a veil between us and the future: and there let it hang." None who heard that address, and but few who read it as it was reproduced in the February number of *The Sword and Trowel*, thought that the immediate future would be for us so heavy with trial, or for him so bright with joy.

On the last day of the same memorable month of January, the dearly-loved speaker, who uttered such wise and weighty words, "fell asleep in Jesus." During the darkness the news flashed round the world, and when February dawned, millions of hearts were saddened to learn that C. H. Spurgeon lived on earth no more.

Many friends will like to know how that last month on earth was spent; and by means of a diary, begun by Mr. Spurgeon, and continued under his direction, much interesting information can be given. In future numbers of *The Sword and the Trowel*, "Mr. Spurgeon's Last Drives at Menton" will be described, with illustrations prepared from photographs, taken either under his personal supervision, or by his special request. The frontispiece of the present volume will be a peculiarly sacred souvenir of the sunny South, for Mr. Spurgeon is there represented as he appeared as late as *January 8th*, when this portrait, *the last that was ever taken of him*, was secured by his friend, Mr. W. C. Houghton. A pathetic interest must ever be attached to this picture, which will be treasured by all his friends, as a parting memento.

MRS. C. H. SPURGEON.

On the first Sabbath evening in January, most of the guests in the *Hôtel Beau Rivage* remained downstairs in the *salon* after dinner. Mrs. Spurgeon played the piano, while the friends sang some of her favourite hymns from *Sacred Songs and Solos,* and Mr. Spurgeon closed the engagements of the evening with a prayer that will be long remembered by all who were present.

Jan. 9.—Mr. Spurgeon completed the revision of the MS. of sermon on Psalm cv. 37, "A Stanza of Deliverance" (No. 2,241). Never did he revise a sermon with greater ease or more delight. His pen seemed to fly along the pages; and many times he paused, that he might tell us of the joy-bells ringing in his heart, as he recounted the glorious story of the wonder-working Jehovah: "He brought them forth also with silver and gold; and there was not one feeble person among their tribes." How little he or anyone else thought that he would never revise another sermon for *The Metropolitan Tabernacle Pulpit !*

Jan. 10.—During the week preceding this Sabbath, several fresh guests arrived at the hotel; and not knowing whether all would approve of hymn-singing and prayer in the public *salon,* the Pastor's friends in the house were invited to meet, after dinner, in his sitting-room. (This room is at the right-hand side of the picture, underneath the lower of the two balconies. Only the top of the window is visible, as the rest is hidden by the palm-trees.) There were nineteen present, and a very hallowed season was spent. Prayer was presented by Deacon Thompson, Mr. S. D. Waddy, Q.C., and Mr. J. W. Harrald. Mr. Spurgeon read and expounded Psalm lxxiii., and afterwards read part of his printed sermon, entitled "LET US PRAY" (No. 288), on the twenty-eighth verse of the Psalm. The portion selected contained the three sub-divisions:—(1) *Prayer explains mysteries.* (2) *Prayer brings deliverance.* (3) *Prayer obtains promises.*

Jan. 15.—A day of mingled gladness and sadness—Mrs.

Spurgeon's birthday, and also the day on which the rumours as to the death of the Duke of Clarence were proved to be only too true. Remembering the kind enquiries of the

HÔTEL BEAU RIVAGE, MENTON.

Prince of Wales during his illness, Mr. Spurgeon telegraphed to express his sympathy with the sorrowing parents; and he was especially pleased when he received a telegram conveying the Prince's "heartfelt thanks."

Jan. 17.—This afternoon, while arranging the hymns for the evening, Mr. Spurgeon said:—"I am going to give a short address to-night." Fearing that he was not well enough to do this, the friends who were present persuaded him to read something that he had already written. They knew that he was doing more mental work than he ought, though he assured them that he was only amusing himself, and that it was much worse for him to be idle than to employ his time in such literary labour as he felt able to perform without effort or weariness. He yielded to their entreaties, though he evidently wanted to have another opportunity of addressing the little company! Mr. Harrald, his faithful "armour-bearer", found out, afterwards, what text he had selected, and the divisions of the subject that he had made. Here is an exact *fac-simile* of the outline he had prepared; what would we not give to know what he would have said then upon this topic, or what he could say upon it now?

"The God of patience."—Rom. xv. 5.

> I. Who exercises patience.
> II. Who claims patience.
> III. Who works patience.
> IV. Who rewards patience.

The first hymn sung was the Scotch version of Psalm ciii.—

"O thou, my soul, bless God the Lord!"

Then the Pastor read and expounded Psalm ciii., and called on his secretary to pray. The next hymn was—

"Jerusalem the golden!"

Mr. Spurgeon then read to the twenty-one friends assembled his exposition of Matthew xv. 21—28, which

MR. J. W. HARRALD, MR. SPURGEON'S "ARMOUR-BEARER."

will appear in his forthcoming "*Commentary on Matthew's Gospel*", a work on which he spent most of his time during the last month. Prayer was presented by Pastor G. Samuel, of Birmingham, and Mr. Spurgeon announced *the last hymn he ever gave out.* How appropriate that choice poem, founded on some words of the sainted Samuel Rutherford, was to his approaching end—

> " The sands of time are sinking,
>   The dawn of heaven breaks,
> The summer morn I've sighed for,—
>   The fair, sweet morn awakes.
> Dark, dark hath been the midnight,
>   But dayspring is at hand,
> And 'glory, glory dwelleth
>   In Immanuel's land.' "

His closing prayer was peculiarly impressive; and well it might be, for it was the last act of worship at *the last service he ever conducted on earth.*

Jan. 20.—Mr. Spurgeon went to Monti for *his last drive* this morning. (See *Sword and Trowel*, May, 1890, for his own description of the scenery along the road.) In the evening, his hand was so painful from gout that he went to bed early; and from that bed he never rose.

The following day, gout in the head gave increased anxiety concerning the beloved patient, and from that time until the end, it was needful that he should be lovingly attended and carefully nursed both day and night. This service was most cheerfully and willingly rendered. No one anticipated that the illness would assume such a terrible form, although the dear sufferer assured those around him that his head ached just as it did when he returned from Essex in the summer, and he feared that he was going to be as ill as he had been at "Westwood" during those anxious months last year.

It was about this time that Mr. Spurgeon said to his armour-bearer, "*My work is done,*" and spoke of various matters that showed that he felt his end was approaching. Still, all clung to the hope that he would be spared, and even permitted to preach again; but on *Tuesday morning, January 26th*, Dr. FitzHenry was obliged to report his patient's condition as "serious." This was for many reasons, a memorable day, for it was the time appointed for bringing to the Tabernacle the thankofferings for the Pastor's partial recovery. (A full account of what took place at Menton that morning and afterwards, will be found in Mr. Harrald's address at the Tabernacle on *Wednesday morning, February 10th*, fully reported on pages 109 to 115.)

Little can be added about the following anxious days and trying nights. Dr. FitzHenry did all that medical skill, constant attention, and loving care could suggest; Mrs. Spurgeon, Miss Thorne, Mr. Harrald, Mr. Allison, and Mr. Samuel, were unceasingly watchful for opportunities of helping the beloved sufferer; but alas! for most of the time he was completely unconscious, and unable to communicate any parting word to the loved ones who waited eagerly for the faintest syllable from his dear lips. He could utter no "dying testimony"; his forty years' ministry made that unnecessary. If there is a regret that he passed away without being able to give any word of farewell, there is also the satisfaction of knowing that there was, on his part, no pain at parting from his beloved wife and family and friends, and no anxiety as to the Church, College, Orphanage, Evangelists, Colporteurs, and the many works and workers he was leaving behind him. At five minutes past eleven on Lord's-day, January 31st, 1892, the beloved Pastor entered heaven.

Home in February.

"*I shall be home in February*," was, for a long time, the Pastor's reply to everyone who asked him when he thought of being back, and *he was home* in February, in a far more real sense than any of us had supposed when we heard the words. Home! How sweet it sounds, and especially for him who, after a sojourn in the South, was ever so eager, when he turned his face homewards, to reach as quickly as possible his happy home on earth! With what intense joy he must have entered his glorious home in heaven!

Mrs. C. H. Spurgeon, who has been most marvellously sustained by the grace of our tender Lord, beautifully says: "His 'abundant entrance', the 'Well done, good and faithful servant!' of the Master, the great throng of white-robed spirits, who welcomed him as the one who first led them to the Saviour, the admiring, wondering angels, the radiant glory, the *surprise* of that midnight journey which ended at the throne of God; all this, and much more of blessed reality for him, has lifted our bowed heads, and enabled us to bless the Lord, even though he has taken from us so incomparable a friend and pastor. All that was choice, and generous, and Christlike, seemed gathered together in his character, and lived out in his life. He was pre-eminently 'the servant of all'; yet he served with such humility and wisdom, that, with him, to *serve* was to *reign*. All are feeling now the power he wielded over men's hearts; and because a prince of God, and a leader of men, has passed away, 'our houses are left unto us desolate.' I must not attempt to speak of his worth ; words would utterly fail me ; but the tears of multitudes, all over the world, testify to the irreparable loss they have sustained.

"I will tell you of one fact which has greatly comforted me in my deep grief; it will ever be a precious memory to me, and a theme of praise to God. It may rejoice your hearts also to have such an assurance from my pen. It is that the Lord so tenderly granted to us both three months of *perfect earthly happiness* here in Menton, before he took him to the 'far better' of his own glory and immediate presence! For fifteen years my beloved had longed to bring me here; but it had never before been possible. Now, we were both strengthened for the long journey; and the desire of his heart was fully given him. I can never describe the pride and joy with which he introduced me to his favourite haunts, and the eagerness with which he showed me each lovely glimpse of mountain, sea, and landscape. He was hungry for my loving appreciation, and I satisfied him to the full. We took long daily drives, and every place we visited was a triumphal entry for him. His enjoyment was intense, his delight exuberant. He *looked* in perfect health, and rejoiced in the brightest of spirits. Then, too, with what calm, deep happiness he sat, day after day, in a cosy corner of his sunny room, writing his last labour of love, *The Commentary on Matthew's Gospel!* Not a care burdened him, not a grief weighed upon his heart, not a desire remained unfulfilled, not a wish unsatisfied; he was permitted to enjoy an earthly Eden before his translation to the Paradise above. Blessed be the Lord for such sweet memories, such tender assuagement of wounds that can never quite be healed on earth! Up to the last ten days of his sweet life, health appeared to be returning, though slowly ; our hopes were strong for his full recovery, and he himself believed that he should live to declare again to his dear people, and to poor sinners, 'the unsearchable riches of Christ.'

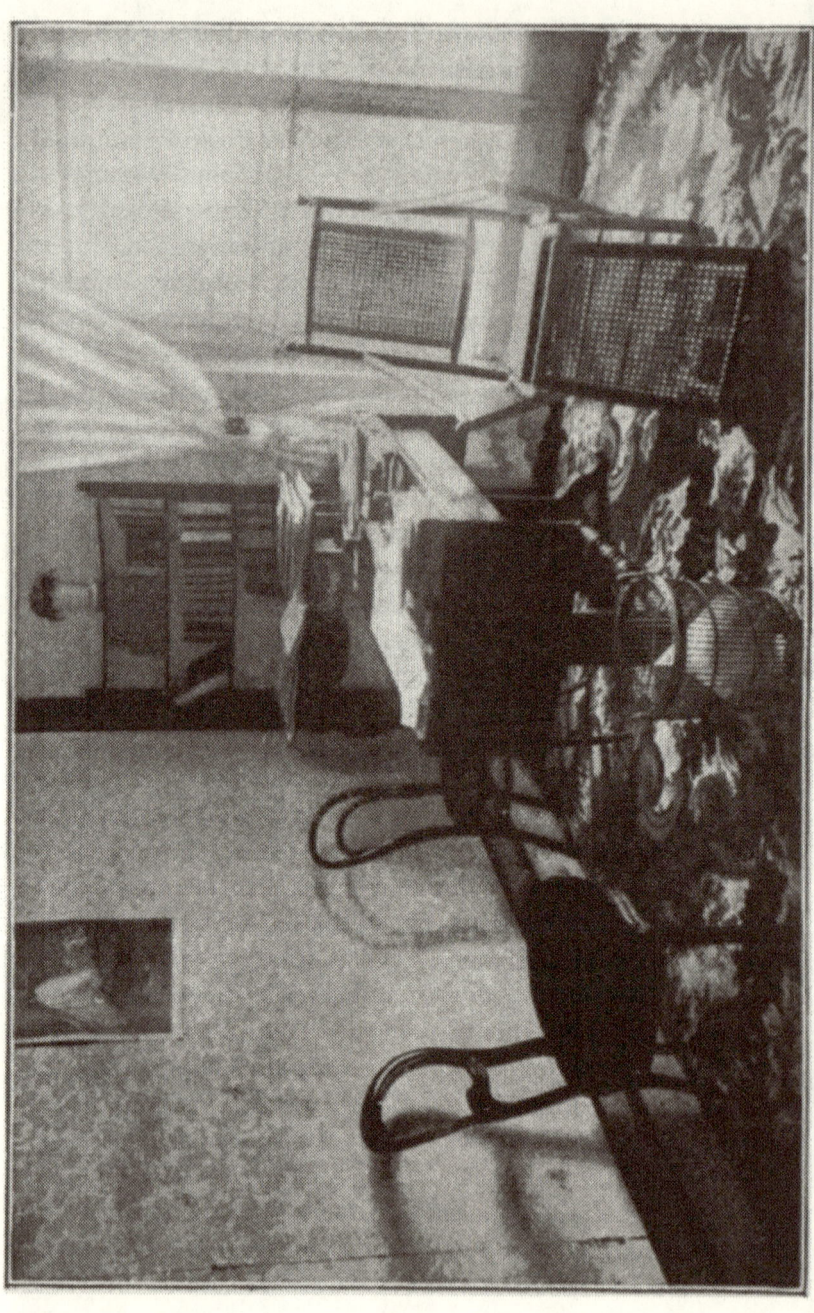

"But it was not to be, dear friends. The call came with terrible suddenness to us; but with infinite mercy to him. The prayer, 'Father, I will that they also whom thou hast given me, be with me where I am; that they may behold my glory,' was answered in his case. His Saviour wanted him up higher, and could spare him to us no longer. He is gone to his everlasting reward, and the hallelujahs of heaven must hush and rebuke the sobs and sighs of earth.'

"Looking up, with tear-dimmed eyes, to the God and Father of our Lord Jesus Christ, we can say, 'Even so, Lord, for thou hast made him most blessed for ever. Thou has made him exceeding glad with thy countenance.'"

A very favourite hymn of the departed Pastor's was, "Come, thou fount of every blessing." It was sung by the little company in the train that conveyed the Pastor and his beloved wife and friends from Herne Hill to Dover, on October 26th, 1891, and during the hallowed service at Menton, on January 10th, it was sung again.

What a new meaning has been given to the second verse :—

> "Here I raise my Ebenezer;
> Hither by thine help I'm come;
> And I hope, by thy good pleasure,
> *Safely to arrive at home*"!

Now, by the "good pleasure" of the Lord, whom he served so faithfully, he has safely arrived at home, and who are we to question the wisdom and love of him who hath taken him to himself?

To the praise of the Lord's providential arrangements, it ought to be recorded, that the very first letter opened by Mr. Spurgeon's secretary, after his leader fell asleep in Jesus, contained the notice of a legacy of £500 for the Stockwell Orphanage. Was not this a gracious indication that the Lord would still continue to provide for the five hundred fatherless children in "Mr. Spurgeon's Orphanage"? God buries his workers; but his work goes on. Doubtless he will move many of his stewards to bring of the substance with which he has entrusted them, that all parts of the work that he inspired his now glorified servant to undertake may be maintained with equal or increased efficiency.

One bright reminiscence may be given. Mrs. Spurgeon had been looking at the planets, Jupiter and Venus, which were unusually bright, even for Menton, where the stars generally shine with a brilliance unknown in our dear dull island-home. Speaking of her beloved, she said, " I wonder what he thinks of those planets now." Mr. Harrald replied, " If they are inhabited, he has asked the Lord to let him go, that he may preach the gospel there." "No doubt of it," she added, "for how often he said that, when he got to heaven, he would stand at the corner of one of the streets, and proclaim to the angels the old, old story of Jesus and his love!" This was his interpretation of the text—"To the intent that now unto the principalities and powers in heavenly places might be known by the church the manifold wisdom of God, according to the eternal purpose which he purposed in Christ Jesus our Lord."

MR. SPURGEON'S BEDROOM AFTER HIS REMOVAL.

Two Characteristic Illustrations.

During the early days of January, Mr. Spurgeon wrote the following short pieces. He was always on the alert for illustrations of spiritual truth; and these last paragraphs, one of them referring to Christian experience, and the other to Christian practice, may well be pondered now that the hand that wrote them is palsied in death. The second should especially remind us that the Institutions, formerly under the care of Mr. Spurgeon, and which will be carried on as heretofore, are still in need of generous support. Let every mercy prompt an offering from thankful hearts. The handwriting of both articles is as distinct as anything the beloved author ever penned; and those who read them will at once perceive that his mental eye was not dim, nor his spiritual force abated, when he wrote as follows:—

New Year's Day, 1892.

"At Menton, the first day of the year was as one of the days of heaven upon the earth. Almost cloudless and windless, beneath the bluest of skies, the day was warm and bright with the glorious sun. Did we draw the inference that, all the world over, New Year's Day was like summer? Did we disbelieve the paragraphs in the daily journals which told another tale of other lands? We were not so foolish.

"A certain brother has an exceedingly rapturous experience, full of confidence, communion, and conquest. Does he, therefore, conclude that all true Christian experience

VIEW OF MENTON, FROM THE BOULEVARD VICTORIA.

From Harper's Magazine.—Copyright, 1883, by Harper & Brothers.

must necessarily be of this delightful order? Does he cast a doubt upon the sincerity of others, whose spiritual weather is clouded, and even darkened with storms? Let us trust that he will not be so uncharitable, so unjust.

"But if a friend, from a land of fogs and frosts, should insinuate that our report of the New Year at Menton was fanciful and fictitious, because he had experienced far different weather, would he not be very ungenerous? So the brother of sombre spirit and troubled experience is not acting as he should do when he judges the cheerful as being frivolous, condemns the rapturous as excitable, and looks upon the confident as presumptuous. He has no right to set up his painful experience as the standard by which to discern the people of God; neither is he justified in denying the possibility of unbroken peace because he has never long enjoyed it.

"We may not judge others by ourselves. We may not infer general facts from individual cases. We must take into consideration a thousand things, and many of these we do not know: wherefore, let us not judge, that we be not judged."—C. H. S.

Provocatives of Generosity.

"The mail from India brings news of the narrow escape from death of the ruler of the State of Morvi, on the 18th November, 1891. It is said that his Highness was at his stables on the evening of that day, and found his grooms searching for a snake that had been seen half-an-hour before. The pursuit was, however, given up, and the Prince drove out as usual. On the way, he suddenly felt a warm sensation on his chest. He had put on an overcoat; and as he unbuttoned it, a black, venomous cobra fell to the ground in a heavy coil, and glided away. His Highness drove back at once to the palace, and distributed a sum of Rs. 500 among the poor, and gave feasts the following morning.

"We, too, have seen a deadlier serpent drop at our feet; but have we been as practical in our gratitude as this Indian Prince? The deadly thing was coiled about our heart, and only by a miracle of grace have we been delivered from its venomous tooth: have we shown our thankfulness to Christ Jesus our Lord by helping his poor people with our substance? Have we made feasts for his saints by the utterance of the Lord's goodness?

"Every time we have a providential escape, or a gracious rescue from temptation, let us think of the Rajah of Morvi, and make haste to celebrate the happy event by bountiful liberality. If such were the case, one could see a new reason for the existence of black cobras, and other dangers: they would become provocatives of generosity."—C. H. S.

Memorial Service at Menton.

When it was finally decided that the remains of the beloved Pastor were to be laid to rest in England, it was felt that there must be a Memorial Service in the little town where he had spent so many winters, and had been so great a blessing to many people in various ways. It was also felt that there was no place so suitable for such a service as the Scotch Presbyterian Church, for Mr. Spurgeon had preached at the opening of that building, just about a year previously, the sermon which was afterwards published under the title of "Redemption through Blood, the Gracious Forgiveness of Sins" (No. 2,207). The minister of the church, Rev. J. E. Somerville, B.D., made all the arrangements, in consultation with Mr. Allison and Mr. Harrald, and in accordance with the wishes of Mrs. Spurgeon.

Thursday, February 4th, was "a real Menton morning"—not a cloud could be seen in the bright blue sky, the sun made the Mediterranean glisten like "a sea of glass mingled with fire", and everything in nature seemed to remind us of the joy into which our loved and lost leader had entered, in the land where—

"Everlasting spring abides,
And never-withering flowers."

There were many sad hearts among the representatives of all sections of the Christian church, who gathered around the olive-wood casket enclosing the precious body. Canon Sidebotham and the Rev. A. M. Topp, the ministers of the two Episcopal churches, were there, with Rev. Talbot

Greaves, M.A., vicar of Clifton, Revs. Arthur W. Phelps, R. Logan, and other clergy from "The House of Rest"; Rev. J. Lings, a constant Menton visitor, and friend of Mr. Spurgeon; Mr. C. E. Faithfull, the sailors' friend, from Marseilles; M. Palmaro, the British Vice-Consul, Dr. FitzHenry (Mr. Spurgeon's medical attendant and faithful friend), Mrs. Hanbury, and all of the Menton circle who could possibly attend.

Many friends sent very beautiful wreaths, for the dear one went home from the land of flowers; but Mrs. Spurgeon contributed *palm-branches*, as the most appropriate emblems of the victory of her beloved, as he stood with the great multitude "before the throne, and before the Lamb, clothed with white robes, and palms, in their hands, and cried with a loud voice, saying, Salvation to our God which sitteth upon the throne, and unto the Lamb."

The hymn beginning—
"Give me the wings of faith to rise,"
was sung. Prayer was offered by Rev. Dr. Murray Mitchell of Nice; and Mr. Somerville read Isaiah xl. 1-8, 1 Corinthians xv. 19-26, and 53-57; 2 Corinthians iv. 17—v. 10; and Revelation vii. 9-17; and then delivered the following address:—

"In the presence of the dead, words of man seem inappropriate, and eulogy is out of place. A prince and a great man is fallen in Israel. We meet, to-day, a company of mourners, and we desire to join in their mourning, the family, the congregation, and that wide circle who have sustained so sore a bereavement; for Charles Spurgeon belonged not to the Metropolitan Tabernacle only, nor to London, nor to England, but to all English-speaking countries, and to many others besides.

"In him, God bestowed upon our *age* and on the *world* a great gift; and we are thankful that for so many years he was permitted to witness with such fearlessness, eloquence, and power, for the Lord, whom it was his delight to serve; and that he was honoured to be the instrument of salvation to multitudes, many of whom never saw his face.

"That active life is over here. No more shall that mellow and wondrous voice (the first that was heard in this church) plead with men, nor the ready pen counsel and delight. The labourer rests. The warrior's 'sword' lies idle, the 'trowel' has fallen from the workman's hand, because the Master has said 'Come.'

"'Charles Haddon Spurgeon is dead,' many are saying to-day; nay, not dead, but entered on life more abundant. The chamber of suffering has been exchanged for the land where the inhabitant shall no more say, 'I am sick.' He has gone from us; but he sees the King in his beauty.

"Shall we lament because another voice has been added to the chorus of the redeemed above, that the servant has been rewarded, that the victor has been crowned? Gone *home*, not gone *away*, he is present with the Lord. In *one more* the Saviour has seen of the travail of his soul.

"Only four days ago we prayed that he might be spared to us, and be allowed to labour longer; but Jesus prayed, 'Father, I will that they also whom thou hast given me be with me where I am, that they may behold my glory.' We cannot now wish that that prayer had been denied.

"Shall we selfishly grudge *the Lord* satisfaction over his redeemed, or *our brother* the blessedness and joy of the Master's welcome, 'Well done, good and faithful servant, enter thou into the joy of thy Lord'?

"He has been called away in his prime, when to us his presence seemed necessary, and when he gave promise of years of usefulness. But his work was done, and we must learn to say—

> 'Just when *thou* wilt, O Master, call,
> Or at the noon or evening fall;
> Or in the *dark*, or in the *light*,
> Just when thou wilt, it must be right.'

FUNERAL CORTÈGE AT MENTON STATION.

So we bow the head, and say, 'The will of the Lord be done. Hallelujah!'"

Pasteur Delapierre, of the French Evangelical Church, spoke in French concerning the great influence exerted by our departed friend over the French-speaking churches, and bore testimony to his fidelity to the revealed Word, his practical charity to all men, and his humility and love, which endeared him to so many. M. Delapierre also offered prayer for the bereaved family, friends, and church. Mr. Harrald delivered Mrs. Spurgeon's message to the congregation: "If you want to tell them anything from me, say—

'HE hath done all things well,'"

and gave some touching reminiscences of his beloved leader's last days. Pastor G. Samuel, of Birmingham, spoke on behalf of the 800 ministers trained in the Pastors' College, and especially referred to the tenderness and gentleness of the departed President. The hymn—

"For ever with the Lord,"

was solemnly sung, and then all stood while the coffin was carried to the open hearse, which proceeded at once to the railway station, followed by probably a larger and sadder company of mourners then ever gathered for a Protestant funeral at Menton.

The Bereaved Church.

Almost as soon as it became known in London that our beloved Pastor had entered heaven, the meetings of the bereaved church at the Tabernacle began. *Monday, the first of February*, had previously, at his suggestion, been set apart as a day of prayer that the epidemic of influenza, which then prevailed, might be removed. The prayer-meetings were held, and a very speedy answer was given, for the disease abated the same week; but little did anyone imagine that the gatherings thus arranged would be turned to such solemn purpose as they were that day. With but little interval, the people met together during the morning and afternoon; and in the evening, an immense prayer-meeting was held, one of the largest ever known, even at the Tabernacle, and, amidst the hush of stricken hearts, God visited his people, and spoke peace to many. Mr. Spurgeon's own version of the thirty-ninth Psalm, often used at these Memorial gatherings, was then sung with deep feeling, for the first time.

Every succeeding day, informal meetings were held, and on *Thursday, February 4th*, Dr. Pierson, who has stood like a giant, strong in faith, all through the trying ordeal, preached from Psalm xc. 16 and 17, a sermon for which everyone who heard it afterwards expressed the utmost gratitude. It was just such a steadying message as was needed at this great crisis in the history of the church. The little-faith of many was rebuked; and new hope born that, though the chief worker was removed, the work of God would be established; and that the beauty of the Lord would yet be given instead of mourning, ay, even in the midst of the sorrow.

Lord's-day morning, February 7*th—the first Lord's-day without a Pastor*—dawned grey and misty. Many an aching heart turned wistfully towards the place of solemn assembly, with mingled feelings of faith and fear. Very early, meetings for prayer were convoked, and the spirits of those who attended them were thus braced for the more public gatherings. A great crowd, dressed in deep mourning, filled the building in every corner.

Rev. JAMES A. SPURGEON opened with the following prayer: "Our Father, which art in heaven, whither thou hast taken the beloved pastor of this church, we cling to thine unseen arm; hold us up.

"Hallowed be thy name; it is everlasting.

"Thy kingdom come; it shall have no end.

"Thy will be done on earth, as it is in heaven—not our will, but *thy* will be done.

"Give us this day our daily bread, for our hearts are hungry. Break, through thy dear servant, our brother Pierson, the bread of life to us to-day.

"Forgive us our trespasses, and let the blood of Jesus Christ cleanse us from all sin; as we here to-day forgive all that have trespassed against us.

"Lead us not into temptation. Though thou hast tried us as silver is tried, yet, with all our trials which have abounded; thy consolations have much more abounded, praise be to thy name.

"Deliver us from the evil one, and from every evil thought, word, or act, in connection with this thy hand and dispensation, or anywhere, life-long.

"For thine is the kingdom; and we bless thee for it, and

PASTOR JAMES A. SPURGEON.

thou shalt reign whose right it is, from sea to sea, and from the river to the ends of the earth. And thine is the power; hold us up in our weakness, and the widow and the fatherless and the mourner everywhere, and specially those on our hearts here to-day. And thine is the glory, for we glorify thee in the fire now and for evermore. Amen."

Though the tension of heart and mind was intense, Dr. Pierson, evidently helped by our Covenant God, upon whom he had cast himself without reserve, was able in the reading, and in prayer, to speak comfortable words to the people, and in the sermon he led the people away from their own loss to their Pastor's exceeding gain.

On the evening of the Lord's-day, such crowds flocked to the familiar rallying-point, that, before the time of service, the Tabernacle was densely thronged with a subdued, black-robed congregation. The number of those unable to gain admission was so great as to fill the open space inside the railings in front, and to reach across the road. Dr. Pierson again preached with great power.

The great Communion Service followed. He who has missed seeing one of these services at the Tabernacle, has missed a sight unique in Christendom. The body of the building, and half the first gallery, filled with communicants, and the rest of the space occupied with interested spectators, is almost an overwhelming spectacle at any time. But now, with the Pastor's chair empty, it was quite overpowering. With few words, and quiet movement, the simple emblems of our Lord's death were taken in token of his body broken and his blood shed for his people. As Christ's death has become the gate of life, it was felt then that perhaps the removal of C. H. Spurgeon might become, by the overruling grace of God, a deep and widespread benediction.

DR. A. T. PIERSON.

At the close of the Communion Service, Deacon Thomas H. Olney read a statement to the church, which gave universal satisfaction. By unanimous voice of the officers, Rev. James A. Spurgeon had been desired and had consented to continue as *Pastor in charge*, and Dr. Pierson had also, in response to an earnest appeal to that effect, expressed his willingness to continue as *Officiating Minister*. Only one sentiment prevailed in reference to this temporary arrangement, and that was deep gratitude. We all thanked God that, though one brother had been taken, the other was left. As we had never known how much we loved our departed Pastor until he was called away from us, we never knew how much we esteemed and valued his brother until he was left alone. Nobly has he fulfilled his part, and as, between him and Dr. Pierson, for whom we devoutly thank God, there exists a most fraternal union; and between them both and the church, the heartiest sympathy; long may the ministry continue, which has so auspiciously begun!

(This arrangement was unanimously ratified at the Annual Church Meeting held on March 1st.)

The Blessedness of the Holy Dead.

A SERMON DELIVERED BY
REV. ARTHUR T. PIERSON, D.D.,
IN THE METROPOLITAN TABERNACLE,
On Lord's-day Morning, February 7th, 1892.

"And I heard a voice from heaven saying unto me, Write, Blessed are the dead which die in the Lord from henceforth: Yea, saith the Spirit, that they may rest from their labours; and their works do follow them."—Rev. xiv. 13.

From the beginning of this great sorrow there is one text, and one only, to which my mind has turned, and which therefore I take to be the message of God to his bereaved people.

Very seldom in the course of human history has a voice ever been heard from heaven, but never unless some most august and important announcement was to be made. Heaven is not opened in vain: and the celestial voice that speaks with divine authority is never heard unless the occasion justifies the utterance. There are three remarkable signs that something is contained in this verse which is of no ordinary moment and magnitude. First, there is the voice from heaven: secondly, there is the command to record the message, for permanence, in the body of Holy Scripture, "saying unto me, Write": and thirdly, there is the "Yea" of the Holy Spirit, as though the Spirit must add his emphatic testimony, that, in the mouth of two witnesses, both of them divine, every word shall be established. One feels a certain sense of awe in approaching a text surrounded by such magnificent evidences of its superlative importance : a voice from heaven ; a command to write ; and the "Yea" of the Holy Spirit. Let us therefore, in the spirit of little children, seeking not so much to frame a discourse, as to open our ears while God discourses, look at the individual phrases of this remarkable text.

I. In the first place, "Blessed are the dead which die in the Lord from henceforth." That latter expression, "from henceforth," is one of the most difficult that exegetes, or expositors of the Bible, have ever confronted. It may refer to a new point of departure with regard to the blessed dead ; it may refer to a new point of departure with respect to the revelation of that blessedness ; and it may refer to a new point of departure in reference to the testimony of the Spirit. We may connect it with the second part of the verse instead of the first. "I heard a voice from heaven saying unto me, Write, Blessed are the dead which die in the Lord ; Yea, saith the Spirit, from henceforth ; that they may rest from their labours." But you perceive that, while there is some doubt as to the application of the phrase, we are in this case embarrassed by riches, for the applications of the phrase are so many and possibly so varied. It may be that, being put in the middle of this verse, it looks both backward to the beginning of the verse and forward to its conclusion, so that it indicates somehow, alike in the redemption of God, and in the revelation of Christ, and in the testimony of the Spirit, a new point of departure—" from henceforth."

Certainly there is one very conspicuous fact, namely, that the resurrection of Jesus Christ appears to mark a new epoch with respect even to the *terms used* about the departed saints of God. Stephen was the first martyr, and, in fact, his death was the first which is placed on record in the pages of Holy Scripture—the first recorded death of a believer in Jesus—subsequent to Christ's resurrection. And, notwithstanding the agony in which he must have died, under the stoning of his enemies, his death is manifestly a typical death, and the description of it has a typical significance. For we read, "He, being full of the Holy Ghost, looked up steadfastly into heaven, and saw the glory of God, and Jesus standing on the right hand of God; and said, Behold, I see the heavens opened, and the Son of man standing on the right hand of God." "And they stoned Stephen, calling upon God, and saying, Lord Jesus, receive my spirit." "And when he had said this, he fell asleep." Three marked features are there, evidently typical: in the first place, a vision of heaven and of Christ; in the second place, perfect peace of mind, even amid the agonies of a violent death; and in the third place, a new term applied to death—"he fell asleep." From the time of the resurrection of Christ to the last chapter of the Apocalypse you will scarcely once find the death of a believer referred to as death, without some qualifying phrase attached to it. There is one exception. In the ninth chapter of the Acts of the Apostles we read of the death of Dorcas, or Tabitha, and the word "died" is used with reference to her, although she was a believer. But the reason is obvious. Peter was about, in the name of Christ, to call her back from death to life, and therefore it was important that the actual fact of her death should be unmistakably stated. Had it been said of her that "she fell asleep," it might have been thought that Peter simply roused her from a trance; but when it was declared that she "died," there could be no doubt of her actual miraculous resuscitation from the dead. But in every other case that I have been able to trace in the New Testament the death of a believer is never once referred to as "death," except with some such qualifying phrase as we find in this text—"die in the Lord," which at once separates such death from the death of an unbeliever.

So important is this fact, as bearing upon the phrase "from henceforth" in this text, that it will amply repay us to examine more fully and in detail the terms used to describe the decease of God's saints.

For instance, take the first epistle to the Corinthians, chapter xv., which contains a long discourse on the subject of death and the resurrection. In the sixth verse we read that Christ "was seen of about five hundred brethren at once, of whom the greater part remain unto this present but some are fallen asleep." Then in the twentieth verse, we read, "But now is Christ risen from the dead, and is become the first-fruits of them that slept." Then, again, in the fifty-first verse, "Behold, I show you a mystery; we shall not all sleep, but we shall all be changed, in a moment." In the second epistle to the Corinthians, fifth chapter, we have another reference to the death of a believer, but again the word, "death," even the thought of death, is avoided: "For we know that if our earthly house of this tabernacle were dissolved"—a tent falling to pieces, and the inhabitants going out to take another habitation. "Not for that we would be unclothed, but clothed upon": the death of a believer is being unclothed as to the vesture of mortality, and being clothed upon with the vesture of immortality. And then, again, in the eighth verse, "We are confident, I say, and willing rather to be absent from the body"—out of home from the body—"and to be present with the Lord"—at home with the Lord. Then we turn to Paul's letter to the Philippians, chapter first, and the twenty-first verse, "For to me to live is Christ, and to die is gain." There the word "die" is used, but in connection with gain; and immediately, as it were, Paul abandons the word "death," and says in the twenty-third verse, "For I am in a strait betwixt two, having a desire to depart and to be with Christ, which is far better." And then, again, in the first Epistle to the Thessalonians, chapter four, thirteenth and fourteenth verses, "I would not have you to be ignorant, brethren, concerning them which are asleep, that ye sorrow not, even as others who have no hope. For if we believe that Jesus died and rose again, even so them also which sleep in Jesus will God bring with him." Then we turn to the second epistle to Timothy, and in the fourth chapter and the sixth verse, we read, "I am now ready to be offered, and the time of my departure is at hand." The Greek word for departure means to let loose, in order to depart, as the cables that hold a vessel to her moorings are loosed, in order that she may sail out for her haven. "I am ready to be offered; and the time when my bark un-loosens from her fastenings that she may enter the eternal harbour, is close at hand"; and yet he was looking forward to decapitation in the arena under the orders of Nero. And once more—without further prolonged study of this topic—Peter says in his second epistle, chapter i. verse 14, "Knowing that shortly I must put off," or lay aside, "this my tabernacle, even as our Lord Jesus Christ hath shewed me."

This somewhat detailed examination may help my fellow believers in this congregation to appreciate the fact, which possibly they have never appreciated before, that the resurrection of Jesus Christ marks a new departure in the death of believers, as least, as to the revelation of the blessedness and the glory into which they have entered; so that, after Christ died and rose again, it was necessary to have a new nomenclature, a new set of terms, to describe the departure of the saint to be with his Lord. It would no longer do to call it "death," for there has been a new apocalypse of the glory of those that "die in the Lord."

II. In the second place, notice that qualifying phrase, "in the Lord." It is no exaggeration to declare of that one phrase, "in the Lord," that no more important single phrase is to be found in the New Testament Scriptures. Any student of the Word of God in the original tongues will know that the little phrase, ἐν Χριστῷ ("in Christ"), is the key to every epistle of the New Testament. The magnificent thought, suggested by those two or three little Greek words, is something beyond the power of any man to set forth properly: "in Christ Jesus." Christ seems to be imagined and pictured forth by the Holy Ghost on the pages of Holy Scripture as a great divine sphere, vast as immensity and eternity, vast as the love and grace of God. And the circumference of that sphere marks the difference between sin and holiness, between condemnation and justification, between hell and heaven. By faith in Jesus, the penitent believer enters into that sphere, and thus crosses the line of circumference that separates between a state of sin and condemnation and judgment, and a state of holiness and justification and salvation. He is now henceforth "in Christ." We have no term to express the grandeur of this thought—insphered in Christ. "Who is he that can harm you if ye be followers of that which is good?" What dart or arrow can penetrate the circumference of that sphere in which the believer is embraced and hidden with his Lord? "The Only Begotten of God keeps him that that Wicked One toucheth him not." And if you are thus in Christ Jesus, you are saved, already saved. The moment that you enter into that sphere you are in God. The world is outside of you, the broken law outside of you, the gulf of perdition outside of you. You are in holiness if you are in him, you are in justification if you are in him, you are in sanctification if you are in him; you are already, virtually, in heaven if you are in him. And so in the epistle to the Ephesians we have that strange expression, ἐν τοῖς ἐπουρανίοις translated into "heavenly *places*." But there is no word for "places" in the original; it is "in the heavenlies." We are not in the heavenly places yet; we are in the earthly places. But if you are a child of God and a believer in Christ, you are introduced to the heavenly states and experiences and joys and privileges; and, when you go to heaven itself, there will be scarcely a joy absolutely new to you, except the actual sight of your Master himself; for you will have had, as in gentle droppings from above, a foretaste and an earnest of what you are going to have in full perfection there.

That phrase, "in the Lord," must have at least three great interpretations. In the first place, a redemptive interpretation, to which we have referred. The penitent believer goes from the world, and from sin, and from Satan, and from condemnation, redemptively, into this divine sphere of safety, holiness and happiness. In the second place, actively and actually; for a believer's life is taken into the life of Christ, his work taken up into the work of Christ, his destiny taken into the destiny of Christ, his life-plan embraced in the eternal plan of God. So the apostle says (Romans xiv. 7, 8.): "None of us liveth to himself; and no man dieth to himself; for whether we live, we live unto the Lord; and whether we die, we die unto the Lord; whether we live, therefore, or die, we are the Lord's." Oh, the magnificence of the thought! Would to God we could rise to it, and feel its glorious reality! While you live you are in this sphere in Christ Jesus. Are you any less in that sphere when you die, when you fall asleep as to your body, and, as to your spirit, you are at home with the Lord? The apostle says, that the disciple that lives unto the Lord, dies unto the Lord; the Lord has not surrendered his control of him when death comes upon him. Neither has the believer lost his identity and unity with Jesus when he falls asleep. We are thus redemptively in the Lord, and actively and actually in the Lord. And what shall I call this other, but being *immortally* in the Lord? We are still in the Lord when we fall asleep, and it is unto the Lord that we die, even as it is unto the Lord that we have lived.

III. But we turn now to look at the concluding part of this great text, "Yea, saith the Spirit, that they may rest from their labours; and their works do follow them." The first part of this statement, "they rest from their labours," is to occupy our thoughts hereafter more fully, and we may pass it now with a word. There is absolute rest, for every believer who is at home with the Lord, from everything of the nature of vexation, of task, of toil, of physical, intellectual, moral, and spiritual limitation; from infirmity, sickness, disappointment, and disaster. All these and all else, which mar the perfection of our service in this world and interfere with the perfection of our joy in God, we leave behind us when, absent from the body, we are present with the Lord.

But let us fasten our thoughts for a moment on the last expression, "and their works do follow them." That is another difficult phrase to interpret: difficult, as has been said before of another phrase—only because of the embarrassment from the various applications which may be made of it. There are three prominent applications which may be suggested. One is that the works, which are done in Christ Jesus, survive the departing saint and remain as his memorial and monument in this world. A second suggestion is, that the works which he has done here follow after him into eternity as witnesses before the throne of God to his fidelity, and as the means of increasing the measure and glory of his reward. And there is a third interpretation, which I venture to propose, and which, I believe, will commend itself to your approval. The Greek word translated "follow" may mean "to follow as one who goes immediately behind and treads in another's footsteps—to accompany." It is like the following of a disciple, close on the heels of his Master just before him; the following of companionship and fellowship. This interpretation is both suggested and confirmed by the difference in the terms of the original, which appears also in the English translation: "they rest from their *labours;*" but "their *works* do follow them." What is the difference between labour and work? Labour, both in the Latin and in the English word derived from it, as also in the original Greek word in this text, suggests the idea of toil amid hindrance and difficulty and weariness—burden bearing. It suggests the thought that one is doing a task that taxes his strength, and fatigues him so that he comes from his work, wearied and worn; it carries the notion of strength unequal to the task, so that one faints at times, or feels himself circumscribed with limitations that he is impotent to throw off. But the word "work" means simply activity, doing, endeavouring, performing.

How blessed is the thought that the Holy Ghost suggests to us! When a saint of God falls asleep as to his body, and enters into the presence of his Lord, as to his spirit for evermore, the *labours*, the toils, the vexations of this world, he leaves behind him; but he carries with him into immortality his *service*. He goes to carry on his work for God, for that is as immortal as God himself. He goes where no limitations exist, where no vexations and hindrances circumscribe his activity, where "they rest not," because they are never tired nor fatigued; where, as they wait on the Lord, they renew their strength, mount up with wings as eagles, run and are never weary, walk and never faint. The tireless and endless activity of a redeemed soul partakes of the tireless energy of an untiring God. Let us not suppose, for a moment, that when a man who has spent his life in seeking to serve God, who has stored his mind with all manner of accumulations, and, with the tension of persistent effort, sought to acquire and achieve all that is possible for his Master; who has laid the foundation-stone of great institutions, has scattered abroad throughout the world the testimony of his faith and his courage for his Master's sake— let us not suppose for a moment that, when such a man falls, as we say, at the blow of death, his service ceases. God is a better οἰκονόμος, economist, housekeeper, than that. He is no such wasteful keeper of his eternal house. When a saint departs to be with Christ, instead of leaving service behind, he enters on a new sphere of service, where, instead of sacrificing acquisitions and attainments, he rather finds an absolutely perfect scope for the exercise of them all; instead of ceasing to work for his Master, he rather begins his work anew in the tirelessness of celestial energy.

What man may think about this is of no consequence; what does the Word of God testify concerning it? I have gathered together some few of the precious testimonies of the Word on this subject for my own comfort, and for your comfort as well. In the twentieth chapter of the Gospel of Luke, verse 38, Jesus Christ, rebuking the errors of the Sadducees, who said there was no resurrection, and no separate existence of angel or spirit apart from the body, says, referring to Moses, who at the bush called the Lord the God of Abraham and of Isaac and Jacob, "He is not the God of the dead, but of the living: for all (even all the dead) live unto him." That phrase, "Live unto him," is used scores of times in the Word of God to express the idea of service. "Whether we live, we live unto the Lord," &c. In this Book of Revelation itself testimonies are massed upon this subject. In chapter vii., verse 15, John gets one of the first and most glorious glimpses into the blessedness of departed saints when the elder answers, when asked as to the white-robed throng, "They are before the throne of God, and serve him day and night in his temple." In the fourteenth chapter of the Book of Revelation we find the text itself: "Blessed are the dead which die in the Lord from henceforth: Yea, saith the Spirit, that they may rest from their vexatious toils: but their activities go with them." In chapter xxii., the closing chapter, we find the sevenfold description of the glory of the heavenly host and the heavenly home. "And there shall be no more curse"—perfect sinlessness. "But the throne of God and of the Lamb shall be in it"—perfect government. "And his servants shall serve him"—perfect service. "And they shall see his face"—perfect communion. "And his name shall be in their foreheads"—perfect resemblance. "And there shall be no night there"—perfect day. "And they shall reign for ever and ever"—perfect glory. In the midst of this sevenfold description there stands that central and commanding sentence, "And his servants shall serve him." Surely service is the centre of the blessedness of heaven, service in its perfection!

This congregation is to-day staggering under the weight of an irreparable loss. It is admitted, on all sides, that the century in which we live has seen no other man that, as a gospel preacher, was the equal of Charles Haddon Spurgeon. I am profoundly convinced that we shall never again see another like him. I should be untrue to myself and untrue to you if I attempted in the slightest degree to conceal the fact that the shadow of an almost inconsolable grief has fallen upon the largest congregation of believers within the bounds of Christendom. But it is not the office of a Christian minister to aggravate such grief. We are bidden to "comfort one another with these words" of God, and I have sought, being providentially thrust into this responsible position without my own will, to point you to the testimony of the Word of God, that it might be possible, leaning on the arm of a divine and unfaltering strength, to avoid being utterly prostrated and wrecked in hope by this unspeakable loss. Suffer me, beside those words of comfort which I have already brought to you from the precious Word of God, to suggest two or three closing reflections.

We are not now attempting to exhaust the testimony to this beloved Pastor. This day is but the beginning of a week of funeral services, at which the tributes to him will cover every department of his character and his career. But just now, in sympathy with the theme we have considered, may I pluck a few sweet "apples" from God's blessed tree of consolation, and put them into your hand?

"The Lord gave, and the Lord hath taken away." It is all "the Lord's doing." A gardener walked through the conservatory and looked upon the valuable plants that had just come into bloom, and, seeing one of the flowers freshly plucked from its stem, he said to his servant, "Who plucked that flower?" The servant said "The master," and the gardener held his peace, and answered never a word. "I was dumb with silence, I opened not my mouth because thou didst it." The Master has plucked one of the fairest flowers of the century, and we must answer never a word. We bow in awe before what is, perhaps, the most mysterious dealing of God with his church that has come to our knowledge in this generation. But, blessed be God! what is a mystery to us is no mystery to him. And he says to us, "What I do thou knowest not now, but thou shalt know hereafter." It is God's doing. It behoves us to keep silence; to accept the mystery and wait patiently for its explanation. But your departed Pastor belongs from henceforth to the blessed dead which die in the Lord. It will go far to wipe the tears away from your eyes, to think of your Pastor as having been seven days in heaven. He knows more to-day than all the philosophers and wise men on the face of the earth. Even the knowledge that he had, in this world, of his Saviour, has comparatively vanished away, for now he stands face to face with him in the glory. He has kissed the feet that were pierced for him; and, full of the ecstatic vision of the Master whom he loved, not even the wants and woes of this congregation would bring him, from that hidden glory, down to the toils and vexations of earth again. His works have gone with him, and they are already rewarding him in the presence of God.

Think of the meeting there at midnight, on the thirty-first day of January, when Charles Haddon Spurgeon heard the voice from heaven, saying, "Come up hither, and I will shew thee things which must be hereafter!" In

1816, William A. B. Johnson, missionary of the Church Missionary Society, went down to Sierra Leone, to labour among the refuse population of that colony of rescued slaves. In 1821, after five years of careful, prayerful toil, he had built his model state and had organized these slaves, gathered from the holds of slave-ships, into a well-ordered and thriving Christian community, where honourable trades and callings and learned professions were represented, and where the colonists, clothed and in their right mind, occupied their own neat, beautiful and well-ordered homes, and assembled in the house of God for praise and prayer. Another cargo of slaves, 217 in number, being landed at the colony, they were sent to Regent's Town, where the model state had been organized, that they might enter as constitutent elements into that colony, under the control of Mr. Johnson. He tells us that, on that day in May, 1821, he saw a sight that, for pathos and for grandeur, eclipsed anything that he had ever seen before. As those hundreds of rescued slaves arrived in the town, the members of the colony, with one mind and heart, rushed forth from their houses to afford these new-comers a cordial Christian welcome; and, as Mr. Johnson was passing along the street, he heard shouts of acclamation that made the very heavens seem to resound with their echo; and his converted colonists came running to him, and one after another said, "Oh, Mr. Johnson! there is my brother! there is my sister! yonder is my father! yonder is my mother! my son! my daughter!" In those freshly rescued slaves, these men and women, who had been redeemed from the filth, the misery, the poverty of their depraved, degraded condition, recognized their long-lost relatives and friends. When the Pastor entered the glory that midnight on last Lord's-day, one can almost imagine that shouts rent the air of heaven, as thousands and tens of thousands who had been brought to Christ, by that loving voice which we are never to hear on earth again, and by those printed sermons that, like leaves of the tree of life, have been borne away as on the wings of the wind for the healing of the nations—that thousands and tens of thousands—and it may be hundreds of thousands—of whom he had never heard, who had found a blessing through his voice or his pen, and had found their way into heaven before him—were at the gate ready with their acclamations to welcome him, through whom they had also "found him of whom Moses in the law and the prophets did write: Jesus of Nazareth, the son of Joseph."

Your Pastor's reward has, seven days ago, begun in the higher and heavenly sphere. Think not that I make light of your grief. God knows I owe too much to Charles Haddon Spurgeon myself for whatever little power there is in my ministry, or strength in my faith, or courage and confidence in my espousal of neglected and despised truths, not to share most keenly in this sorrow. But the time has come for us to look up; we must not look down; we shall go down if we look down. And if we look up by faith we may see the door opened in heaven, and see there that beloved man who shall never more know weakness or infirmity, from whose eyes all tears have been forever wiped away, who shall never henceforth find it difficult to serve his Master, and whose work shall never more be a vexatious and wearisome toil. To him already there have been disclosed the sheaves of a vast harvest, whose seed he sowed beside all waters; much of the seed that he thus scattered was borne away from his own sight, and the results of his own unselfish husbandry were disclosed only when he stood before his Master in the ecstasy of the heavenly life.

"Blessed are the dead which die in the Lord from henceforth: Yea, saith the Spirit, that they may rest from their labours; and their works do follow them." God is saying to this congregation to-day: "Be up and doing;

work while the day lasts; whatsoever thy hand findeth to do, do it with thy might." And especially is God saying to the unconverted members of this congregation, " Remember the words that he spake unto you, being yet present with you." If his voice did not bring you to Christ while he lived, will you not let that voice which speaks to you from his coffin persuade you to come to the Christ that he still presses on your believing and affectionate choice? Will you not help to accumulate his reward, even now when he has gone from you, by coming within the circumference of the great sphere of grace, in Jesus Christ? " Being dead, he yet speaketh "; he beseeches you with celestial earnestness to live unto the Lord from this day, and die unto the Lord when the summons comes to you. Then, with him, you shall fall at the feet of your common Saviour in the ascriptions of endless praise. Amen.

A Door Opened in Heaven.

A SERMON DELIVERED BY
REV. ARTHUR T. PIERSON, D.D.,
IN THE METROPOLITAN TABERNACLE,
On Lord's-day Evening, February 7th, 1892.

"After this I looked, and, behold, a door was opened in heaven: and the first voice which I heard was as it were of a trumpet talking with me; which said, Come up hither, and I will shew thee things which must be hereafter."—REV. iv. 1.

This book is called the "Apocalypse," because it is the opening of hidden things, the revelation of mysteries kept secret from the foundation of the world. The first three chapters are prefatory and introductory. They contain a salutation, and then an account of the personal vision of the ascended and glorified Christ, with a record of the messages which he dictated to his servant John to be written to the seven churches of Asia Minor. This fourth chapter opens with the words, "After this I looked, and, behold, a door was opened in heaven." That is to say, at the beginning of the fourth chapter we start with the Apocalypse proper, or the unfolding of the marvellous mysteries of heaven. "A door was opened in heaven"—it is the first time a door was ever opened into those great mysteries, and a believer bidden to "come up hither and behold the things that shall be hereafter": the first time, except, perhaps, when the apostle Paul was caught up to the third heaven. Certainly to the same degree and with the same explicit declaration of these mysteries, we have no other such vision of heaven in the

Word of God: if a believer had ever before had knowledge so complete of the marvels of that celestial world, he had never come back to earth to reveal them to men. Here is "a door opened in heaven"; a celestial "voice" that speaks with divine authority; and a "shewing" or revelation of the hereafter.

The scene is thus transferred from earth to heaven, from the present to the future, from the here to the hereafter. And if you will follow, step by step, the nineteen chapters that constitute the remainder of this book of the Apocalypse, you will find that everything proper to be communicated or possible to be communicated, concerning that marvellous and mysterious sphere of life, has been at least outlined on the pages of this holy record. Surely it is not strange that, in the midst of a great sorrow like this for you, and a great triumph like this for him who has departed, we should gladly get a glimpse of the abode where he is, and the joy that in the future state awaits all fellow believers. So may God help us to get out of this word of revelation the balm of a divine comfort! Let us look through this open door, and see what John saw.

First of all he saw a throne and him that sat upon it, and a rainbow round about the throne in sight like unto an emerald. The central object, and the central glory in the vision of heaven, is God; and if we have not learned to think of heaven as, first of all, not the place where our departed friends, however dear, are gathered, but, first of all, as the place where God dwells, we lack the fundamental conception of heaven. The first thing that John saw, and the first thing to be seen, was the throne of God. The light and glory of that divine presence makes every star grow dim, and fills the whole horizon of heaven and the whole vision of the redeemed.

What is the significance of the rainbow round about the throne? The rainbow was the first sign of covenant promise. When God set the bow in the cloud, he called the attention of Noah and his family to the fact that it was to be the sign of covenant relation. Whatever else the "rainbow round about the throne" represents, it seems to say to me, as a believer, that the God that sits on the throne is "my God" in covenant, and that I need not be afraid to approach him if I approach him under the shelter of the covenant sign.

There is another equally conspicuous object that John saw there, a very curious and complex object, too—a Lion-Lamb—the "Lion of the tribe of Juda," and the "Lamb as it had been slain," combined in one. A lion for majesty, a lamb for meekness; a lion for strength, a lamb for weakness; a lion as the reigning sovereign, a lamb as the atoning sacrifice. God's Lion is a lamb, and God's Lamb is a lion; and if any of you have ever doubted the equality of Jesus Christ with God the Father in essence and in glory, I beg you to notice how, through these nineteen chapters of this book of the Revelation, there is no worship paid, or honour ascribed to God the Father, on the throne, that is not equally offered and ascribed to that Lion-Lamb, that Lamb-Lion.

And, as there is a rainbow round about the throne, which reminds me that God is my God in covenant, so that Lion-Lamb has about him blood that interprets the sealed book; for in the next chapter we read of the book, written on the surface and on the backside, and sealed with seven seals, and that no man was found worthy to open the book, or unloose the seven seals; but this Lion-Lamb of God prevailed to open the book and unloose its seals; and the ascription of praise and of worship testifies that he was found worthy and competent both to unloose the seals and to interpret the record. Oh, the interpreting power of the blood of Christ! Is prophecy a sealed book to you? You have never applied the blood to it, for there is not a seal there that the blood does not dissolve and unloose. Is human history a sealed book to you? Touch the seals with the blood, and the history is found to be the record of God's redemptive plan. Is the providence of God a sealed book to you? Touch the seals with the blood, and the mysterious providence of God is explained. Is this your present bereavement an event inexplicable to you? The interpreting power of the blood shall reveal to you its meaning in God's good time. Is the Bible a sealed book to you? From Genesis to the Apocalypse, Christ is the light that illumines its darkest pages. And so we have God on the throne, with the rainbow of the covenant assuring the soul; and we have the Lion and the Lamb, with the power of his blood to interpret the Word of God—the book of prophecy, of history, and the oftentimes more mysterious book of God's providential dealing.

Then round about the throne there is a countless host of angels. Numbers are exhausted to express the vastness of their multitude. "And the number of them was ten thousand times ten thousand, and thousands of thousands." That is, ten thousand times ten thousand, which is one hundred millions, and thousands multiplied into thousands, which gives us another multiplier of millions; and so we have, at the lowest figure, hundreds of millions multiplied by millions: in other words, absolutely countless myriads, or multitudes of angels. According to the literal interpretation of these figures, they would more than sixty times outnumber the entire population of the globe! Sixty spheres like this, each inhabited by fifteen hundred millions of human beings, would give us only the equivalent of these numbers if we take them at the lowest reckoning, and disregard the plural form of the multipliers.

Within the circle of these angels, as though nearer in relation to God than even the angels themselves, there is a multitude besides.

In the first place, there are those four mysterious living creatures (ζῶα) which remind us of the cherubic vision of Ezekiel. We know not what those living creatures represent, but if I may give my personal "judgment as one who has obtained mercy of the Lord to be faithful," I am more and more satisfied that they represent the great ruling attributes of God, such as wisdom, and power, and love, and grace, in their relation to the salvation of the lost race of man. But, as this matter is encumbered with mystery, we pass it by.

In close connection with these four living creatures, there are twenty-four elders, and we shall have less difficulty in recognizing in them the representatives of the body of believers in the Old Testament and in the New; that is to say, the twelve tribes and the twelve apostles, twenty-four representative elders signifying the entire body of believers, both in the Jewish dispensation and in the Christian dispensation. Their viols and their harps, their palms and their songs, all indicate their individual connection with the scheme of redeeming love.

Beside these, we have, in the seventh chapter of this book, an account of the "hundred and forty and four thousand" sealed from among the tribes of the children of Israel. It is wonderful how the Bible interprets itself, for, in a subsequent chapter (xiv.), where these hundred and forty-four thousand again appear, we are told they are the "first fruits unto God and the Lamb." First fruits are those first gathered out from the harvest field, the specimen of the harvest to come, but only a specimen; and these virginal redeemed ones that have never been "defiled with women,"—and are therefore in marked contrast with the followers of adulterous Babylon—and who, so far as they have been defiled by sin, are washed in the blood of the Lamb and follow the Lamb whithersoever he goeth,—these are "the first fruits"; and so, after this, the apostle John beheld "a great multitude, which no man could number, of all nations, and kindreds, and people, and tongues," sorrounding the throne of God. They represent the final harvest, of which the hundred and forty-four thousand are only the first fruits.

As has been said, the twenty-four elders and these hundred and forty-four thousand, and the multitude that no man could number, all stand inside of the circle of the angelic host, as though nearer to God than the angels themselves. And it is no exaggeration to say that a believer in Jesus Christ, in his finally redeemed estate, will stand in closer relation to God than even the angelic hosts; for, among all the angels, none are accounted worthy to constitute the bride of Christ, but that bride is to be gathered out of all peoples of the earth, and to enter into relations of espousal with the crucified but risen Jesus.

So much for the inhabitants of heaven.

Let us go a step further. What is revealed about the employments and enjoyments of heaven?

First of all there is endless worship. Worship means worth-ship, the ascribing of worth to Almighty God. "Thou art worthy, O Lord, to receive glory and honour and power." And, in all parts of this book of the Apocalypse, there is the same tireless, endless, heart-felt, adoring worship. Let us stop to consider a moment, that, if you do not love worship, you never can enter heaven. If you do not love worship, you are unfitted for the main activity and ecstacy of heaven, which is endless ascription of glory and praise to God and the Lamb!

And then, besides this worship, there is endless and tireless activity, as we have already seen. "They serve him day and night in his temple." "His servants shall serve him;" their activity ennobled, and strengthened; their activity, in its nobler and grander sphere of service, knowing nothing of present limitations of strength and knowing nothing of present hindrances to activity. The service of God in heaven will be the perfection of service.

And, then, how many elements, even beside these, enter into the enjoyments of heaven!

First of all, the presence of God. God is in the midst of them, and is their God. "The Lamb who is in the midst of the throne shall feed them, and shall lead them unto living fountains of waters." How wonderfully does John describe by the Spirit the perfection of bliss! There is all in heaven that could be desired, for God is there, and Christ is there; the saints are there, and the angels are there; heavenly society, and perfect fellowship with God and the redeemed and the angels. What opportunities for the enjoyments of the mind and the heart! for increasing experience of divine things! What opening of the inmost soul to be absolutely filled with the divine incoming and indwelling!

And as everything is there that is to be desired, so is nothing found there that is not to be desired. "They shall hunger no more, neither thirst any more; neither shall the sun light on them, nor any heat." "And God shall wipe away all tears from their eyes." "And there shall be no more death; neither sorrow nor crying; neither shall there be any more pain." Such words as these mean nothing less than absolute renovation! "Behold I make all things new." It is the passing away of everything that curses this world. The slime of the serpent is on all human joys and pleasures; but there is no track or trace of the serpent there! The blossoms of our human Edens all fade and fall even before we pluck them; but the blooms in that garden never fade and never fall. Satan is cast into the lake of fire and destroyed. Nothing enters that defiles or works abomination or makes a lie. Sin for ever banished! No death, for death itself shall die! Perfect bliss! We can say no more about it. The Bible says no more about it. The probability is that the things that are there, beyond what intimations we have, are simply "unlawful to utter." The voice that spoke to John said, "Come up hither, and I will shew thee things that must be hereafter." They must be seen to be known. They cannot be brought down to this sphere, even in inspired description, for we have nothing to interpret them. We must ourselves be lifted to that sphere and look through that open door, or we can have no appreciation of these great things of God.

Our examination would be seriously incomplete if special attention were not called to the vision of "the holy city," which John records in the twenty-first chapter; and that it may be before us more completely, let me read a few verses from that chapter:—"And I John saw the holy city, new Jerusalem, coming down from God out of heaven, prepared as a bride adorned for her husband. And I heard a great voice out of heaven saying, Behold, the tabernacle of God is with men, and he will dwell with them, and they shall be his people, and God himself shall be with them, and be their God."

In the tenth verse also we have "The holy Jerusalem descending out of heaven from God, having the glory of God: and her light was like unto a stone most precious, even like a jasper stone, clear as crystal; and had a wall great and high." And the city had twelve gates; on the east three, on the north three, on the south three, and the west three. "And the gates of it shall not be shut at all by day; for there shall be no night there."

What does all this mean? There is a heavenly city, "a city which hath foundations whose builder and maker is God;" and what does "city" mean, but an organized community, a place prepared, an everlasting habitation? There is a place prepared for those who love our Lord, and when God prepares a place it is sure to be just what is needed, absolutely adapted to all the wants of his dear children

What a place that will be for us intellectually! We are

told, in the thirteenth chapter of the first epistle to the Corinthians that, "Now we see through a glass, darkly; but then face to face." The bulk of our knowledge in this world, which does not come to us by the observation of our senses, we get through the inductive processes of the reason. For example, we reason from cause to effect; and so we discover truths, as we say, "by inference." But there we shall not reason doubtfully from cause to effect. All knowledge will be instinctive and immediate, like the intuitions of the human mind and soul. Intelligence will flash on us as a lightning glance reveals objects hitherto in the darkness; and so the present measure of our knowledge shall absolutely flee away as the dimness of day-dawn departs when the mists of the morning flee, and the glorious, full-orbed sun shines forth in cloudless and matchless splendour!

And, as the intellect will find in heaven a home perfectly fitted for it, so will the heart of man, and his moral and spiritual nature, find in God's city everything that is needed for perfect satisfaction and bliss; the union of the æsthetic and of the moral, beauty and virtue, boundless perfection in all surroundings with boundless perfection in our own nature and capacity to enjoy.

Notice also that the gates of this city are always open, and there are twelve gates—three opening toward each point of the compass. What a rebuke to bigotry! Is there any church that would pretend to say that the only entrance to heaven is through its particular communion? Is there anyone that dares to say that entrance to heaven is only through his particular form of theological dogma? How John's vision of the Holy City rebukes all such intolerance and uncharity! From all directions they come, but always moving in one direction! Mark that. The gates face toward every quarter; but from all quarters of the horizon the lines of march which pass through those twelve gates *meet at one point!* It matters not whether believing souls come from Asia or from Africa, from America or from Europe, from remotest lands or islands of the sea. It matters not whether they come from Jewish, Pagan, Heathen, or Moslem tribes, or from denominations of the Christian church in Christian lands. If you have found God in Christ, if your heart has been turned from sin towards holiness, if you have felt after God, if haply you may find him who is not far from every one of us; if in any way you have learned to rely on God's appointed sacrifice, and have been taught of his precious Spirit; from whatever quarter of the earth you come, you have equal right to enter through whatever gate of the city, and you will find your way to the throne of God and the Lion-lamb, and have an equally assured welcome.

The gates will not be shut at all by day, and as there is no night there, they are never shut. What is the use of a shut gate? It is to keep somebody out or to keep somebody in; and those gates will be always open, for in heaven there is no occasion to keep anybody out, and there is no occasion to keep anybody in; those that are within do not desire to go out, and those that are outside could not be induced to come in. I had lately put into my hands an infidel tract which seeks to make ridiculous the Christian doctrine of hell; and the basis of this, as with almost all these infidel assaults, is found in a misrepresentation. God is conceived as drawing an arbitrary line between one class and another class, so that, like a despot, he admits some to heaven, and remands others to hell; whereas the Word of God teaches us that, whatever may be said about divine sovereignty in human salvation, there is a law of spiritual affinity, which is inseparably connected both with heaven and hell. When Judas by transgression fell, he went "to his own place"; and, the disciples, "being let go" from the presence of the Jewish Council, "went to their own company." God ordains in this world a mixed society, the good and the bad together, that the good may restrain the bad, and that the bad may even discipline the good, and so help to perfect the goodness of his own children. But, when we leave this world, everyone of us, being loosed, goes to his own company: and the company of impenitent and rebellious sinners is enough to make a hell, as the company of penitent believers would make a heaven. We must never overlook the fact of this affinity, and its importance in its bearing upon eternal destiny. God may, with impunity, leave the gates of his celestial city for evermore open. There is no danger of any redeemed souls desiring to go out, unless perchance there were some message of mercy or errand of grace still to be accomplished for our Lord and his Christ. Nor will there be any lost soul, outside of heaven, that would desire or even consent to come in. In my youth I heard a sentimental clergyman say, as he concluded a sermon, "If I could stand on the battlements of hell and preach this gospel to lost souls and fallen angels, what a jubilee there would be in hell, and what a universal acclamation of praise to Almighty God!" There would be no such thing. Not a lost soul or fallen angel would enter heaven if full permission were given, for unless the Holy Ghost inclines you to worship, what would you do where worship is the eternal and universal employment? And unless the Holy Ghost gives you a spirit of willing and loving service for Christ, what would you do where only his servants are found, who serve him day and night with tireless energy? And unless you have a heart that goes out to God in the affinity of a spiritual nature like unto himself, what would you do there, and how could you be happy there, even though you were there? Do not deceive yourselves. There are some birds whose eggs are laid in another bird's nest, and, when the little birds are hatched and begin to mature, and their wings begin to grow, if they hear the voice of the mother bird, though they may never have seen their own mother before, they will leave the nest of the stranger and alien, and fly to the shelter of the mother.

> "Rivers to the ocean run,
>   Nor stay in all their course;
> Fire ascending seeks the sun;
>   Both speed them to their source.
> So a soul that's born of God,
>   Pants to view his glorious face,
> Upward tends to his abode,
>   To rest in his embrace."

If you have such affinity and attraction toward God, you could go nowhere else but to heaven; and if you have not that affinity for God, you could not go to heaven, and you could not and would not stay there if you were there.

Will you not seek now the preparation, that makes it possible for you to enter through the gate into the city, and go no more out?

There appears to be no building in the holy city, not even a temple! If there were buildings seen there John has not left it on record. He tells us of the city, of walls and gates, but there is no hint of any buildings. This is a mystery, and I can only venture to suggest a possible solution. When the Feast of Tabernacles was kept, the Jews were accustomed to go upon the roofs of their houses and celebrate that feast by building booths to commemorate their pilgrim sojourn in the wilderness. And, when their numbers became too great and the house-tops became too small, they gathered in the temple courts, or in the open spaces, such as the street that was before the water gate, of which we read in the eighth chapter of Nehemiah. In some large open vacant space they erected their booths and abode under them for eight days, that they might commemorate their journey in the wilderness with the tabernacle of God in their midst. When they built these booths they were directed in Deuteronomy to build them of various materials, and four sorts of branches seem to have been interwoven into their structure. First, there were fruit trees; second, palm trees; third, willow trees; and fourth, evergreen trees. If we rightly interpret this record of the Old Testament we may find types in all these. The fruit tree represents fertility of life in service. The palm tree represents a life of victory over temptation and trial. The willow tree, that grows only by the brook, represents patient endurance of sorrow and suffering. And the everlasting green seems to speak to us of a life in Christ that never fails or fades. And may not the booth of the pilgrim have been itself a type of our future reward? Is it not possible that, within those magnificent walls, John saw only an open space, because, so to speak, every believer who enters heaven through the blood of Jesus Christ nevertheless *builds his own booth?* Will it not depend upon the measure in which, by grace, you have triumphed over trial and temptation, the measure in which you have patiently borne the sorrows and the sufferings which God has sent upon you, the measure in which you have yielded fruit in the service of a holy and active life for him, the measure in which you have in yourself represented and manifested the undying life of the Holy Spirit; may it not depend in some measure at least upon your earthly triumphs and services and endurances what kind of a booth you build within the walls of the heavenly Jerusalem in that last great Feast of Tabernacles?

In that mysterious parable in the sixteenth of Luke we are told, "Make to yourselves friends of the mammon of unrighteousness; that, when ye fail, they may receive you into everlasting habitations." With all the obscurity that surrounds that parable, there is at least a plain suggestion in it that we should take even material possessions, like money, that have in themselves no moral quality, and so use them, with a consecrated spirit for the glory of God, that, by-and-by, when heart and flesh fail us, we shall find that they have gone before us and constructed for us everlasting habitations. In other words, while salvation is all the free gift of grace, your work has its wages, your service has its reward, and the measure of your reward will depend on the quantity and the quality of your service. There is an old Latin maxim which finely represents this, affirming of good works, "*non causa mercedis, sed regula retributionis*"; which in substance teaches that, while grace is the entire ground of our salvation, our good works in Christ Jesus determine the measure of our reward —the rule of recompense, not the ground of acceptance.

It is now a week ago, since that devoted man of God who has long preached in this pulpit, heard that voice, " Come up hither," and, obedient to that voice, not only looked through, but went through, the open door into heaven, and now knows as he is known. Extended reference to him will be made hereafter. But consider what a reward he has! What a booth was built for him by his long and unselfish ministry to souls, even before he went into the presence of his Lord. Think of his triumphs over temptation, and of the palm branches entwined in that booth! Think of his patient endurance of suffering, and of the willow branches woven into that booth! Think of the manifested life of God in him, and the evergreen branches that helped to build that booth! Think of the fruits of his long and consecrated ministry, and of the fruitful branches that complete that booth!

I never knew a man whose personal love for Jesus was more tender and beautiful than his. When he sat in this house of God, or on the platform of great public assemblies, and brethren, of whatsoever denomination and from whatsoever parts of the earth, spoke the language of Canaan and paid their tribute to the personal majesty and glory of his Redeemer, the tears that ran down his face, and the smiles that illuminated and transfigured it, showed how his heart beat in response to every such tribute of personal love to his

Lord. What must have been the rapture of that Pastor of yours who has been withdrawn into the glory, when for the first time he looked on the face of Jesus ! His ecstacy must have surpassed words and even surpassed imagination. He now stands with the white-robed throng, and has struck his harp to a nobler song than was ever sung on earth. He loves somewhat as he was loved. He has dropped sin in the perfection of holiness that knows no blemish ; sorrow, in the perfection of bliss that knows no alloy ; pain, in the perfection of the health that knows no disease ; and for him death has died !

Oh, let us, through this solemn week, look from the open grave to the open heaven, and turn our eyes away from earthly ashes to heavenly beauties ; let us seek to get up where, through this open door, we may get a glimpse of him who sits on the throne, come within the shelter of the Bow of the Covenant, and touch the Blood that has redeeming and sanctifying power ; let us henceforth do whatsoever we can in the Name and Power of God to accomplish the whole will of our Master, and so accumulate for heavenly service and heavenly blessedness all those good works which, wrought in Christ Jesus, prepare everlasting habitations for God's saints !

The First Day of the Second Week.

At eleven o'clock, on *Monday morning, February 8th*, the precious burden from Menton was expected to arrive in London. The officers of the church and a few friends gathered at Victoria Station in good time; and as the appointed hour drew nigh, many of the public began to loiter about. A plain hearse and a few ordinary carriages were in waiting, and a very few minutes past the time the train from Newhaven drew slowly up to the platform. The coffin, which had crossed from Dieppe during the night, and, in answer to the prayers offered the previous evening, had arrived safely, had been taken from its outer case at Newhaven. There, and also at Lewes, informal meetings were held by the ministers of the town. As the beautiful olive-wood sarcophagus was quietly and reverently lifted into the vehicle, the crowd eagerly pressed forward to look at it. With bared heads, and, in many cases, with streaming eyes, the people stood, while the magnificent palm-branches, which had been sent by Mrs. Spurgeon all the way from the South of France, were placed above the coffin. Then, through the crowd, which now numbered thousands, the solemn procession passed on its way to the Pastors' College. The rain soon came down in torrents, and those who were weeping thought it meet that the English skies should weep, too, for him who had fallen in the fight. Along the route there were many who recognized the meaning of the hearse and palm-branches, and when the *cortège* turned into Temple Street, immediately at the back of the Tabernacle, there was a great hurrying to secure a place near the College gates.

The beloved body was at once borne to the Common Room of the College; common, that is to say, in the sense of being open to all the students, but not "Common" even in that sense that day, and in any other sense common nevermore, since it was the first resting-place in England of the mortal body of *the late* CHARLES HADDON SPURGEON. The room had been beautifully prepared for the reception of the remains, plants of the palm species, and white arum lilies being placed in profusion around the room; and now there lay that most suggestive olive-wood casket, with the official black seals of the Vice-Consul and the Commissary of Police, which had been placed upon it at Menton, still clear: within it—ah! how the tears came—there was all that was mortal of the beloved Pastor, the honoured President, the revered friend; the "man greatly-beloved", who had the seal of God so clearly upon his forehead, that all owned the sanctity of his life.

Immediately there was held a short and simple service, attended only by the officers of the church and a few invited friends. The time was chiefly spent in prayer, bowing low before our God. Then a few of the students of the College were admitted to gaze upon the coffin, and pay homage to the memory of their leader.

In the afternoon, another short service, specially for the members of the bereaved family, was held.

Of the Tabernacle prayer-meeting, *in the evening*, little need be said, except that it was very largely attended, and was filled with a sense of God's presence. We turned away saying, "How awful is this place!" Dr. Pierson made a personal statement as to the remarkable leading of God with reference to his present sphere; and, after reading the Word of God, urged strongly that when God took away Moses, he always had a Joshua to lead his people; and it was now the attitude of the hour to wait expectantly on him, who never fails those who put their trust in him.

Several earnest prayers were offered for the remaining services of the week. It was desired of God that hundreds might be blessed by means of them, and special petition was made that the great throngs which would gather might be kept calm, and free from any accident. Hearty thanks were also rendered for all the streaks of light in the midst of the darkness, and for the last favour, in that the sacred dust of the dear Pastor had at length been safely brought to the scene of his many labours. Mr. Chamberlain sang the late Pastor's favourite solo, "Show me thy face": a prayer already abundantly answered in his case.

As "devout men carried Stephen to his burial," it was appropriate that, towards ten o'clock at night, a band of the students of the Pastors' College should carry the sacred burden from the College to its place in the Tabernacle. They counted it an honour to be entrusted with the task; and some pews at the front having been removed, the lifeless clay was deposited in the great building, where the living voice had so often been heard in loving persuasion, and in outspoken defence of the truth.

Only those who have taken part in the arrangements for the memorial meetings which were to follow, can have any conception of the labours involved in carrying them so safely to a satisfactory issue. Everyone about the Tabernacle was busy from morning to night, and sometimes all night long. Each vied with the other in helping forward the necessary preliminaries. Until Monday night everything was spontaneous, and without much definite pre-arrangement; but the dimensions of the matter in hand required, for the future gatherings, the most careful judgment and the greatest precision. Nothing was lacking. Both the cool, clear head to plan, and the warm, eager hand to execute, were available; and events have proved the wisdom of the plans, and the completeness of the organization. Letters poured in literally by the thousand, demanding an answer. A most miscellaneous assortment of tickets had to be allotted; careful arrangements for the comfort and safety of the people had to be devised, and all the other necessary funeral fixtures had to be made. Now, when all is over, let it be said, to the praise of the presiding Spirit of God, that not one thing seems to have been forgotten; not a single accident has happened; not a jarring note has been heard. All those who shared in the services are greatly indebted to the earnest workers who so willingly and efficiently conceived and carried out the excellent arrangements.

Tributes of Affection.

From seven o'clock in the morning of *Tuesday, February 9th*, until seven in the evening, the Tabernacle was open, and two continuous streams of people passed up the aisles to view the coffin enclosing the body of him who had been the greatest spiritual force of his generation in London, or perhaps in the world. All classes were represented, from the very poor to the well-to-do artisan, and from the tradesman to men of the city and suburbs. Passing the coffin, over which were triumphantly placed Mrs. Spurgeon's palm-branches, many were moved with evident emotion. It is variously estimated that 50,000 to 60,000 persons must have visited the spot during the day. This was a very memorable day, and a remarkable preface to the days still more memorable which were to follow.

The precious body was enclosed in a leaden casket, and the outer coffin of Menton olive-wood had plates at the head and foot, bearing the following inscription:—

In ever-loving memory of
CHARLES HADDON SPURGEON,
Born at Kelvedon, June 19, 1834,
Fell asleep in Jesus at Menton, Jan. 31, 1892.

"I have fought a good fight, I have finished my course, I have kept the faith."

Around the coffin were many beautiful tributes from loving hearts. First came a graceful anchor, composed of lilies and hyacinths, from the Rev. John Robertson and the congregation of Gorbals Tabernacle, Glasgow, with the quotation from one of Mr. Spurgeon's most recent letters, " The sun shines at length." Next to this was a beautiful wreath, " In loving and grateful remembrance," from the children at the Stockwell Orphanage. Side by side with this testimony of affection was the large floral harp, formed of lilies, with golden strings, one of which was significantly broken, which had been sent from the sister isle. It was inscribed, " 'He being dead yet speaketh,' Hebrews xi. 4. A loving tribute to the memory of Pastor C. H. Spurgeon, from the Baptist churches of Belfast." Attached to this were a sword and trowel fashioned in violets, and accompanied by the following extract from a memorial poem written by Mr. Maxwell:—

> "Oh, master-builder thou, on Zion's wall
> Thy busy *Trowel* knew no cankering rust !
> Thy *Sword* was keen and double-edged withal
> To smite th' invading foemen to the dust."

Pastor A. G. Barley, on behalf of Pasteur R. Saillens and Christians in Paris, brought a magnificent wreath.

Flowers and wreaths would have been sent in almost incalculable numbers, but it was specially requested that the memory of the glorified Pastor should be honoured by gifts to the College and Orphanage. In many instances this has been done right heartily, and doubtless other friends will yet be moved to present similar tokens of esteem and gratitude.

At the coffin sides were several cards, which attracted the notice of many.

That from Mrs. Spurgeon read : " 'With Christ, which is far better.' I will follow thee, my husband. Undying love from ' the wife of thy youth.' "

On behalf of his departed brother, Mr. James Spurgeon had a card, " Behold, I die, but God shall be with you," Gen. xlviii. 21.

On behalf of himself and his wife, Pastor J. A. Spurgeon had another card, " So an entrance shall be ministered unto you abundantly into the everlasting kingdom of our Lord

THE OLIVE-CASKET UNDER THE PALM-BRANCHES AT THE TABERNACLE.

and Saviour Jesus Christ," 2 Peter i. 11 ; " If we believe that Jesus died and rose again, even so them also which sleep in Jesus will God bring with him," 1 Thessalonians iv. 14.

Pastor Charles Spurgeon's card read : " His," Rom. xiv. 8 ; " Now he is comforted," Luke xvi. 25 ; " In fondest memory of the dearest of fathers, from his son Charles."

The next card read : " Within the veil," Heb. vi. 19 ; "Absent . . . . present with the Lord," 2 Cor. v. 8 ; " In affectionate remembrance of dear father, from son Tom." This was attached to the coffin by Mr. Charles Spurgeon on behalf of his brother in New Zealand.

Mr. Harrald's card read : " In fondest memory of my dearest earthly friend, my beloved Pastor and father in the faith, and 'the good soldier of Jesus Christ', whose armour-bearer desires to be faithful unto death as his captain was."

The card of Miss E. H. Thorne (Mrs. Spurgeon's companion) read : " In loving memory of the best and kindest friend I ever had on earth."

On the black drapery of the upper rostrum was the very significant admonition, " Remember the word that I said unto you being yet present with you ; " while, on the lower platform, the text, " I have fought a good fight, I have finished my course, I have kept the faith," was inscribed. None could question that it was a true description of the life of the man of God whom they had come to honour ; a marble bust of whom looked down upon them from between the one platform and the other.

On Tuesday, as the people passed in file to view the coffin, a copy of Mr. Spurgeon's sermon for the previous week, "GOD'S WILL ABOUT THE FUTURE" (No. 2,242), was given to each, as an appropriate memento of the occasion.

Memorial Meeting

FOR MEMBERS OF THE CHURCH.

On Wednesday morning, February 10th, 1892, commencing at 11 o'clock, the service arranged specially for members of the church and its organizations was held, the Tabernacle being filled. The chair was taken by the Rev. J. A. SPURGEON, pastor in charge.

Deacon S. R. PEARCE, Superintendent of the Metropolitan Tabernacle Sunday-school, opened the meeting with a sympathetic prayer, which gave a fitting key-note to the meeting which was to follow; after which

Rev. WILLIAM STOTT, formerly assistant pastor, announced the hymn, "All hail the power of Jesus' name," which was sung with solemn feeling.

Rev. JOSEPH ANGUS, D.D., Principal of Regent's Park College, who was introduced by the Chairman as "a former pastor of this church, my venerated tutor and lifelong friend," then said: "Of all meetings connected with these services, I deem it the greatest privilege to be allowed to take part in this. You are assembled to-day as a Christian Church, and you have reckoned me as still, in some sense, one of your members. I believe, that on your church-roll, my name will be found at the close of the year 1837. I was then only a lad; had just finished my course in Edinburgh; and was invited to become your pastor. For two years the pastoral relationship was sustained, amid the kind love and prayers and counsel of a devoted people. At the close of those years my happy pastorate closed with deep regret on my part, and with very hearty sympathy on the part of the people. In those two years one hundred and twenty members were added to the church.

"There were then, I remember, in connection with the church, the families of Warmington, Richards, Gale, Pewtress, Olney, and Burgess—names still fragrant in this place; their children and their children's children have been for years connected either with this church or with sister churches. Nothing done in those days can be compared with your recent history; but in the faith, the love, and the devoted work of that day, there was everything to cheer the heart of the pastor. When I was called to become secretary of our Mission it was one of the severest wrenches I have ever known. For fifty years now I have been severed from the church, working elsewhere, but I have been in constant touch with some of its members and with its pastor. I have shared your sorrows, and your success; and I feel that it is a fitting thing that I should be here to-day, in this deepest sorrow of all, to commend the church and all its agencies to the guidance and blessing of our divine Lord. As I stand here I see before me the faces of the dead almost as distinctly as the faces of the living; it is a blessed memory and a blessed spectacle!

"I have been struck by the appropriateness of the Scripture text which you have inscribed over your beloved friend: 'I have fought a good fight, I have finished my course, I have kept the faith.' As soldier, as runner, and as steward, he has no reason to be ashamed. We thank God for all his faithfulness, and we gather from his life fresh incentive to completer consecration. May I venture to suggest a motto appropriate to your condition as a church, which, I trust, may commend itself to your hearts : ' Remember them who are your leaders, who have spoken to you the word of God, whose faith copy, considering the end of their conversation.'

"One thought besides. We are here this morning to show our affection and respect for all that was mortal of our beloved friend. We mean to follow his bier to-morrow to the grave, but please remember, now, that your pastor is not here at all. All that was mortal of him is here; but he himself has become immortal. Sometimes men speak of following Christians to their tomb; sometimes they adopt language still more heathenish, and speak as if our loved ones were resting peaceably in their graves; but I affirm that the Christian man is never put into his grave at all. 'Absent from the body,' he is forthwith 'present with the Lord.' We cannot but feel the deepest affection for all that was mortal of our dear friend, and pay our homage to his name; but he is no more here: he is 'for ever with the Lord.'

"I believe that he misses his family; I believe that he misses his orphans so dear to his heart; I believe that he misses his students who are so greatly indebted to him. He misses his church, which was, in a large degree, the source of his strength; he misses the enquirers and the converts who were the joy of his heart, as they are the joy of the heart of every true minister. I cannot but believe that he misses them all, and it may be that in that land he knows as little about them as we know about him. But whatever be the disadvantages of the loss of the earthly relationship, to be with Christ is far better. His sins are behind him; his weakness is behind him; his cares and distractions are behind him; and he is for ever with the Lord. 'Wherefore comfort one another with these words.'"

Rev. A. T. PIERSON, D.D., announced by the chairman as "My dearly loved colleague in the service of this great people, a man whom to know is to trust up to the hilt," said :—

This is a unique gathering. It is the one meeting that I would rather be at, of all the gatherings of this week, for now the family meet round the bier to weep and pray and talk together about the spiritual father and brother who a few days since was in the land of the dying, but is now in the land of the living. I thank you that you have included me in the family gathering, if not as "one born out of due time," yet as one that you have so gently and generously adopted into your family circle, and who shares deeply in your profound grief. But, before I say what God has put in my heart, I must unburden myself of the last message at hand from dear Mrs. Spurgeon, who cannot be here to-day, and from whom, perhaps without design on her part, I have only this morning received a beautiful, tender, and sisterly letter, a portion of which certainly belongs to you. I will omit all the personal references in it, and read only what she says about her beloved and herself. The letter was written last Lord's-day, and is as follows :—

MRS. C. H. SPURGEON'S LETTER TO DR. PIERSON.

"I want to tell you how perfectly happy my beloved was during the three delightful months of his residence here. The joy of bringing me to the place he loved so well, and showing me eagerly all the beautiful scenery in which he so delighted, was greatly enhanced by the assurance that you were standing in his place at home. How little we thought what God meant to do with his dear servant when he called you from beyond the seas! but our faith shall not fail. 'He hath done all things well'; and though the future, both to you and to me, may seem clouded and uncertain, we will trust and not be afraid. With me it is an absolute necessity that I keep looking up. 'He is not here; he is risen,' is as true of my beloved as of my beloved's Lord. To-day he has been a week in heaven. Oh, the bliss, the rapture, of seeing his Saviour's face! Oh, the welcome home which awaited him as he left this sad earth! Not for a moment do I wish him back, though he was dearer to me than tongue can tell. I shall pray much for you all during the week of grief. I feel myself like a shipwrecked mariner who has with difficulty reached the shore, and now looks with streaming eyes and fainting heart on others still struggling through those awful waves of sorrow. With Christian love and intensest sympathy,

Your grateful friend,
SUSIE SPURGEON."

We have shut the doors this morning against the world and the churches at large, that this great family may have a little familiar and close intercourse about the dead. This beloved man of God was to us in this family circle a preacher of the gospel. What a preacher! I am persuaded that the century has known no man that was his equal in the simple and persuasive utterance of the gospel message. It was a heroic resolve on his part 'not to know anything amongst you, save Jesus Christ, and him crucified.' But it was a rarer success on his part that, knowing nothing but Jesus Christ, and him crucified, he gathered and held the largest congregation within the bounds of the Christian world, for over forty years.

There are some, in these days, that would depreciate him, as a man that had no broad horizon—as a man whose range and scope were narrow. But such a verdict reacts upon those who depreciate him, for it shows how little they appreciate the genius of his ministry. The Campsie fiddler, when he heard Paganini, went home and broke and burned his own fiddle, not simply because that master violinist had brought out of his wooden box the most marvellous melodies and harmonies that he had ever heard, but because on one string he had executed melodies and harmonies that no other living performer had been able to bring out of all four strings. And the glory of Charles Haddon Spurgeon in his preaching of the gospel was that, from one string, 'Christ, and him crucified,' he evoked the melodies and harmonies to which a whole orchestra of intellectual instruments is not equal. The vibrations of that chord ran from the depths of the most profound mysteries to the heights of the most celestial glories. The combinations and the variations that he executed upon that one string have held the church of God entranced, and the world in awe. I pray you to notice that the limitation of his ministry was the glory of his ministry. He had the bravery not to know a thousand things that he might have known. He had the bravery to make the Bible the one book that he studied, and the Christ of God the one theme on which he discoursed. And you who for forty years have listened to his ministry will have found that out of that one string he brought every strain of instruction, every voice of consolation, every message, tender, pathetic, sublime, and beautiful, that is needful for the mind, the heart, the conscience, or the spirit, of a child of God.

And I would have you notice also, in uttering these simple tributes to his memory, that he was not only a great preacher and evangelist, he was also a great Pastor. There are many evangelists that have the advantage that they only preach, and that they preach to audiences so different that they can use the same material over and over again, repeating, and completing as they repeat. Whitefield preached the same sermon over, fifty or one hundred times, improving it at every delivery; but Charles Haddon Spurgeon could not in this manner repeat himself. For thirty-seven years he has given his sermons to the public, and when they have been pronounced in this place they have been, in a sense, lost to him for future use, for they have been given in the wider pulpit of the press to a more magnificent audience than it was possible for him to reach even here. Notwithstanding the fact that the conditions of his ministry thus forbade the ordinary repetition of sermons, he has gone on speaking with perpetual freshness on this one perpetual theme; and yet the ministries of the last year among you were more precious than the ministries of any previous part of his life.

Was not the secret of his ministry in two little utterances that he emphasized in his words, and especially in his life? When Dr. McAll went to Paris to begin his great work for the evangelization of the French people, he could speak only two sentences in French, and those not with Parisian accent either. One was 'God loves you,' and the other was 'I love you.' Upon those two sentences Charles Haddon Spurgeon built his ministry. His whole gospel preaching was a proclamation, 'God loves you;' and his whole pastoral and personal life was the affirmation, 'I love you.' The people learned of the love of God through his lips, and were drawn to him by the personal love that he had to souls, as exhibited in all that he did and in all that he said.

I would remind you also that he was a great organizer and leader. Fifty mission halls or benevolent organizations, in some way or other connected with this church, yet survive, which owe their existence, under God, to his suggestion and organizing power. I need not remind this family of God, of his dear brother, James A. Spurgeon, who has been so marvellously fitted to complement and supplement all his labours, and has been so closely associated with him, as John Wesley and Charles Wesley were associated, a little more than a century ago. Nor need I remind you how these two beloved men of God, like right hand and left hand in the service of the Master, have founded the Pastors' College, which has had eight hundred students in its halls, and is represented on every continent of the globe. I need not tell you how these two brothers have likewise originated and maintained, through God, the Stockwell Orphanage, which at present has over four hundred boys and girls within its walls, doubly orphaned now that another father has been taken from them. Nor need I remind you of the Almshouses and the multitude of other noble and philanthropic works which owe, if not their existence, their subsistence, to this manly and Christian heart which now has stopped beating.

We have nothing to say to-day about the work accomplished by our departed brother beyond the bounds of this church. That will come in review on some subsequent occasion. I limit myself now to what he was to this church, with its organizations and its institutions.

There was nothing in which C. H. Spurgeon shone more than in his character as a true Christian believer. First and last, what he was as a preacher, what he was as a pastor, what he was as a worker, he owed to what he was as a believer in Christ Jesus. I do not wonder that the children in the Orphanage and in the Sunday-school were all drawn to him. I do not wonder that they understood him, for I never knew a Christian believer who was more, in the very best sense, himself a little child. Yes, it was a *child* that died on the 31st of January, nearly fifty-eight years old. He never lost his child-likeness, though he had lost his childishness; he carried all that is most sublime from childhood into the period of his manhood and into his maturer years.

Do you ask me what was the secret of his power as a Christian believer? I think that the answer to that question is exceedingly simple. We shall not lose it even in analysis, for, at the bottom of all, it was that he had an overwhelming sense of the powers of the world to come. The invisible things were visible to his faith. The future and eternal were like present and temporal to him. He went into his closet and handled God, he saw that it was he himself, and he came out with the vivid impressions of communion with the invisible and the eternal. If you will take that single secret you will find that it underlies every other secret of his personal life and personal ministry. We need not look very far to find out why he was what he was. He took the Bible, and the whole Bible, as the inspired book of God; he took Christ, and the whole Christ, as the justifier, sanctifier and redeemer; he believed with all his heart; and every utterance was a speech born of deep conviction. To the ingenuity of intellectual genius, he added the ingenuousness of moral genius, and produced first and foremost, upon all who heard him, the impression that what he said he believed, and what he believed he believed with all his heart. Hence, as a great ocean steamer draws smaller craft in its wake, even unbelievers and sceptics were in a measure brought to fall into the line of his teaching, because of the positiveness of it, which was born of a defined and confirmed faith.

Suffer me to say one word more. I may the more fitly speak of his sick and dying bed, because I belong to another nationality and to another branch of the Christian church in a distant land. Round about that sick and dying bed, from May last to the end of January of this year, for more than eight months, the whole Christian church was bowed in solicitude, as round about his bier to-day, from all quarters of the earth, Christian believers bow in tears. I think that not since Christ ascended has there been a more pathetic illustration of the power of one believing child of God to attract to him millions upon millions of believers, upon whose faces he has never looked. Ten thousand messages and letters of sympathy, sets of resolutions and telegrams of enquiry came to his home here and in Menton during the time I have specified. There was not a branch of the Christian church that did not furnish representatives in this pathetic instance of condolence, either by personal calls or by communications through telegraph or post. From the Archbishops of Canterbury and York, down to the humblest vicar and curate, tributes have been paid to him ; from all the branches of the Baptist, Methodist, Congregational and Presbyterian churches, and from every other denomination of Christians, expressions of sympathy have been received. Yea, even the Jewish rabbi begged him to understand that the Jews were lifting prayer to the God of Abraham, of Isaac, and of Jacob for his restoration. There has never, I repeat, been a scene, of which I have any knowledge, so pathetically sublime in the course of the eighteen hundred years of Christian history. Verily 'prayer was made without ceasing of the church unto God for him.'

O my beloved friends, you do not know all you have had in him, and you do not yet know what you have lost. But, blessed be the name of God, what is your loss is his great gain.

What, in this great crisis, are we to do ? We must go and stand by the Jordan, where he stood ; take the mantle of the ascended man of God ; smite the waters with that mantle, and say, 'Where is the Lord God of Spurgeon! *He* still survives, and is ready to interpose for us.

Be sure that you take these Orphans to your heart, and see that in their comparatively fatherless condition they find the whole church here like a nursing mother. See that you take the Pastors' College to your heart, and ensure a generation of noble and faithful ministers of Christ to carry out the line of teaching, and to defend the gospel, that has made this pulpit illustrious. See that no work under which the shoulders and heart of Charles Haddon Spurgeon stood as a support shall fall to-day because that support has been withdrawn. I venture to prophesy that, if such is the spirit of your faith and your consecration, God will, in some mysterious manner, bless to you the departure of his servant, even as he has blessed his long presence among you.

Mr. J. W. HARRALD, Private Secretary to Mr. Spurgeon, to whom the chairman paid a just tribute, calling upon him as "A dear friend, one of my brother's dearest helpers, who put wisdom and strength, gentleness and tenderness unrivalled, at my brother's disposal by night and by day, in life and in death," announced the hymn,—

> "Servant of God, well done!
> Rest from thy loved employ;
> The battle fought, the victory won,
> Enter thy Master's joy.
>
> "The voice at midnight came;
> He started up to hear:
> A mortal arrow pierced his frame;
> He fell, but felt no fear.
>
> "His spirit with a bound
> Left its encumbering clay;
> His tent, at sunrise, on the ground
> Without a tenant lay.
>
> "The pains of death are past;
> Labour and sorrow cease;
> And life's long warfare closed at last,
> His soul is found in peace.
>
> "Soldier of Christ, well done!
> Praise be thy new employ;
> And, while eternal ages run,
> Rest in thy Saviour's joy."

Being peculiarly appropriate to the circumstances of the beloved Pastor's entrance into rest, this hymn was sung most heartily by the whole congregation.

Mr. HARRALD, to whose words a special interest attached, as he had been by the side of the beloved sufferer to the end, then said: "I feel that I am here to-day as the representative of our dearly-loved and deeply-lamented senior Pastor, and of his beloved and bereaved wife. We meet to-day, as we have been reminded, in the capacity of a family. Therefore, speaking to you as members of the family, I wish to bear testimony, for dear Mrs. Spurgeon's sake and on her behalf, to the sustaining grace of God which has been granted to her, and to all of us who have sorrowed with her, away in the sunny land. The hymn which we have just sung speaks of 'the call at midnight', and close on midnight the call came to him whom we mourn. Many of you perhaps know that our beloved Pastor said to everyone who asked him when he thought of being back, '*I shall be home in February*,' and nearly an hour before the time that he had himself fixed, *he was at home*, not at 'Westwood', but at his heavenly home, 'for ever with the Lord.' As the five of us knelt by his bedside, in the little room at Menton, after he had entered into rest, I felt that I ought to lead the little company in prayer for all who had been bereaved; but we were touched beyond expression, as we still continued on our knees, to hear the voice of the loved one so sorely bereaved, thanking God for the many years that she had had the unspeakable joy of having such a precious husband lent to her. You have heard from her beautiful letter something of what the past three months have been to her. We could go farther back, and speak of the past seven months; for seven months ago she gave her husband up to his Lord, but the Lord lent him to her a little longer. His dear wife always reckoned that those seven months were all extra, and so she was ready when the Master wanted the loan back again for ever. If there could have been any wish of his heart that otherwise would have remained unsatisfied, it was, as she tells you in the letter, that together they might sit under the palm-trees of his lovely Menton; that they might walk beneath the olives that flourish there; and that they might sojourn a little while by the tideless sea, beneath the cloudless sky, and amid those scenes he so dearly loved, mainly because they reminded him of 'Thy land, O Immanuel!' Those last three months seemed to make their earthly bliss complete; husband and wife often said that it was their honeymoon over again. They celebrated together at Menton their thirty-sixth wedding-day, also Mrs. Spurgeon's birthday, and from the family standpoint—and that is where we meet to-day—it was all that one could have desired. And oh, though it was sad for us to lose him there, we felt that, at least, one regret would be spared to us; had he stayed at home we should all have said, 'If he had but gone to Menton, he might have recovered!' But that was not to be.

"You cannot tell all that those three months at Menton mean. Little by little it will come out, and you will be thankful as you see how true is the text which has been placed on one end of the coffin. The question has been put to me already, 'When did the Pastor say to you, "I have fought a good fight, I have finished my course, I have kept the faith"?' Let it be known, as distinctly as possible, *the Pastor did not say it at all.* I have taken every opportunity I could get to say that the last message he was able to deliver to the congregation, or to anyone, was that remarkable message telegraphed to you on the very day that you were bringing in thankofferings for his partial recovery. Read that message again, in the light of what I am certain he knew at the time, and then see how characteristic it was.

"He and Mrs. Spurgeon were talking together, and they called me into the bedroom. They said, 'There is a little matter of business for you to attend to,' and then our dear Pastor dictated to me a telegram to be sent to the Tabernacle. He began, '*Self and wife, £100, thankoffering*'; but altering the wording, he said, 'No; put it, "*£100, hearty thankoffering towards Tabernacle General Expenses. Love to all friends.*'

"I waited for more, but he had fallen asleep. That terrible unconsciousness, that soon seized him in its dreaded grasp, was already beginning to affect him. I waited, perhaps half an hour, and when he awoke, I said—

"'You did not finish the telegram.'

"'Hasn't it gone yet?' he asked.

"'No,' I replied; 'there is plenty of time. They do not meet at the Tabernacle till four this afternoon; and I could not send it off without telling them how you are, for all will be anxious to know about you.'

"In his own characteristic way, he said, *Let them find out; that is all I am going to say.* Was it not just like him? Of course, I put a few words at the end of his telegram, that the friends at home might know how ill he was; but his last message was in harmony with his whole life—all for others, and not a word about himself. Was not his action characteristic even to the end?

"In most solemn conversation with me, several days before that, he had said, *'My work is done'*; and he began talking of certain matters which no man would speak of, least of all such a man as he, unless he was certain that his work was ended. Yet, knowing that he was upon his dying bed, and perhaps, for aught one can tell, knowing that this was the last message he would ever send, he only said, *'Hearty thankoffering.'* Notice that he did not say *'for recovery'*; every word was carefully weighed. *'Love to all friends.'*

"This was his last message to you, and it is no use asking for any other. There is no other. We watched day and night with him. Oh, what would we not have given if we could have had another word? We hoped against hope that there would have been some other final message, but no other was given. There you have it: *'Hearty thankoffering. Love to all friends.'*

"Do you ask, how did that text, 'I have fought a good fight, I have finished my course, I have kept the faith," come where it is? It was my sad and mournful duty to submit to dear Mrs. Spurgeon certain matters which needed attention, and amongst other things, I took to her the inscription I had prepared for the coffin. It ended with this text. As soon as I read it, she said, in her own inimitable way—

"'How is it that you always think of just what I have been thinking? There is no other text for him.'

"So the text was placed where it is; but our dear Pastor would never have thought of applying those words to himself.

"'*I have fought a good fight.*' You know how true that is.

"'*I have finished my course.*' It is no broken column that we have to rear to his memory. His work is finished.

"'*I have kept the faith.*' And everyone here and throughout the whole world knows how bravely he did it.

"You may know something more also. Many voices will say this—but none ought to say it more distinctly than I do—that within that olive-casket there lies all that is mortal of *a martyr for the truth's sake.* If you will look in your *Sword and Trowel* for February, you will see a note on 'The Bible and Modern Criticism', and at the end you will read what the Pastor wrote with his own hand but a few days before he told me that his work was finished. Concerning that great controversy, which has now cost him his life, he says there that he does not regret his action, 'even though an almost fatal illness might be reckoned as part of the price.' We must now take out the word 'almost', for 'part of the price' paid by our beloved Pastor, in his contention for the faith, was his own life. For the truth's sake he counted not his life dear unto him; and again and again he has said, in the presence of those who can bear unflinching testimony to the fact, that, if necessary, he would gladly have laid down his life a thousand times for the sake of the gospel, for the defence of which he was 'set' as much as the apostle Paul ever was.

"You may imagine how much there is that one would

wish to say to you personally; but I must say to the officers and members of this church and congregation, and to other friends throughout the world, on dear Mrs. Spurgeon's behalf, how deeply thankful she is for all the tokens of love she has received during the last eight or nine months; first the loving messages of sympathy, then of congratulation, and now of condolence. They have been simply overwhelming; and she can but ask that through every public channel her thanks may be conveyed throughout the whole world, for all the love and all the sympathy which have been showered upon her so royally.

"But has not our dear Pastor a last word for us? Ay, that he has; and here again I must link his name with that of his beloved wife. You know what, by a most remarkable overruling of the providence of God, last week's sermon was—('GOD'S WILL ABOUT THE FUTURE,' No. 2,242). Even more remarkable, the Pastor's message for this very week is what Mrs. Spurgeon has herself entitled, 'HIS OWN FUNERAL SERMON' (No. 2,243). The text is, 'For David, after he had served his own generation by the will of God, fell on sleep.' That sermon is his special message for to-day.

"But among peculiarly tender memorials of our glorified Pastor, there are some words, written by his own hand, as clearly as ever he wrote, in this little book, which I hold in my hand. It is now a very precious treasure, for it tells us something of what he wanted to say before he was taken. I do not say that these words are all his own composition— some evidently are not—but they are gathered together, and some of them doubtless composed by him. They were put just where I should be the first to find them, in order, doubtless, that they might come as his message to you. Put these couplets together, and listen to the Holy Spirit's message to you, for by these words, 'he, being dead, yet speaketh.'

"'No cross, no crown; no loss, no gain;
    They first must suffer, who would reign.'

"'He best can part with life without a sigh,
    Whose daily living is to daily die.'

"'Youth builds for age; age builds for rest:
    Who builds for heaven, will build the best.'

"'Poor they may live, but rich they die,
    Whose treasure is laid up on high.'

"'Oh, the sweet joy that sentence gives—
    "I know that my Redeemer lives!"'

"'We cannot, Lord, thy purpose see,
    But all is well that's done by thee.'

"The last word is—

"'Prepar èd be
    To follow me.'

"Oh, may every one of us follow him, as he followed his Lord!" To which the congregation responded with a hearty "Amen."

The Rev. V. J. CHARLESWORTH, called upon to read the Scriptures, as a long-tried helper and friend, the Head-Master of the Orphanage, said: "There are lingering echoes which will now find a voice in the words of the inspired apostle, and which all must feel so truly applicable to the beloved Pastor who has gone.

"'I determined not to know anything among you save Jesus Christ, and him crucified.'

"'His grace which was bestowed upon me was not in vain.'

"'But as God is true, our word toward you was not "Yea" and "Nay." For the Son of God, Jesus Christ, who was preached among you . . . was not "Yea" and "Nay," but in him was "Yea."'

"'I have not shunned to declare unto you all the counsel of God.'

"'The gospel which was preached of me is not after

man. For I neither received it of man, neither was I taught it, but by the revelation of Jesus Christ.'

"'By grace are ye saved through faith; and that not of yourselves: it is the gift of God.'

"'Hold fast the form of sound words which thou hast heard of me in faith and love, which is in Christ Jesus.'

"'Therefore, my beloved brethren, be ye stedfast, unmoveable, always abounding in the work of the Lord, forasmuch as ye know that your labour is not in vain in the Lord.'

"'O, come let us worship and bow down; let us kneel before the Lord our Maker, for he is our God, and we are the people of his pasture and the sheep of his hand.'

"'The Lord of hosts is with us; the God of Jacob is our refuge.'

"'He that spared not his own Son, but delivered him up for us all, how shall he not with him also freely give us all things?'

"'For whether we live, we live unto the Lord; and whether we die, we die unto the Lord: whether we live therefore, or die, we are the Lord's.'

"'Precious in the sight of the Lord is the death of his saints.'

"'He asked life of thee, and thou gavest it him, even length of days for ever and ever. His glory is great in thy salvation: honour and majesty hast thou laid upon him. Thou hast made him most blessed for ever: thou hast made him exceeding glad with thy countenance.'

"'Make us glad according to the days wherein thou hast afflicted us. Let thy work appear unto thy servants, and thy glory unto their children. And let the beauty of the Lord our God be upon us: and establish thou the work of our hands upon us; yea, the work of our hands establish thou it.'

"'Pray for the peace of Jerusalem: they shall prosper that love thee. Peace be within thy walls, and prosperity within thy palaces. For my brethren and companions' sakes, I will now say, Peace be within thee.'"

Rev. T. W. MEDHURST, who was the senior student of the College, entering in the year 1855, and who has been ever since an honoured minister of the Word, being called upon, led in a heartfelt and heart-moving prayer.

Deacon T. H. OLNEY, the treasurer of the church, one of the eldest of the officers whom Mr. James Spurgeon, in introducing Mr. Olney, spoke of as "a band of men whom God has touched; the excellent of the earth in whom we all delight," said :—" In the presence of the great sorrow and the crushing calamity which have come home to the hearts of each one present, there is no need to-day to set aside seats for special mourners. We are all special mourners. I desire your sympathy and your prayers at this time, for I am not a practised speaker, but I have been selected on the present occasion because for so many years I have had the privilege and the honour of being associated with our dear Pastor in his work. My brethren in office have asked me to be a witness on their behalf of the loving esteem and reverence in which we have always held our beloved leader. We never had a difference of opinion with him. What happiness that is to look back to! There was never a strife, and never an unkind word.

"I do not wish in any way to be thought a critic of our dear pastor. I loved him too well for that. George Herbert says, 'The minister should be the judge, not the hearer,' and I agree with his sentiment. But I would add my honest testimony to the worth of our beloved friend.

"My opening remark about him is that he was first of all a man of faith, a man of humble trust. He retained much of the child in his nature. God was his Father, and his trust was as simple and childlike at the end of his career as it was at the beginning. I had the honour of hearing his first sermon in London, and he then struck the keynote of his ministry. The sermon was from the Epistle of James, the first chapter, and the seventeenth verse: 'Every good gift and every perfect gift is from above, and cometh down from the Father of lights, with whom is no variableness, neither shadow of turning.' It was a marvellous sight, that morning at New Park Street Chapel, when he came into the pulpit. He had the dew of his youth upon him then. Few of you can remember him as the wonderful youthful preacher; but he spoke with the same confidence in the first sermon, and with the same eloquence, as in later years. He spoke afterwards, perhaps, with riper judgment, but never with greater power than when he spoke to those eighty or one hundred people in 1853.

"My next remark about him is, that he was a man of prayer. He did not depend merely upon his own prayers, but he always invited the prayers of his people. When the prayer-meeting was well attended, he expected a blessing. I will try to prove that to you in his own words. When the congregations of the church began to increase at New Park Street, did he say, 'I am a popular preacher. I am a successful man?' No; this is what he wrote to me: 'The house was filled with hearers; many souls were converted; and I always give glory to God first, and then to praying people.'

"My third testimony about him is, that he was a grateful man. He was grateful not only for the prayers of his people, but for their offerings. When he was away from home, I used to send him a telegram every Monday morning with an account of the proceedings of the previous Sabbath, and he wrote to me that he valued those telegrams very much. This postcard was sent to me from Menton in answer to such a telegram: 'The news of the offering rings the bells in my heart. What a good people I have.'

"The fourth testimony I have to bear is, that the greatest joy that our dear Pastor ever experienced, was in the salvation of souls, in the increase of the church, and in the glory of Christ's kingdom. I will read you an extract from a private letter sent to me: 'Your telegram was one of the grandest ever transmitted on the wires. It made my heart sing, "Hallelujah!" Blessed be the Lord for the care of his church! Dr. Pierson has sent me the outlines of his sermons, which prove that he deals in the finest of the wheat.' My telegram had told him that forty-nine had joined the church; I think it was in December; and his reply shows the joy with which it filled his heart. He adds, 'May the forty-nine new friends be a real accession of strength.' To which we all add, 'Amen.'

"I bear record of him, in the fifth place, that he had a very kindly esteem of the church officers by whom he was surrounded. An extract from another letter will make this clear:—'May the Lord richly bless you. Never man had a kinder company of friends, or felt more bound to them. Let us pray for a blessing exceeding all that we have hitherto known. It may be had. It will be had.'

"I must also bear testimony that he inspired very great confidence in us all. Whatever he recommended we accepted at once. I can remember the building of this great Tabernacle, the opening of the Stockwell Orphanage, and other things which we have not time to refer to. Many of the great undertakings might, at first, have seemed imprudent; but his plans were always well matured. They were always thought over beforehand, and prayed upon, before they were introduced to us. We, as Deacons, had very little to do but to back him up.

"In the next place, he drew out very devoted service. I do not think that he had many drones about him, they would not have been happy in his company. He always set us to work, and started us in such a happy way that we have kept on at it. You know for how many years I have been the treasurer of the church, and you know with regard to the other officers associated with him, how continuous their labours have been. My dear brother, Mr. Joseph Passmore, has been with him from the beginning. The Pastor won our affection and kept it.

"The last point is very tender ground, but we can bear a true witness. He was a most charming companion. You in the church knew many of his excellences, but those of us who were intimate with him and were able to enjoy his private friendship, know what a rich treasury of conversation he possessed. His humour was always humour without baseness. For instance, note one of his remarks to his Deacons. He said, 'You are the best Deacons that any minister was ever blessed with, but do not be proud. You are no better than you ought to be.' This will give you a sample of the terms on which we were. Whenever we met together we were a happy, united band, with confidence in our leader, that he was trusting in the Lord and would lead us to fresh victory. Some of those who have been here with him have gone on before, and I have thought with what pleasure they would welcome him on the eternal shore. Earth is poorer, heaven is richer, for his loss. May it tend to draw our hearts and affections heavenward. If so, the death of our Pastor will be blessed to us, indeed.

Elder J. T. DUNN, on behalf of his fellow officers, said:—
"There are two brethren my seniors. One is laid aside on the bed of sickness, and the other is too feeble to make his voice heard in so large a congregation; therefore I have been asked to speak to-day. My personal reminiscences of our beloved Pastor have only helped to endear him more

and more as the years have rolled on. For some thirty-four years I have been identified as his helper in the work of the church. My recollections of him, so far as regards his tender sympathy and his kindness, which is beyond expression, are very vivid to-day. He was thoughtful in the highest degree, and hearty in all his expressions of brotherly feeling and Christian love. His letters, his words, and his actions speak of a man whose heart was large. Following his dear and blessed Master, he always sought to do unobtrusive acts of kindness, many of which never can be known or spoken of here, but all of which will be known in 'that day.'

"When persons came to enquire concerning salvation, or to confess their faith in the Lord Jesus Christ, how his eyes would brighten; and how heartily he would welcome them. It mattered not to him what the character of the clothing, or what the age of the candidate. He could always meet their condition, and tenderly sympathize with them. Many a one have I seen go into that vestry with a tearful eye, who has returned with joy on the countenance. The Lord has struck the fetters from many a sin-bound soul while upon his knees in that hallowed room.

"His tenderness towards the poor and the afflicted was very noticeable. If, in the morning of the day, he had a communication that some member of the church, or even someone who was not a member of the church, was laid aside, he would turn out of his way, in order that he might call upon the sick one, to help and comfort them.

"Let me say one word concerning my brethren, the Elders whom I represent. We are of one heart and of one mind. Our hearts were knit to the beloved Pastor, and we have pledged ourselves to hold together in the name of the Lord, whom we serve; whatever may be the future history of the church, you will find the Eldership standing as one man for the faith of the Gospel of our Lord Jesus Christ."

The CHAIRMAN here interposed, and touchingly said: "I am sure that you will spare me the minute required to read a telegram, which has just arrived from my dear sister at Menton.

"TELEGRAM FROM MRS. C. H. SPURGEON.

"My heart bleeds with yours, but our beloved's joy is full. We shall see him again, and our hearts shall rejoice. Death shall be swallowed up in victory, and the Lord God will wipe away tears from off all faces.

Spurgeon, Menton."

Rev. W. CORDEN JONES, "a trusted servant and helper in connection with the Colportage Association," gave out the hymn commencing, "Oh, God of Bethel," which was heartily sung, after which it was announced that Principal Gracey, who was to have represented the College, was, to the regret of all, too ill to be present, and that only one other name, reminding us worthily of the text, "Instead of the fathers shall be the children," remained upon the programme.

Deacon WILLIAM OLNEY said: "I have been asked to speak this morning on behalf of the many missionary workers. Our dear Pastor, whom God has taken to himself, had a remarkable power of infusing his own love for souls into the hearts of others. In response to his 'Trumpet Calls to Christian Energy,'* from this platform, men went out of this congregation in hundreds, to fling themselves into the slums of the South of London, and bring in members to this church out of some of the lowest parts of the neighbourhood. As a consequence of this, there are, to-day, twenty-three mission stations, and twenty-six branch schools, and at these places there are every Sunday evening about one thousand of the members of this

---

* The title of one of Mr. Spurgeon's admirable books.

church working for the Lord Jesus Christ amongst the poor. Just before Mr. Spurgeon was taken ill last summer, with that illness which has ended fatally, he used to recount, sometimes in his addresses at the prayer-meeting, sometimes in private conversation, a little incident in mission work which was very touching. A dear brother who, I expect, is present here this morning, wrote to his Sunday-school class in a mission school, and in consequence of those letters, some half-dozen of his boys were brought to a knowledge of the Lord Jesus Christ. Our dear pastor used to tell that story with tears, and to ask all his Christian hearers to be as earnest in telling the story of the love of Jesus by tongue and by pen.

"How was it that our dear Pastor had such a love for mission work, and had such a great influence in spreading it? I think, perhaps, most of all, because he valued the souls of poor men. He looked upon the soul of a poor man as equal in value to the soul of a rich man; he knew that for all eternity the soul of a scavenger, cleansed by the blood of Christ and sanctified by the Holy Spirit of God, would shine as brightly in the crown of the Lord Jesus Christ as a soul of any peer of the realm, who might be brought to the knowledge of the Lord.

"Another reason for his great interest in mission work was his wonderful kindliness of heart. How full of love he was—real charity—not the name of the thing, but the very spirit of it! I remember a dear friend, a poor widow, going up from Bermondsey to join the church. She came back and said, 'Oh, Mr. Spurgeon was so kind to me. He not only spoke in words and received me into the church, but he gave me half-a-crown.' I confess that I was very much alarmed to hear it at the time, for I feared that all the poor widows in Bermondsey would want to come and join the church. But it was an illustration of his kindliness of heart towards the poor.

"The South of London in this mission work is poor, inexpressibly poor, to-day, because of the loss that we have suffered. I beseech you, brethren, men of position and influence and riches, connected with this church, to do for the home mission work, as far as you can, what the Pastor did for it. And let my fellow soldiers of the cross working in South London missions, go forward as led by his spirit, still believing that the gospel which was powerful in his lips shall be powerful in ours also."

The service closed with the Benediction.

Memorial Meeting
FOR MINISTERS AND STUDENTS.

On Wednesday afternoon, February 10th, 1892, commencing at three o'clock, the Memorial Service for Ministers and Students of all Denominations was held, a magnificent congregation assembling, representing all sections of the visible church.

Rev. DAVID DAVIES, of Brighton, after prayer by Dr. PIERSON, announced the opening hymn,—

"Come, let us join our friends above
 Who have obtained the prize,
And on the eagle wings of love
 To joy celestial rise.

"Let all the saints terrestrial sing,
 With those to glory gone;
For all the servants of our King,
 In earth and heaven, are one.

"One family we dwell in him,
 One church above, beneath,
Though now divided by the stream,
 The narrow stream of death.

"One army of the living God,
 To his command we bow;
Part of his host have crossed the flood,
 And part are crossing now.

E'en now by faith we join our hands
 With those that went before;
And greet the blood-besprinkled bands
 On the eternal shore."

The singing by such a number of cultivated male voices, accustomed to congregational praise, was of a most inspiring character.

Rev. ALEXANDER McLAREN, D.D., the Chairman of the meeting, then said : " Dear brethren and comrades in the ministry of the Lord Jesus,—We gather this afternoon united in one sentiment of affectionate reverence for the greatest preacher of his age. I suppose that such a gathering as this, of men more or less directly and exclusively engaged in the ministry of the gospel, differing widely from one another in opinion, forms of government, casts of mind, methods of discharging our work, and yet giving one unanimous suffrage as to the supremacy of our departed brother, is an unheard-of thing. It was not only the genius that we admired; it was not only the splendour of his popular gift, or the diligence with which he cultivated it and offered it to his Master ; but it was the profound faith, the earnestness, the devotion, the self-oblivion, which endeared him to many hearts, and were the secret of his power. Instead of eulogizing the dead preacher, I venture to ask you, with myself, to try to draw lessons from that extraordinary career, which has ended, so far as we are concerned, to-day. It seems to me, meditating on the loss of my dear friend and brother, your brother and friend, that I have learned for myself some lessons, which I venture, with all respect and deference, to press upon you.

"Thinking of C. H. Spurgeon's life, I have learned what is *the staple of a successful ministry*. I would not narrowly construe the word. I would make all allowances for diversities of natural temperament, and for differences of audience to whom we have to speak; but, making all allowances for these, and remembering likewise that no one man is capable of all things, I still point to that coffin, and say that, to myself, it proclaims that if a man desires to reach, and to hold, and to bless, the largest number of his fellow-men, he must keep fast to the great central verities of the Christian faith—salvation through Jesus Christ, the Incarnate Lamb of God; life through the Divine Spirit; faith in Christ, the uniting bond; and simplicity of good works, the manifest token. We do not need—we shall be unwise if we seek—other sources for the power and blessedness of our ministry than the adherence to the regnant facts of man's need, and the all-sufficient supply of that need in Jesus Christ our Lord.

"There is one thing in which all the world is alike, and that is, sin and misery. There is one message that will find its way to all hearts, and that is, the message which our dear brother consecrated his life to proclaim. This needs and implies the consecration of the loftiest intellect, and will reward the energies of the most sedulous cultivation. For there is no greater mistake than to suppose that plainness and efficiency can be secured without toil and pain.

"Our brother was gifted with a natural genius for forceful utterance, which sets him by the side of the greatest masters of the English tongue; but it was not because of natural genius only, but because he had set himself to be 'understanded of the common people,' that his words crystallized themselves into proverbs, that they flashed and glowed with illustration, and never transcended the possibilities and comprehension of the lowest of his audience. That is an ambition which the most learned amongst us, and the most cultured and refined among us, may well set before themselves. I do not believe that any truth is so deep that it is not capable of expression in the English tongue which John Bunyan and C. H. Spurgeon wielded. I do not believe that we Christian ministers have got anything much worth saying to-day which cannot be said in language, that the old women in their garrets, and the little children in their nurseries, can understand and remember. And so,

I say, let us take the lesson of the staple of a successful ministry.

"Will you bear with me while I go a step further, and venture to crystallize another set of thoughts into words, that we may all learn here to-day, what is *the spirit of a Christ-taught and therefore successful ministry?* I know nothing more beautiful, as there was nothing more winning and powerful, in our brother's work, than his utter self-forgetfulness. No affectation; no contortions; few exaggerations; a rich variety of tone and subject; and all made mighty because you could see that the last thing that he was thinking about was himself. The least stain of the opposite thing spoils everything. The harp-string, when it is struck and touched so as to make melody, vibrates and becomes invisible when it is musical; and you and I, dear brethren, must consent to efface ourselves if we would set forth Jesus Christ. The wall on which the pictures hang must be of a neutral tint; and the men who will glorify Jesus must forget themselves.

"Nor is the accent of conviction and the spirit of robust and unfaltering belief less needful. Our friend was little touched by questions and difficulties which torture some of us; but let a man preach the things that he is sure of, be they few or many, and let him keep to himself his doubts. 'YEAST,' the title of a book well-known in its day, was self-condemned, by its title, for yeast is meant to be kept till it has passed through a process before it is fit for human lips. So what we have to set forth is the belief, which, by God's grace, we have won; if we stick to that, we shall not fail to learn and find more. From this bier there comes a voice, 'I believed; therefore have I spoken.' Brethren, let us answer, 'We also believe, and therefore speak.'

"May I say, before I sit down, that *the hidden spring of a successful ministry* is no less taught us to-day than its staple and its spirit. No man will forget himself, or preach with supreme power the great truths of the salvation that is in Christ Jesus, unless in many a silent and secret hour he himself has fed upon these, and unless the way into the holiest of all is very familiar to his willing feet. We know that the marvellous power of fusing all this mighty mass of people, and bearing up their hearts to the throne, which our brother possessed, and which some of us think yet more helpful than his ministry to men, was not gained or kept except by the simple, childlike, continual, close, penitent, aspiring, and yearning communion of his own heart with the Father in the heavens. Brethren, the river that has to fertilize a continent must rise up on the mount of God, and be fed with the pure snows that lie there.

" Pardon me that I have occupied so much of your time, but I sought, if I might, by my humblest and truest testimony of love and of loss in this great grief, to make you share in the lessons which I hope it has taught me."

A hearty " Amen " from many in the audience showed how deep was the response to these words.

Rev. CANON FLEMING, B.D., being next called upon, said :—" There are times when our hearts are quite too full to find utterance, and this is one of them. Even if I could speak as I wish, I could not pretend to embalm your grief for your pastor and friend to-day. As the Chairman has told you, I am with you in a double capacity. I am here as Honorary Secretary of the Religious Tract Society—a society which owed much to the pen, and also to the voice of Spurgeon—a society which he loved, because he loved everything that was catholic, good, and evangelical. I also stand here as an old personal friend who enjoyed his friendship for more than five-and-twenty years, ever since I came to the metropolis and began to work near to him in South London. It goes without saying that he loved his friends; you have only to recall the grasp of his warm hand, and the ' God bless you!' that leaped to his honest lips, to be sure of that.

"I am also glad to stand here as a clergyman of the Church of England, not taking upon myself in the slightest degree to represent my own church, but taking the full responsibility, as one of its working clergy, to say that I feel honoured by being invited to take part in this memorial service. I have not forgotten words which I heard Mr. Spurgeon speak many years ago in South London. He said, 'I would not give a headless pin for a man who did not belong to that denomination which he conscientiously believed to be the best; but I have learned to love truth better than any sect, and Christ more than any church.' Those were strong words. Yes, and in order to Christian union, which we all desire to-day, and which the Church at large, with all its differences, desires and longs and prays for, we must be one in Christ, holding those great cardinal truths which cluster round the cross; which bring men to God, and draw man to man. There are differences of administration, but there is one Lord. There are diversities of opinion, but there is one body. We are under different standards; but I feel that as ministers of all denominations, assembled here to-day, though we may be ranged under very different banners, with names that we love and cherish and honour inscribed on them, yet we have one sovereign standard under which we all rally, and upon which is inscribed the name that is above every name—the name of Jesus.

"Our friend was called for a long time to pass through the baptism of pain. The whole world watched his sick bed; and the letters that he then wrote to you, and the messages that he then sent to you and to others, made that sick bed the best pulpit from which he ever preached. He is now in the Father's house, where are many mansions, and there is no sick room there. No tear can fall within the crystal gates of that kingdom; no pain, no sorrow, no sin, no death can enter there.

"His life had no evening, not even a twilight. His end was so gradual and so gentle, that we may say of him, as our Master said of Lazarus, 'Our friend Lazarus sleepeth.' Who of us, I ask, except those who have a right to personal and domestic sorrow, can mourn for a man who died so happily, his nobly-used faculties possessed up to the last, his life lived out from birth to death like a fruit which blossomed in his youth, and then fell ripe and mellow before the frosts of winter had even touched it? There is no idea of incompleteness resting upon his work. He would have been great in any calling to which he might have devoted himself, but he was greatest of all in that which was the passion of his life—to preach the gospel in order to bring souls to Christ.

"He had the endowment of a surpassing memory, and that, humanly speaking, was a wonderful key to his power and his success. Not only did he forget nothing, but he could command and use whatever he had learned. Yet all the gold, and myrrh, and frankincense of his genius were laid at the feet of Christ, with the humility of a little child, and he was wholly unconscious of the gift that he carried in his hand. He has gone, as a writer has said, a little nearer to the Master of all teachers, himself a great teacher; not always polished, sometimes rugged, plain, homely, but always sweet and pure. His sermons and his books always carry diamonds in disguise.

"How much do all the students here owe in gratitude to him? The old students, many of you now enrolled in the ranks of the ministry, can never forget the depth of his piety, the tenderness of his spirit, the fertility of his illustrations, the power of his prayer, and the sympathy of his marvellous voice, hushed now here below, but richer than ever above. He taught you what it was to be teachable, and not censorious towards others; to be large-hearted, yet true and firm and discriminating, never tampering with truth, and never parleying with error. He made you feel that the Bible is a book not to be suspected, not to be apologized for, but to be believed, trusted, and received with docility as the very Word of God. How are you all, and especially the young men of this generation who are to take up the standard, and carry on the great work to which he devoted his life, to pay him the debt which you feel in your hearts, you owe to him? You can only try to do it by imitating him, and by following him in the spirit of those lessons to which we have just listened from our Chairman. But I venture to suggest that a man will best imitate Spurgeon by not attempting to imitate him at all, and he will best follow him by following HIM whom he loved and served.

"The world to-day is colder, darker, duller, poorer, for his absence; but heaven is fuller, warmer, richer for his presence."

Rev. WILLIAM CUFF led the assembly in a very earnest prayer in which, beseeching God for the present power of the Holy Spirit in the lives of many of the ministers of the Word, he evidently touched a chord which gave a ready response.

Rev. JOHN BOND announced the next appropriate hymn,—

"Far down the ages now,
  Her journey well-nigh done,
The pilgrim Church pursues her way,
  In haste to reach the crown.

"No wider is the gate,
  No broader is the way,
No smoother is the ancient path,
  That leads to light and day.

"No sweeter is the cup,
  No less our lot of ill;
Twas tribulation ages since,
  'Tis tribulation still.

> "No slacker grows the fight,
>   No feebler is the foe,
> No less the need of armour tried,
>   Of shield and spear and bow.
>
> "Still faithful to our God,
>   And to our Captain true;
> We follow where he leads the way,
>   The Kingdom in our view."

The singing was again phenomenal, surging around the building like the voice of many seas.

Rev. J. MONRO GIBSON, D.D., Moderator of the English Presbyterian Synod, then said:—"If the angel of this church—and that title from the Apocalypse seems to be the fittest for him now—were with us once again, guiding this meeting, as he has guided so many in this place, and having it according to his own heart, I am sure that he would forbid that the prevailing tone should be a tone of lamentation. While he was yet alive we fasted and wept, for we said, 'Who can tell whether God will be gracious unto us, that his servant yet may live?' but now that he is dead wherefore should we fast? Can we bring him back again? We shall go to him, but he shall not return to us. Like David, in his great sorrow, we have come to worship him who gave, and who now has taken away. The honoured and beloved widow has given us the true key-note in that beautiful message of hers, which so touches all our hearts, showing, as it does, that she is strong in faith, even as her husband always was: 'He hath done all things well.' Never were palms more appropriate than they are here to-day. Never with more emphasis could the song be sung in Zion, 'O death, where is thy sting? O grave, where is thy victory? Thanks be to God, who hath given his servant the victory, through our Lord Jesus Christ.'

"But then there comes the thought of loss, immeasurable and unspeakable loss. We cannot express nor realize it.

Still we do not forget that, measureless as is the loss, just so measureless was the gift. Forty years of such service! And shall we murmur because it was not lengthened to sixty years, as it might have been? Before we murmur let us consider how rarely in all the history of the church, if ever, there has been just such forty years as this, so real, so full, so world-wide in reach and power.

"We have spoken of the loss as immeasurable, but we may not speak of it as irreparable—not at least in the largest sense. To the dear ones in the home, to those who called him Pastor, and to those who called him friend, it is irreparable; not till the morning of the resurrection can that loss be repaired. But let us not imagine or suggest in our unbelief that God cannot repair to his cause even so great a loss. Is not 'the residue of the Spirit' with him? It is not within the bounds of probability that those of us who have silver in our hairs will ever look upon his like again; but is there any reason to believe that there cannot be such another raised up in the coming generation? May there not be among the young men in this assembly to-day many Spurgeon-like souls? May we not hope and pray that, in this very hour, the petitions which we have been offering may find an answer, perhaps beyond what we have imagined, and that God by his Spirit may already have touched, may be touching now, or may touch ere the service closes, some young hearts with that same fire which began to burn in the soul of Charles Haddon Spurgeon long ago, and has without failing burnt on all these forty years? Oh, may God answer that prayer, and grant his Spirit to many of the students gathered here! Though it is not possible that any of the older men may attain to the measure of the stature of our dear friend, may not everyone of us add just a little to his stature? To the natural stature we cannot add a cubit by taking thought, but to the spiritual stature we can most unquestionably add by the grace of God. How great would be the power if there were just now some increment of spiritual force all over this vast sea of hearts that mourn to-day for Charles Haddon Spurgeon!

"And why should we not expect it? Suppose that, just in proportion as the spirit of sympathy and love has been poured out, there was a spirit of grace and supplication poured out? If only we continue in prayer, and have our hearts open to receive the answer to our prayers, might it not be that the spiritual forces available for the cause of Christ would be even greater now than in the days when the pastor of this church was in his prime? Then it may well be that, marvellously as Christ was magnified in the life, he will be still more marvellously magnified through the death of his great servant, who made his gospel ring out from this spot where we stand, even to the very ends of the earth."

The Rev. HERBER EVANS, D.D., Chairman of the Congregational Union, said:—"Little did I think, when I came here on a Thursday night in May last to hear my friend Mr. Spurgeon; to have another touch of his hand; and to pay my first visit anywhere after I was elected to the chair of the Union; that I should be called upon by the Committee of that Union to attend his funeral, and to express a tribute to his memory. We unite in the unspeakable grief which we all suffer by his departure. Some of us thought, in coming up from the country, that we should look once more upon his face, but perhaps it is better that we should not, because we should be obliged to say for the first time, 'He will not speak to me.' But we are here, in the presence of death, to take a look over into the unseen. It has been said that our dear friend could always preach better on the Sunday, if, on the Saturday, he had been to see the dying, and to have just a look over the brink. I hope that this meeting will help us preachers of the gospel to carry with us home to our different spheres of labour some of the secret power which enabled him to wield such influence, so that we, too, may serve our Master with greater devotedness and earnestness.

"All men, as far as I know, admit now that at the back of all Spurgeon did and all he said there was a man, a true man, a large-hearted man, or, as Milton said of Cromwell, a man of men. He was possessed by the gospel, and he had the deepest conviction of its power to save men, because he knew that it had saved him. He once said in this Tabernacle, 'Next to the Holy Spirit who sets us praying and sets us working, I owe prosperity in preaching the gospel to the gospel that I preach.'

"Everybody who came to hear him, of late years anyhow, would, I think, confess, 'Here is a man that preaches from the bottom of his heart. He believes, without a doubt, what he says.' Dr. Charles Stanford once said, 'Whatever use there may be in doubts, they are not good to preach.' God could not have conferred a greater blessing on this age, than by giving us this man—a man with a great soul, and that soul fully possessed with love towards God and the gospel. He lived not only his own personal life; he moulded the lives of thousands. His character was not like a watch hidden in a pocket, to tell upon the life of one man, but rather like a great clock in a high tower, directing and correcting the lives, shall I say, of millions; showing them time by the light of eternity.

"We must not be misled by the way which some critics have of explaining his great influence. They say that he had a beautiful voice. So he had. They say that he had great humour and great dramatic power and unique eloquence, which is quite true. But his sermons did not carry those things with them when they were printed, and you must therefore explain their success in some other way. Neither did the work that he did as a Christian philanthropist come from those gifts. They must therefore have had another source. This is the grand chapter in Charles Haddon Spurgeon's history, and it is this chapter of philanthropy which has compelled men outside the Christian church to admit that at any rate he was no hypocrite. No, my dear friends, there is only one force sufficient to account for all that this man did. He was a man of God, 'full of faith and of the Holy Ghost.'

"I have heard it said too often to please me, of late, that Mr. Spurgeon had no great advantages of birth and training. I do not believe that. Was it not a great advantage to be born of godly, prayerful parents? Was it not a great advantage to be able to trace his pedigree back for two hundred years to a martyr for Christ in Job Spurgeon, and to a long and unbroken line of preachers who preached because they believed in the gospel? From such a line came this grandest preacher of the age, who preached the word of God without a single hesitation, and who preached all of it. I think he had great advantages of birth and training. Was he not trained in the way he should go? And when he became old, did he depart from it? Was he not led in 'the way everlasting'? And is he not on it now, only a turning or two farther on?

"But there was one thing that he did not inherit, and one thing that he could not transmit—his personal piety. It was from this that his enthusiasm for Christ arose. It was this that kept his life and his zeal kindling to the very last. Let us thank God for such a preacher in our day. He suffered more than many a martyr, but he 'endured as seeing Him who is invisible.' He never could have had such sympathy for orphans without homes, for students without means, for widows without friends, had he not been made perfect by great suffering. The high price which everyone must pay for the power to be a great healer is to suffer even to agony. The old principle is still true, that we can only heal one another with blood.

"There are two Charles Haddon Spurgeons. One is to be buried to-morrow in the midst of great sorrow and grief, in the heart of this city which he loved so well, and which he gave his life to save. Many a man from distant parts will come to that grave, and will say, 'I read his words far away in my distant home, and they turned me to Jesus; and I vowed that when I came to London I would drop a tear over his grave. It is not a tear of sadness, when I think of him it falls as naturally as April rain.' Mothers will take their little children to that grave, and tell them quietly the name of the man that turned them heavenward, and changed their earthly home to a place of peace."

Here the speaker almost reached his native Welsh *hwyl*, and hundreds of strong men in the congregation sobbed like little children.

"But there is one Charles Haddon Spurgeon whom we cannot bury; there is not earth enough in Norwood to bury him—the Spurgeon of history. The good works that he has done will live. You cannot bury them.

"Mr. Spurgeon was the strongest believer in prayer that I ever met. I have preached for him in this place several times, and I have gone away each time with this one conviction: 'This is the greatest believer in prayer I ever met.' His deacons and elders are also men of prayer; it is prayer throughout the place. And that is the reason that Spurgeon was not only a preacher, but a prophet. He was always waiting upon God for his message, and he came to his people with the message he had freshly received from his Lord.

"He has gone, but his works remain. What a grand thing it is, that when we do good it remaineth for ever. I know not from what tree the rail on this platform was cut, but I know that every little leaf that grew upon the parent tree helped to make it strong and helped it to grow. Oh, it is a very sad thing, in one sense, that we Christian ministers and Christian workers pass away so soon, like the leaves of autumn before the blast. But the work remaineth for ever. The world is richer to-day because Daniel opened his window to pray towards Jerusalem. Yes; and the world is a richer inheritance for our children and grandchildren who shall come after us, because Charles Haddon Spurgeon lived. Sleep on, then, dear brother after thy great toil, in that dreamless bed, until the time shall come which thou hast prayed for—the resurrection of the body. Friendship and love will cast their garlands on thy memory, and good men and women here and hereafter shall bless thee for the noble work which thou hast done so well."

The Rev. T. B. STEPHENSON, D.D., President of the Wesleyan Conference, said:—"'If you would find his monument look around.' Those words have been in my mind ever since I looked upon this sea of faces to-day. I refer now not so much to this building, which will always be associated with the memory of our brother, as to this wonderful gathering, one gathering only amongst many wonderful gatherings. This meeting is unique; it will be historical; and it answers to all the world the question, 'What was Spurgeon's place in the Christian Church?' People are already asking whether Spurgeon was a great man, and with their lilliputian measuring-rods they are trying to find the size of his faith, of his work, and of his character. How idle it all is. Men, even in the hour of their death, are not always appreciated at their real greatness, but no man, who was not in the noblest sense a great man, could have won, or have deserved, such a testimony as your presence here to-day is giving to his memory.

"I am here on behalf of the Methodist churches, which desire, through my poor lips, first of all to give glory to God for the abounding grace which has shone through the words and life of his servant; and secondly, to pay to his honoured and fragrant memory our tribute of affection, of admiration and gratitude. He did not belong to us except as he belonged to all the churches, but he did belong to us because he belonged to all.

"Like the loftiest and strongest servants of God, he was a denominationalist. He believed in something; he believed it strongly, and he believed it intelligently. Therefore he belonged to a defined and recognizable section of the Holy Catholic and Apostolic Church. But because his was a lofty spirit, his brotherly affection flowed far and wide beyond the boundaries of his own church. His quick eye recognized the essential truth wherever it was found, and he called every man brother who was true to the Master, Christ, and who desired that all his work should find its centre at the cross of Calvary.

"Even when ministering to his own, as we all know well, his influence was never confined to his own. Out of him, because of his great faith, flowed rivers of living water, and the streams thereof found their way to the very ends of the earth. He belonged to us all. We were all the better because of him. To this church, of course, he belonged in a more special and intimate sense; but it has shown by the arrangements in which we have been suffered to take part, that it does not grudge to any of us that we should claim our heritage in his great work and life.

"In his early years he spoke of the Methodist theology with some tartness, not to say severity. We have always thought that then he did not quite understand us. As his career progressed, he came to find that we were nearer a good deal to him than he thought in those earliest days. At all events he loved us much; he served us nobly on many occasions; and he showed that he was not to be divided from those who earnestly and honestly loved the Lord Jesus Christ, by any of those minor points of division which he held to be light indeed, in comparison with the great central truths. But if he had spoken of any views which we may hold far more severely than he ever did, we would not think of it, we could not think of it to-day. We think to-day only of his exultation of his Master, Christ; only of the passionate fervour with which he besought men to come to Christ and be saved; only of the Spirit of Christ which shone in all his works throughout his noble life.

"Many things have been said to-day which will, I am sure, dwell in your memory, and which I will not attempt to repeat; but there are two thoughts which I venture to suggest to you in reference to our dear friend who has gone. I think that he rendered a great service to his age, and to the coming age also, in that he upheld during so long a life the majesty of preaching. Men say that preaching is played out, and that the pulpit is superfluous. The editor is to be the great minister of God in the future, and the people are to get their gospel from the newspapers. God grant that they *may* get gospel from the newspapers, and that the editors may be equal to the duty which some of them are prepared to accept. But with that coffin before us, none of us can doubt that the pulpit is the power in the world still—that still by the foolishness of preaching God is pleased to save men. And I am quite sure that in the fact that from this place there rolled forth over the world a voice which it was willing to hear, and which it listened for—yes, listened for, even through the strife and din of politics, of commerce and pleasure—there has been maintained a testimony to the power of the simple preaching of the gospel, the value of which it is impossible for us to estimate now.

"I confess to one thing that always drew me very strongly to our dear friend, and which, I think, has accounted for the wonderful hold that he has had upon, not religious circles only, but upon the mass of the people throughout this country, and that is the fact that with all the gracious and abounding unction which attended his words and ministry, there was a healthy and natural manliness. It is not always easy when we are speaking of the deepest things of God to avoid a look and tone which the world is very ready indeed to misinterpret. Sometimes it is difficult for us ourselves to keep clear, altogether, from the unreal in thought and feeling when we are dealing with those subjects which lie deepest in our hearts; and the world is not slow to call by the ugly name of 'sanctimoniousness' that which we very often are delighted to recognize as the working in us and out of us of the Spirit and mind of God. Mr. Spurgeon, though he delighted to speak of the deepest things, and though he allowed his delight in speaking of those deepest things to be obvious to everybody, yet, when he was speaking of his closest and deepest relations to the Lord Jesus Christ, he always had in tone and manner a naturalness, a brightness, a cheeriness, which went to every man's heart, and which made men say, 'That is a true man. However, he may be talking about things that are beyond me, and belong to a region that is higher and farther than I have yet penetrated, yet he is a true man.'

"In showing to the world the glorious example of a fine, healthy, natural manliness in connection with the sweetest evangelical doctrine, and the richest evangelical experience, he has also rendered very great service to the Church of God. During the last two or three days, those words of the Saviour, applied to the Baptist, have been running very often in my mind with reference to our departed friend.

"'What went ye out to see? A reed shaken with the wind?' No, this was no reed shaken with the wind. This was a man who knew his mind, and had a will of his own, and could not be bent hither and thither by every passing breeze.

"'What went ye out to see? A man clothed in soft raiment? behold, they that are gorgeously apparelled and live delicately are in kings' courts.' No courtier was this man, seeking carefully for the word which would not grieve his patron. This was a man who dared to speak the truth to anybody, even to the great king 'Mob.' This man was ready to take the consequence of his deed. His life was not devoted to having the softest bed, the pleasantest place, the healthiest work, and the largest honour. He was ready to bear the consequences of his faith and duty—ready to suffer and endure, rather than to be false to his convictions, or negligent of his opportunities.

"'But what went ye out to see? A prophet?' Yea, a foreteller, a messenger whom God sent, and who, because he was a true messenger, was, above all other things, anxious to deliver his message. If the prophets whom God raises up even now have ever a message given to them —something that comes from the divine mind and must pass through other minds to the people—happy is he who is willing and content to be the messenger of God.

"Those wonderful lips, upon which many of us hung so often with delight, are closed now, and we shall hear the silver voice no more: but we thank God that we have heard it. We glorify God for the grace that dwelt so constantly upon those lips; and, amid all the sorrow of to-day, we rejoice in this consolation, that the voice, though stilled on earth, is already heard in praise before the throne of God."

The Rev. A. T. PIERSON, D.D., who was the next speaker, said:—

When the whole Church of Christ gathers about the bier of a saint, it is very proper that America should be represented, and I am here, inadequate as I am, as such a representative, to lay the garland of American Christians alongside of this grave.

I am not one of those who share the faintest hope that

Charles Haddon Spurgeon will be reproduced in this age, or in any other. God never reproduces a man; and when he made Charles Haddon Spurgeon he broke the mould. But we may, from this blessed and sanctified life, learn something about the way to live. The alabaster flask has been broken, and the whole house is full of the odour of the ointment. But, if we cannot construct another alabaster flask like this which is shattered, we may, at least, by the odour that fills the whole Church of God to-day, learn what it is that makes a life fragrant to holy men, and even to a gainsaying world.

I think that I never felt the responsibility of speaking for a few moments, more than in this marvellous assembly, in which, I presume, more ministers of Christ and students of the Word are represented than, perhaps, in any single assembly that has met in the British Isles for half a century.

One danger in reviewing such a life as this is, that we shall hastily dismiss our own responsibility by simply saying of such a man, " He was an inimitable genius." Has it ever occurred to us that Mr. Spurgeon was great, not so much on account of any single faculty, or achievement, or peculiarity, which was so colossal as to overtop all else; but rather that he was great by the rare combination of beautiful and useful characteristics? And, if we may not aspire to the like combination for ourselves, may we not, from the individual peculiarities, learn something of what is possible to be embodied and illustrated in our own individual lives?

I am deeply persuaded that, whatever we may say about this marvellous man, there is for his greatness, a basis, both natural and supernatural, which it is possible for us to understand, and in some measure to reproduce.

For example, as to *the natural basis of his usefulness*, I would remark, first of all, his love of truth—of what was genuine, of what was honest, of what was outspoken. He reminds me of Seneca's pilot, who, in the midst of the stormy waves, looked out on the waters, and said, "Neptune, you may sink me, or you may save me, but I will hold my rudder true!" You may not have agreed with Mr. Spurgeon in the course which he lately pursued with regard to his convictions of doctrine and of duty; but no man is here present who can withhold his hearty admiration from one of the most heroic acts known in the century. There are very few men that make new friends after the age of fifty years. When a man cuts himself loose from the friends of his manhood and his maturer life, and stands virtually isolated and alone because he feels that in some matters, which others consider minor matters, but which he himself thinks are major matters, he is called upon to suffer, for the truth's sake, such heroism would have led a man to the stake in the days of martyrdom.

And then, dear Mr. Spurgeon, besides having a love of truth, was never afraid of hard work. We speak of "a man of genius" as though genius need not be allied with industry to accomplish results. I am not so much a believer in genius as some men are; but I am thoroughly a believer in the genius of industry. He spared himself no effort, down to the last days of his life. Even in the midst of the weakness and suffering at Menton, within the last few months, he painstakingly revised a considerable portion of his forthcoming Commentary on the Gospel according to Matthew. Spinoza, among many things that are false and fallacious, says very many true things; among others he says this: "There is no hindrance in the way of personal advancement that is more fatal than simple self-conceit and the laziness which self-conceit begets." To think that we have accomplished anything, and to lie by on our oars and let ourselves drift, because, forsooth, something has been achieved that lies in the past, is the death-blow to all real progress. My brother, the best work which you did ten years ago will not take the place of the best work you can do to-day, any more than the nutritious bread that was baked a month ago will answer for your present appetite. We must have new experiences, fresh accumulations, and higher exaltations of spirit, if we are to keep up with the demands of the multitude about us, nay, with the demands of our own souls.

Then I greatly admired in dear Mr. Spurgeon the marvellous singleness and simplicity of his aims. Archbishop Whately said, that "many a man aims at nothing, and hits it with remarkable precision." We must have something to aim at if we want to secure results in this life of ours. Charles Haddon Spurgeon aimed at something desirable to be accomplished, and by the grace of God attainable in the way of accomplishment, and steadily pursued his aim; therefore he was the man that he was.

And what zeal such singleness of aim gave him. I was taking up yesterday a little analysis made by Dr. Andrew Bonar, when he sat down in his study to contemplate modern zeal. He felt compelled to write that he believed, in his own case, oftentimes what he would call zeal for his Lord, if it were analyzed and divided into a hundred parts, would be found to consist of—

Personal ambition	23 parts.
Love of praise	19 parts.
Pride of denomination	15 parts.
Pride of talent	14 parts.
Love of authority	12 parts.
Bigotry	10 parts.
Love of God	4 parts.
Love of man	3 parts.
Making in all	100 parts.

Here ninety-three parts are carnal, leaving but four parts for love to God, and three parts for love to man. When we come to submit our zeal to this awful divine chemistry, how fearfully humbling are the analysis and the result!

As I am speaking to fellow ministers, I want to say here, that because of this singleness of aim, among other things, he never lost sight of the oratorical character of a sermon. I pray you to notice that *sermo* is speech, whose means is eloquence, and whose end is persuasion. A sermon is not an essay; it is not a theological discussion; it is not a poetic production. It is, first of all, something that has an aim. That aim should be to bring men to Jesus Christ, the Justifier, the Sanctifier, the Redeemer. The oratorical character of a sermon depends on the supremacy of a practical aim, an aim outside of self, an aim so unselfish and absorbed in God that it shall lead a man to say, what Ignatius said, when he stood in the arena at Rome, awaiting the onset of the Numidian lions: "I am grain of God. I must be ground between the teeth of lions to make bread for God's people."

We may not have the genius of Charles Haddon Spurgeon, but, if we will imitate his love of hard work, his love of the truth, his love of souls and the singleness of his aim, we may attain to results of a similar kind to his, even though not in a similar measure.

But now in full view and sense of my responsibility I want to say, before I close, a word on *the supernatural basis of his power;* and may God give me special grace in th most important duty. The supernatural basis is the only one that will account for the marvellous character or the marvellous career of that man whose ashes are before you.

Mr. Spurgeon believed first of all in the full infallible inspiration of the Word of God. To him the Bible was God's book *par excellence*, not pre-eminently God's book, but solely God's book, inspired in such a sense as makes the word *inspiration* applicable to no other book ever put before the human race.

He believed, in the second place, in the inspiring Spirit as a personal Spirit; that, when God revealed his will in ancient times, holy men of old were moved to write the Scriptures by the Holy Ghost, so that the product was essentially the product of the Spirit of God, and not of the spirit of man. I speak emphatically on this subject, for the modern theories of inspiration are so constructed as to let out entirely the supernatural element. When we are told, for instance, that a prophet, knowing certain fundamental principles of God's moral government, and being himself an accurate observer of human affairs, and a close student of human nature, was thereby enabled to predict the future of his people, I would like to know what is to hinder any other man who knows God's great moral principles, who is an accurate observer of events, and who is a student of character, from being himself a prophet and uttering predictions! But what does Peter say concerning the prophets themselves? "Searching what, or what manner of time the Spirit of Christ which was in them did signify, when it testified beforehand the sufferings of Christ, and the glory that should follow." I pray you, intelligent, educated, cultivated brethren, to notice the two intelligences which Peter recognizes: the spirit of the prophet, and the Spirit of God that was in the prophet; these two intelligences being actually engaged in a sort of conflict among themselves, so that the inferior intelligence searches to know what the superior intelligence indicates in the unintelligible words which the prophet writes and speaks. Now, Mr. Spurgeon believed in those two intelligences— the Spirit of God and the spirit of man; and in his preaching and study of the Word of God, he sought to rise into the atmosphere of the superior Intelligence, that he might bring down the thoughts of God to the level of man. That is, more than any other assignable cause, the secret of his preaching.

In the third place, he believed in the personal indwelling of the Spirit of God in the soul and body of the believer, constituting him a temple of the Holy Ghost.

Put these three things together, and see whether any man can heartily believe in them without being a mighty and spiritual preacher. See the effect in the interpretation of the Word! If human authors produced the Bible, then how are we in interpreting the Bible to secure the aid of the authors? Can we go into the catacombs and summon from their tombs the dead whose pens were concerned in the production of the Scriptures? But if the Holy Ghost is the author of the Scriptures—if the handwriting is the handwriting of God, though the hand is the hand of man, then I submit to you, that in the interpretation of the Bible, we may reverently call the Author himself to our aid. What is the consequence? Mr. Spurgeon found out, and others who believe like him have grasped the same truth, that the originality of sermons depends not on our invention, but on our discovery. That is to say, instead of inventing a discourse out of our own minds, and attaching it by the artificial hinge of a text to the Holy Scripture, we search to know what the Holy Ghost means in the Word of God; and when, by his gracious aid, we have discovered his meaning, we unfold that meaning in the discourse. So the greatest sermon is that which unfolds the greatest discovery of the hidden Spirit.

Now, Mr. Spurgeon had to cultivate his own individual life of piety, or all this would have become impossible to him. If the Spirit of God dwells in a man, and is to illumine the pages of the Word, the clearness of such illumination will depend on the unobstructiveness of the media through which his light shines. If we would have fellowship with God which is constant and uninterrupted, we must keep the panes of glass, in the windows, clear. Then the Spirit's light, burning within us, and shining through the undimmed medium upon the pages of Scripture, will unfold to us the wondrous things of God. But if we close those windows with dark shutters, if our failure to realize divine communion and to live in fellowship with God intercepts and hinders the Spirit; if, in other words, as Paul says, we "quench the Spirit," how can the light of the Spirit which must shine through our own experience, illustrate and illuminate the pages of the Word that we are to expound and explain?

Oh, my brethren, we need in these days, more than all else, one more touch of the supernatural in our individual lives! Give me the man that preaches with a deep personal sense that God lives in him by the Spirit, and that this Book is a living book, which the living Spirit inspired, and in which the living Spirit still dwells; then bring the man, who is himself a living temple of the Spirit of God, into contact with the Book, which is the living utterance of the Spirit of God, and how can there but come from such a ministry power to convert, power to sanctify, power to edify, and power to redeem?

This is the message which your American brother brings in humility and simplicity this afternoon to this great assembly of ministers and students of the Word. God give us the spirit of Charles Haddon Spurgeon, for that spirit was the Spirit of God!

D. L. MOODY sent his greeting by telegraph from Paisley. The message was read at this juncture, and ran, "Heartiest sympathy with sorrowing friends in London. 'Jesus Christ the same yesterday, and to-day, and for ever.'"

Rev. F. B. MEYER, B.A., the last speaker, was called upon when the time for the meeting had expired, and when already the crowd was gathering at the doors for the evening service. He spoke amid interruption, caused by some who were compelled to leave, and said :—" In the midst of a great campaign, one of the leading officers may suddenly fall fatally wounded, and for a moment his comrades in arms may call a halt around his body, but there is not a thought of renouncing the campaign in which they with him were engaged. Every man feels himself once again called by that event to more entire consecration to the great ends for which his leader died. Surely it would be a mistake if we were to allow the feelings which have been called out by this memorial meeting to subside, without our gathering around this coffin with these remains, and once again pledging ourselves, one and all, to renewed devotion to the Captain of our salvation, and to renewed energy in the preaching of his holy gospel. The prophet may have been taken up into heaven, but it is not wise for us to stand gazing thither, we must seek again to be clothed about with the power that made him what he was. Then let us betake ourselves along the lonely way to the Jordan, to the sons of the prophets, and to the work that still remains to be done in the land. The man of God who has been taken from us was indeed a golden vessel, and the most of us are but of earth or wood; but it was not because he was gold that he was what he was, but because the Master used him. If we to-day will only once again put ourselves into the hands of the Master, and seek an enduement of that same Spirit, surely from this gathering there will go forth a tide of holy influence that shall touch, and illuminate, and fill many a church with new power. I ask you, therefore, to join with me in a few moments of solemn dedication, that we may again lay ourselves on that altar that sanctifies the gift, and that we may seek a fresh enduement of the Holy Ghost. Then men shall say of us, 'The spirit of Elijah doth rest upon Elisha,' then Jordans shall part before the mantle, then we shall go forth to follow our departed brother in his works of healing and salvation."

Mr. MEYER then led the assembly in a dedicatory prayer, in which occurred the following passage:—" We know how rich thou art, else thou hadst not been able to spare from this earth so rare a man as this. How royal thou art, how full thy hand is of those ascension gifts, unexhausted by the flight of ages, and the demands of thy Church, since thou art able to give men like this, and then to take them to thyself again." Thanking God for Mr. Spurgeon's unblemished, stainless character, and for his sweet humility so unaffected, the speaker mourned the years in our own lives which the cankerworm and the caterpillar had eaten, and besought renewed grace which would enable all to fight the good fight, to finish the course with joy, and to keep the faith unto the end.

Rev. J. McEWAN, D.D., pronounced the Benediction, and this remarkable meeting was at an end.

Memorial Service

FOR CHRISTIAN WORKERS.

On Wednesday evening, February 10th, 1892, the service specially designed for Christian workers of all denominations, and church members, other than members of the Tabernacle, commenced at seven o'clock. George Williams, Esq., presided.

Mr. W. J. ORSMAN, of the Golden Lane Mission, opened the meeting with prayer, in which he thanked God that, as a wayward youth, he heard Mr. Spurgeon in the Surrey Music Hall, and that there his feet were turned into the way of life. He voiced the feeling of many when he said : " We are sore in heart—troubled, stunned, bowed down with great sorrow, blinded with the bitterest tears we ever shed. Many of thy children are learning the awful mystery of heart-breaking, — carrying griefs they cannot speak, their lives curtained with darkness and suffering; but we pray that in this starless night thou wilt come over the troubled waters, speaking peace to our souls. Thou loving Binder and Healer of torn hearts, in thy pitifulness strengthen us that we may say—' He hath done all things well.' "

Mr. A. H. BAYNES, Secretary of the Baptist Missionary Society, announced Mr. Spurgeon's own version of the thirty-ninth Psalm, so appropriate to the occasion. With great solemnity these verses were sung—

> "Behold, O Lord, my days are made
> A handbreadth at the most;
> Ere yet 'tis noon my flower must fade,
> And I give up the ghost.
>
> Then teach me, Lord, to know mine end,
> And know that I am frail;
> To heaven let all my thoughts ascend,
> And let not earth prevail.
>
> What is there here that I should wait,
> My hope's in thee alone;
> When wilt thou open glory's gate
> And call me to thy throne?
>
> A stranger in this land am I,
> A sojourner with thee;
> Oh, be not silent at my cry,
> But show thyself to me.
>
> Though I'm exiled from glory's land
> Yet not from glory's King;
> My God is ever near at hand,
> And therefore I will sing."

Mr. GEORGE WILLIAMS, President of the Young Men's Christian Association, said: "Charles Haddon Spurgeon was the gift of the great Father to the church universal. The Metropolitan Tabernacle was the great centre of his labours, but the result of his labours could not be contained within these walls. They flowed over like a fountain; bubbling up here, they reached the whole metropolis, the whole of England, all over the world where the English tongue is spoken, and in many countries where it is unknown. Therefore it is that we are exceedingly grateful to this church for giving us, the outside Christian public, the opportunity of coming and expressing our devout gratitude to Almighty God for having raised up Charles Haddon Spurgeon to be a blessing to the whole world!

"What a welcome he must have received in heaven ere this! What an abundant entrance into the kingdom of our Lord and Saviour Jesus Christ must have been his! What shouts and Hallelujahs! What palms of victory and triumph! We are left sorrowing, but we will rejoice that God lent him to the church militant so long. With what power, with what force, with what strength of will he laboured here! A very Samson, he slew the Philistines right and left! Like David, no Goliath was too large for him to encounter and to overcome in the strength of the Lord!

"Now that he has gone, we desire that his mantle might fall upon us. What was the secret of his strength? Was it not his nearness to his dear Lord, the communion which he had with his Master? Was it not the intensity of his love, the steadfastness of his faith? Is not God saying to us, through his beloved servant, 'Be it unto you according to your faith'? I remember hearing of a conversation which he had with a minister who came to him depressed because of the lack of conversions as a result of his ministry.

"Mr. Spurgeon said to him, 'But surely you do not always expect conversions when you preach?'

"'No, of course I do not,' the minister replied.

"'Well, then,' Mr. Spurgeon said, 'be it unto you according to your faith.'

"I believe that dear man of God, as he stood in this pulpit, expected conversions, and what he expected God gave him. May the implicit faith which he had in God, dwell also in us.

"His will be a great name in the history of England for this century. As the names of Whitefield and Wesley have such a sweet savour amongst us, so will his be for ever fragrant. We shall speak now of Whitefield and Wesley and Spurgeon as the three great departed leaders in the evangelical cause.

"We praise God for this gift, which we have not yet fully appreciated. What good cause did not dear Mr. Spurgeon help? How often he put new life into a meeting by his presence. Wherever he went the people came, and his great sense, and love, and faith inspired all with confidence. How the British and Foreign Bible Society valued his presence at their annual gatherings! How the London City Mission benefited by his aid! How the Young Men's Christian Association relied upon the advocacy of his voice and pen! How the various missionary societies were stimulated by his enthusiasm! When we think, too, of what he did for other churches and other denominations, what a focus of power for good is seen in his life.

"I desire, on behalf of the multitude outside of the Metropolitan Tabernacle, to give expression to the intensity of our admiration, and love for your beloved Pastor. All of us—the Church of England, the Congregationalists, the Wesleyans, the Presbyterians, and every other congregation —saw in him a champion, a holy, mighty man of God, ready to stand in the front, and to maintain those blessed doctrines of the old gospel, which had won his heart, and which he knew would win the hearts of other men. Therefore, it is that we desire to express to the beloved wife, and to the dear sons, our intense sympathy. How rejoiced he must have been to have had such sons! God bless them! May the mantle of their father fall upon them, and upon his dear brother and sisters may the blessing of God abundantly rest. God be praised for sparing them. We pray that the dear friend from America, who is ministering in holy things in this place, may be preserved and guided in all the future; that the crowds who have been in the habit of attending here, may continue to attend, and that benefit and blessing may continue to flow out from this congregation to the ends of the earth."

Sir ARTHUR BLACKWOOD, K.C.B., President of the Mildmay Conference, said:—"If the beloved brother whose remains lie here to-night could speak to us, I believe that he would say, 'Speak not of me, but of my Saviour; or, if you must speak of me, speak of the great God who was magnified in me.' He ever loved to hide himself, so far as his strong personality permitted, behind the Saviour whom he preached. Wrapped in the folds of the banner of the Cross, which he so courageously, so steadfastly, so persistently waved, his main desire was to be nothing, that Christ might be all and in all. We shall honour him most truly, we shall express our love most fittingly, we shall justify our regard for his person most really, if we seek to do as he would bid us do.

If our brother has desires concerning the work of God on earth, surely they are that, by his entrance into the kingdom of glory, multitudes might find their entrance to God's kingdom of grace on earth. As with zeal, he ever delighted to draw the sword of battle against the enemies of the truth, that they might become its friends; and as multitudes have fallen beneath the weighty strokes of that weapon, so he would wish that those whom he slew in his death should be more than they whom he slew in his life. If perchance it was permitted to Elisha to know and to rejoice in the fact that his very remains possessed such life-giving power that the man whom they were burying hastily in his grave no sooner touched them than he came to life, well may our beloved and departed brother rejoice, if it be permitted to him to know, that by his death many have entered into life eternal. And as for him to live was Christ, in this sense to die will be most certainly gain. Thus we can rejoice with him and thank God; and if we weep we will look upward through our tears, and rejoice as we think of the perfect bliss and ineffable enjoyment which is now his. He has entered into rest by the side of the River of the Water of Life, whose streams he has ministered in such fulness to thirsty multitudes on earth. He has also entered upon a career of service which no pain, nor weakness, nor sickness, can ever interrupt. The hand that, like Eleazar's, clenched the sword with such a grip that it could not be unloosed, now waves the triumphant palm; and the voice that told out with such inexhaustible fulness the unsearchable riches of Christ his Lord, now sings that new song with multitudes around the throne.

"What was it that gave Charles Haddon Spurgeon his power? What may we learn from the testimony of his life? Is it not this above all things, that the glorious gospel of the blessed God which so permeated his whole being, and which he so rejoiced in preaching, lives on, and has undying power within it to turn the hearts of the disobedient to the wisdom of the just; to fascinate the humble, to abase them that sit on high; to lift up the beggar from the dunghill, and to set him among the princes in the very presence of God? What was it that, when our brother lay stricken by mortal illness last summer, evoked such anxious solicitude from the very steps of the throne, from the bishop's bench, from the great, the noble, throughout the land, and from millions of unknown folk who had hung upon his lips and read his writings? What was it that made this man so great? What is it that now causes princes to send their telegrams of sympathy to his bereaved widow? that causes the Bishop of this diocese, with true brotherly Christian love and respect and esteem for his memory, to follow him to his grave; what makes millions upon millions mourn to-night throughout the whole world? What is it that made this man the object of such respect, such veneration, and such love? Was it his wide range of philosophy, his extensive scientific knowledge, his soaring intellect? No; the cause lies deeper than these. Was it his mother wit, his command of his native tongue, his genial face, his loving grasp? No; it was the firm grasp that he had of the gospel of Christ, the unflinching earnestness and faithfulness with which he preached it, the valour with which he stood in the gap when men fled on all sides, his adherence to the doctrines of grace, and his determination to know nothing among men save Jesus Christ and him crucified. This it was that gave him his hold upon the hearts of thousands.

"I may well quote the eloquent, truthful, and noble words that, but three days ago, were uttered by the Archdeacon of London, in St. Paul's Cathedral, as he said that it was 'the unswerving strength, the exuberant vitality of his faith in God's revelation to man through his Son Jesus Christ, combined with the weight and warmth of his zealous love for souls, that gave him that unbounded power which he exercised so loyally for Christian belief among the classes who are the very backbone of England, and throughout the English-speaking race.'

"'When he left the pulpit,' said Lord Houghton, 'whatever your impressions might have been as a mere critical hearer when you came in, he left it an inspired apostle.'

"He has now left the pulpit for ever, but his apostleship lives on in the quickened hearts and lives of innumerable hearers, and his inspiration is acknowledged of all men. That is why his funeral will be made almost a national occasion, and why all good and devout men among his countrymen, without distinction of faith or sect, will stand in spirit around his grave.

"A sympathetic, yet not uncritical writer, has lately observed, 'Mr. Spurgeon had but one sermon, but that sermon was always new. To him, Christianity was not an argument but a message, and a message to be believed at once by those who heard him.' No higher praise than that can be given to a minister of Christ's gospel. He took for his style and dignity, the apostolic words, 'We are ambassadors for Christ.' He trod in his footsteps who, amid all the vapourings of the schools, poured contempt upon the philosophies, falsely so called, that filled the air, and said,

'I am determined to know nothing among you save Jesus Christ and him crucified.'

"When we think of the universal sorrow, of the world-wide feeling of respect and love that his deeply-lamented removal from us has aroused throughout the whole world, is it not a token for good that God's Spirit yet remaineth among us; and that in these days of darkness, doubt, difficulty, unbelief, and intensified worldliness, wherever the gospel of Christ is firmly held and purely preached, multitudes are won and God is still glorified among us.

"Speaking for myself, highly privileged to stand here to-night, I feel as one who has lost a very personal friend. We did not meet often, but when we did, how refreshing it was to look him in the face, to grasp his hand, and to hear his cheery voice. What a lift up he gave at Mildmay Conference not once nor twice only; how he carried us with him in his enthusiastic and eloquent utterances of truth! I remember what good it did me when, some years ago, after he had preached in some country church, I ventured to speak a word with him in the vestry. Putting his hand on my shoulder, he said, 'Well, brother, we always know where to find you.' That cheery word of kindly commendation made me feel six inches taller than I had ever felt before, and sent me on my way rejoicing.

"Still more do I feel that in him I have lost in common with you all, a trusted leader, one to whom we instinctively looked for words of counsel when days were dark. He had almost intuitive, because God-given, discernment of the things that Israel ought to do in times of perplexity, and often uttered a word of vigorous cheer, loud and plain above the din of battle, which sent courage into all who could catch its notes.

"It seems as if a light that had burned brightly and savingly on a stormy coast, and had lighted many a ship safely into her haven, had suddenly been quenched. But we look up and forward. We know that he who fitted Charles Haddon Spurgeon for the work to which he called him here on earth is well able to supply his place. It may not be exactly in the same way, for God has no duplicates in his museum; it may be by men of other gifts and other powers; but surely that life is a token that God has not left his people; and that, as the century waxes old, and the coming of the Lord draweth nigh, he will send forth labourers into his vineyard.

"Upon us, however feeble our strength, however small our sphere, lies the responsibility of holding aloft, with all the vigour that God shall give us, the torch of truth which he has put into our hands; of following, though it may be at a distance and humbly, the steps of that valiant leader and champion of our Lord Jesus Christ's cause on earth. To us it remains to defend his truth in our measure as he defended it; and then, when we shall see our brother again, it shall be with the joy of feeling through God's grace that we have endeavoured to carry on the work that he has commenced His work will never end, his voice echoes still; by his printed page, circulated in every land, and by thousands and thousands of souls whom God permitted him to win for Christ, Charles Spurgeon's voice will go on and on as long as this world shall last. As long as the names of Latimer and Ridley, of Baxter and Bunyan, of Wesley and of Whitefield are known and loved, so long will the name of Charles Haddon Spurgeon be esteemed and remembered. God grant us grace to follow his steps, for Christ's sake."

Mr. IRA D. SANKEY said: "I feel it a very great privilege to meet here with the thousands who gather around this bier, to pay some little note of homage to one who has done so much for me. That voice is silenced for ever on earth, but who of us here cannot recall its clarion tones as it has moved us from time to time in this great temple.

It has always been my custom, when coming from my own land to this country, to visit this Tabernacle, to have my torch lighted anew for the work in which I have been for years engaged; and never have I come into this building without receiving a blessing from that grand man whom I remember so well standing in this honoured spot, proclaiming the glorious gospel of the Son of God. I have now come from Scotland, where, for over three months, Mr. Moody and I have been holding services throughout the country, preaching the same old gospel that fell from the lips of that honoured man; and I bear testimony to-night in the name of my Master, that the old gospel has not lost its power.

"For years we have watched England and Scotland from our own shores, and a few lighthouses along this coast always attracted our eye. None shone so brightly as the torch that was burning continually in this Tabernacle. When darkness seemed to be spreading over the religious world, we would often cast longing eyes to London, and watch what this great captain was saying and doing. We always found inspiration from this pulpit, and always felt that in him we had a friend who would stand against all foes, a leader that we could safely follow. Many a prayer has come across the sea for him, from those who never had the joy of hearing his magnificent voice, and they are in sympathy with us to-night. Our land loves Charles Haddon Spurgeon. The Church of God on yonder shore has looked to him for years; and now he has gone, they will continue to pray that God may bless the people at the Tabernacle, and send them a man after his own heart to preach the old gospel, the power of God unto salvation.

"I learnt from the Pastor of this church, how to use the voice that God had given me, that I might preach to thousands who have assembled in our great congregations throughout this country and our own land. I might almost say that he taught me how to sing the praises of God. I have held him up as an example to hundreds of congregations, as a man who could inspire his people to worship in hymns of praise, by devoting time to the reading of the hymn, and then himself standing and singing with the people. I hope this example may be largely followed by the ministers of the gospel. The praise of God is a part of the worship, and should not be slighted.

"I bring to-night, to this great congregation, loving messages from Mr. Moody. When he heard that this great man of God had passed away, the first thing he said was, 'I want to go to London to stand by the grave of him who has done so much for me.' C. H. Spurgeon has been a constant inspiration and joy to D. L. Moody. He wanted to come to the funeral, but we could not both of us come away at once, so he said, 'You go, Mr. Sankey, and sing a hymn in honour of that dear man of God.' He remains yonder preaching the gospel, winning souls to Christ; just where dear Mr. Spurgeon would have him to be.

"I will not take up time further, but sing a little hymn that I think may be appropriate for this occasion. It is said that the early Christians, to express their certainty of seeing their friends who had passed away, only bade them 'Good-night,' so sure were they of meeting them on the Resurrection morning. I will sing a little hymn based on that fact, and may God bless the singing to all our hearts."

Mr. Sankey then sang, with exquisite feeling, the hymn beginning—

> "Sleep on beloved, sleep and take thy rest,
> Lay down thy head upon thy Saviour's breast;
> We love thee well, but Jesus loves thee best,
> Good-night! Good-night! Good-night!"

Rev. Canon Palmer, M.A., Rector of Newington, in which parish the Tabernacle is situated, said:—" It requires some courage to attempt to make you hear my voice after the pathetic sounds to which you have just listened. The Pastor for whom you mourn, if he was remarkable for one thing more than another, it was for his fearlessness in speaking the truth. He spoke the truth through evil report and good report, without caring either for praise or blame of men, but only for the opinion of his Master. I am sure, therefore, that you, in this great Tabernacle, have been taught by him not merely to hear truth, but to bear truth; and you will bear with me if, at the outset, I venture to speak some words of truth with respect to myself. I cannot but remember the only other time that I stood in this place. The occasion of my visit was the return of a missionary of the Church of England from Japan, who came bearing a message from a missionary in Japan connected with your own communion—he had, I believe, been educated in your Pastors' College, at any rate, he looked to your Pastor for sympathy and for guidance. The missionary of the Church of England, Mr. Wright, had formerly been curate in the parish of St. Mary, Newington, and, as he was charged to deliver the message from your own missionary to Mr. Spurgeon himself, he wrote to me and asked if I could arrange an interview for him. I wrote to Mr. Spurgeon, and the answer I received to my request was:—

"' Dear Sir,—At this present time it is still an effort to get in and out of the carriage, will you therefore come to me? I think it most kind of you to write to me. Would you like to come to my vestry at the Tabernacle on Monday at six, or on Wednesday at three? Would you send word to the Tabernacle on Sunday morning, for, as I am going away, everybody wants to see me during the next few days, almost as if I were going " to that bourne," etc.'

"I came to the Tabernacle, and spent several hours here, and in the course of a very interesting conversation with Mr. Spurgeon, our remarks turned in the direction of the Church Catechism. He said to me:—

"'I learnt that when I was a boy, and there is a great deal in it which I think very good.'

"I playfully rejoined, 'If you had thought it all very good perhaps you might have been Archbishop of Canterbury.'

"Now I am sure you will suffer me to say that I, at least, think it all very good, and you would think the worse of me, as a minister of the Church, if I did not. For if there are parts of the Church Catechism with which Mr. Spurgeon did not agree, and with which you do not agree, there are parts of it, at least, with regard to which we are one. I am sure that everyone in this Tabernacle would repeat, if it were necessary, the answer to the question, 'What dost thou chiefly learn in these Articles of thy Belief?' 'First, I learn to believe in God the Father, who hath made me, and all the world; secondly, in God the Son, who hath redeemed me, and all mankind; thirdly, in God the Holy Ghost, who sanctifieth me, and all the elect people of God.'

"There are many things in which I agree with you as well as in that. I agree with you in admiration for a Pastor from whose eloquent lips thrilling and heartfelt words shall be heard in this life no more. I agree with you in sympathy as to the perplexity which you must feel in finding someone to be, at any rate at once, all to you that he has been to you. He was no doubt the greatest preacher of this century. In the pulpit at St. Paul's last Sunday there was testimony to that. There is no one whom I can think of who could have held these thousands together Sunday after Sunday, and year after year, as he did. And as the rector of this parish I am here to testify that he was a benefit to every denomination, for he was the great foe to indifference. When the voices of other men would deepen apathy, his voice, like the voice of a trumpet, aroused men and compelled them to think. The gospel which he preached was that saying which is 'worthy of all acceptation,' and which all Christians accept, that 'Christ Jesus came into the world to save sinners'; and if I should not agree with the definition of election which you might give, I should at least be in accord with you in heartily believing that he whose earthly tabernacle lies before us is one of the elect.

"Who had a heart of compassion amongst men if such a heart did not beat in the breast of your Pastor? That heart which beats no more was ever warm with compassion. No one could speak to him, no one could hear the tender thrill of his voice, without at once recognizing the compassion in his heart. Let the Almshouses, which he founded; let the Orphanages, where the fatherless found shelter regardless of the creed of their parents, testify for many a long year to the greatness of the compassion which beat in that great heart of his.

"Here, perhaps, it will not be ungrateful to you if I refer to another of his letters, the first one which I ever received from him. I was reminded of it just now when I entered this assembly by the sound of the bell. It was out of that bell, not a musical sound I admit, that our intercourse arose. This was the letter Mr. Spurgeon wrote to me. The year is not put down, but 'July 6' is the date upon it. It was a particularly hot and sultry July.

"'NIGHTINGALE LANE.

"'DEAR SIR,—I beg to call your attention to the great disturbance caused by the ringing of the bells at St. Gabriel's, while the congregation at the Tabernacle is engaged in prayer. I reminded your predecessor that no right of bell-ringing belongs to any but a parish church, and informed him that I really must appeal to the law to stop the needless nuisance.

I am sure it is far from me to wish to interfere with the peculiarities of my neighbours, but when we are disturbed by the clanging of a loud bell I am obliged to complain. The hours at which we are at worship are after 6.30 on Sunday, from 7 to 8.30 on Monday, and 7 on Thursday. Wishing to be on good terms with all in the parish, I trust you will not allow the bell-ringers to disturb us further, and will substitute a few strokes for the many which are now given.'

"I have no copy of my answer, but I think I could remember its effect tolerably well. It was, that I did not know what the law might order, but I was quite sure of what the gospel required. *It* required that my neighbours should not be unnecessarily troubled, and I would give orders at once that the bell-ringing should be confined to a few strokes, and that I had no doubt that the bell ringer would be very much obliged to Mr. Spurgeon for mitigating his labours in that extremely hot weather. He wrote me at once.

"'DEAR SIR,—I am exceedingly obliged by your prompt and Christian reply. I felt it needful to make my protest against the bell-ringing somewhat strong, that I might not appear to be asking a favour merely, but claiming a right not to be disturbed. Otherwise the lapse of years gives right to a custom against which no protest is entered. This, and no unfriendliness to you, prompted what you considered to be a threat. I can only hope that future correspondence may be, on my part, on a more pleasant subject, and, on your part, may be in the same generous tone.'

"I had occasion to write to him afterwards, but I find that his replies are not all in my possession. They have been carried off by other people. One, I know, is in the possession of a bishop, and another in the hands of an archdeacon, so that I am afraid I shall never be able to get my correspondence again. But I afterwards referred to this little incident of bell-ringing, and he wrote to me and said :—

"'I have been very ill since I returned, but I am now better and ready for work. I am so glad the bell-ringing led to your hearty letter. God bless you.'

"Now, I ask you, was not that a man worth knowing? Does not that show his kindness of heart? He was perfectly right to protect his congregation from disturbance, but, mark his generosity. Directly he saw that I was ready to look at the matter in a reasonable way, his heart overflowed with kindness. When the Secretary of the Hospital Sunday Fund proposed that we should have a joint meeting to promote the cause of hospitals, I want you again to mark your late Pastor's considerate kindness. He at once supposed that I should not like to come to the Tabernacle, and so he said to the secretary :

"'I do not think the Rector would like to come to me, but I should be very glad to come to him, if he will invite me.'

"So I wrote at once and invited him to have dinner with me beforehand on the evening of the meeting. He answered :—

"'Right joyfully would I have accepted your hospitality, but my own meeting does not close till 8.30, and it is a very special one. Its speciality I was not aware of till this week. I hope I may come and see you at some other time, and take a cup of tea with you. This time I must decline. This is unavoidable, and not of my choice. It would give me great pleasure to have an hour with you at the Rectory or here.'

"There were other letters, but I will only refer to one more, as it relates to an important movement, and it aptly illustrates his humility of mind. Some of you may remember that I was appointed by the Bishop as Secretary to a movement for having some lectures on Socialism at the Lambeth Baths. I wrote to Mr. Spurgeon, seeking his co-operation. I asked him, at any rate, if he would put up some bills at the Tabernacle, and he wrote at once—

"Send the bills to the Tabernacle for our lobbies; they shall be put up there. I find notices to be given out at divine service are not congruous, and in making a discriminating choice I might give offence; so I give out only our own needful ones, and wish to dispense even with these. I rely upon the lecturers not to give way to the Socialistic idea, for this means the utter subversion of society. Faith in the eternal verities will come through the force of truth, by the Holy Spirit, and not through any yielding to popular remonstrances. The subject will need careful handling. I feel refreshed, but I have stern work before me. What should I do without my Divine Helper?'

"Our Lord says we are to know the elect by their fruits, and Mr. Spurgeon put on all those Christian virtues and excellencies which are indications of the elect in an eminent degree. It was not that he wore them for a short time, but that he wore them for a long time. When he was at Menton, I had occasion to write to him. Having an impression that he was of the same age as myself, I put the question to him, and at the bottom of the post-card, which came in reply, he wrote these words—'Yes, fifty-seven is my number until June 19, 1892. May *you* make it seventy-seven at least.'

"His preaching, unlike the preaching of many others, was eminently illustrated by his practice. You will remember not only the lessons of his words, but the lessons of his life. I trust that I shall remember them also. I have that hoary head which is referred to in the text of one of Mr.

Spurgeon's first sermons; and, therefore, I hope that my fellow ministers who are near me will pardon me if I say, that, great as may be the difference between ministers of one denomination and another, there is one thing which belongs to us all, which Mr. Spurgeon has helped to teach me, and which, I trust, I shall never forget, that over all that belongs to us, over our orthodoxy, over our eloquence, and over our energy, we must put on that one cloak or dress to which the apostle referred, if we too are to be considered amongst the elect—namely, that charity which the apostle calls, 'the bond of perfectness.'"

Colonel GRIFFIN, President of the Baptist Union, said:—"We are gathered here to-night under the shadow of a great sorrow. A prince and a great man has been called from our midst, and we sorrow most of all that we shall see his face no more. It is now at least twenty-five years since I first entered this great Tabernacle a stranger in London. I came here in common with thousands of strangers who visit this great metropolis. My first and great desire upon the first Sunday of my stay was to hear Charles Haddon Spurgeon. Little did I then think that I should ever get to enjoy anything like intimacy with the great man who occupied this platform. But, in the providence of God, my stay was prolonged, we became acquainted, we became fast friends, and although my intimacy with Mr. Spurgeon has not been that which many have enjoyed, I learnt to love him and to revere his memory. He has gone from us, gone to his eternal rest, but his works shall long follow him.

"It was his delight to preach Christ Jesus and him crucified. He had but one text, but what a marvellous text it was, from which over 3,000 separate sermons could be preached, which have been scattered far and wide throughout the length and breadth of the world. One text, but it was the text for which the world was longing, 'Christ, the Saviour of the world'; Christ and his cross was his song here on earth, and to-night he is rejoicing with Moses and the Lamb above. One text he had, rather let us say one Book, and from that Book he preached his thousands of sermons. One Book, in which he believed most fully, and which he accepted in all its entirety. In that Book he found first the promise of a Saviour to redeem; then the prophecy regarding that Christ; then the realization of the prophecies by Christ on earth; his grand mission, his glorious work: his sufferings and his death. This was where Mr. Spurgeon found his power; it was in telling the 'Old, old story of Jesus and his love' that he won the multitudes. Those who knew him best, and enjoyed close intimacy with him, can rejoice that they were ever privileged thus to hold communion with an 'honest man, the noblest work of God.'

"There were some that differed from Mr. Spurgeon. He and I, although occupying different positions, and sometimes apparently antagonistic, have never had an unfriendly word, nor has he ever breathed aught else than a spirit of Christian love and fervent charity. It is my privilege to stand here, not for my own worth or individual merit, but because of my official position representing the Baptist Union of Great Britain and Ireland. Mr. Spurgeon thought fit to sever his relations with that Union. We honoured him for his sincerity of purpose, although we were sorry he saw it wise to withdraw from us. Amongst the members of that Union to-day, throughout the length and breadth of this country, there is but one common thought, one common feeling of intense love, and earnest respect for him who was a prince in Israel.

"He is not dead; no, brothers, he still lives! There is no death to such as he!

> 'The stars go down
> To rise upon some fairer shore;
> And bright in heaven's jewelled crown
> They shine for evermore.'

Mr. Spurgeon has left us, but we rejoice that his spirit still lives. Even if you were to close this mighty Tabernacle, to dissolve the College, to stop the ingathering of the orphans, to blot out the thousands of sermons that have been scattered far and wide, Mr. Spurgeon would still live, and his influence would still be felt thoughout this great universe. Generation after generation, the tradition will be handed down of him who laboured here, and whom God enabled to be a minister of his eternal truth.

"We mourn, and yet we mourn not as those who are without hope. The God whom Mr. Spurgeon served is still 'God over all, blessed for ever.' We will trust him; and while he, who was our leader, has gone before, we will seek to follow in his footsteps, when God shall call us to our eternal rest, that we may be meet for that inheritance which is above. My heart is full; there is much that I could say, but time will not permit. Oh, may all in this mighty assembly, with those who have preceded us to-day in the other services, and the more than fifty thousand who passed by this bier yesterday, remember, as we think of him who has gone, that his power and strength came from the God and the living Saviour, whom he so faithfully represented! May we be led to imitate the example of him, who, through faith and patience, now inherits the promises; and who, while we are meeting here, is rejoicing in the fulness of that light, which comes from the throne of glory on high!"

Rev. A. G. BARLEY, of Paris, said: "As one of the most humble and unknown of the many workers whom our beloved President enabled to take their place in the Lord's vineyard, I come to speak on behalf of the Baptists of France. Until yesterday I fully expected that my honoured colleague, M. Saillens, would have performed this sad duty. He was, however, yesterday stricken by evident signs of the dread epidemic, and I have therefore to stand in his place and to speak in his name. Being an Englishman, I felt that I should not be able, in my own words, to express the feelings of French Christians, and therefore I asked that a French message might be written for me to read. The address is as follows :—

"We, the pastors, evangelists, and members of the French Baptist Churches, desire to bring our homage, and the tribute of our respectful love, to the memory of the great man whose loss is mourned to-day.

"It seems to us appropriate that our voices, though few, should be heard at this sorrowful hour. It was to our country that Mr. Spurgeon came for many successive years, to seek rest and recuperation; it was on French soil that his last days were spent; his glorious soul has ascended to heaven from France. He loved our clear sky, our blue sea, our fragrant flowers—he loved our people.

"There are other and higher reasons for which we feel a right to claim Spurgeon as partly our own. This great Puritan of the nineteenth century bore a strong resemblance to the greatest Frenchman who ever lived—John Calvin.

"The same attachment to the divine revelation; the same strong, firm faith in the sovereignty of the all-wise God; the same disdain for mere human theories, traditions, and fashions; the same rock-like fidelity to the truth, however difficult to believe, however hard to practise—these characteristics will make Calvin and Spurgeon appear before the eyes of posterity as men of the same mental and spiritual mould. Men such as these, moreover, are too great to be monopolized by any single church or nation; they are possessed, in their own degree, of the great cosmopolitan spirit of Christ himself, who, though a Jew by natural birth, is the elder brother of us all.

"The influence of Spurgeon upon modern Christianity in

France, though indirect, has been great. Only once was he able to comply with our oft-repeated requests to preach in Paris; the manifold demand of his ministry and his physical weakness compelled him to hurry through our country, in every city of which he might have had large and eager audiences. But though he did not speak, his voice was heard through the printed sermons, many of which were translated and have been a means of salvation, of comfort, and of joy to thousands of souls. Some of us remember how, when we were still young, the marvellous report of God's blessing upon the youthful English preacher made a great impression upon us. The crumbs which fell from your richly-spread table were eagerly sought by isolated Christians, who, thirty years ago, lived under the persecuting hand of the Empire, when no dissenting place of worship was allowed to be opened; when meetings of more than twenty persons were prohibited; when the Baptist pastor of Paris was even forbidden to read the Bible in private houses with his friends. Who can tell how much, in those trying times, Spurgeon's sermons helped to maintain the faith, the patience and the courage of God's scattered people in France?

"The recent attitude taken by Mr. Spurgeon with regard to the New Theology has been a wonderful encouragement to those French Protestants, who still hold the faith for which their fathers suffered. The struggle between Faith and Reason, between the Bible and 'Science falsely so-called,' is raging in France even more than in England. The controversy has been long enough to show us where the new doctrines will surely lead their followers. How thankful, therefore, felt the few witnesses of the Truth among us, when Spurgeon's voice was heard—so clear, so uncompromising, so full of assurance! That doctrine *must* be true which is preached by a man on whose altar the heavenly fire has so often and so unmistakably descended.

"One of the last productions of Mr. Spurgeon's indefatigable pen (now laid aside for ever), viz., *The Greatest Fight in the World*, has created a profound interest in our French Protestant Churches. One of our religious periodicals has characterized it as 'Spurgeon's Swan Song.' More of his works will, we trust, be made accessible to our people, and thus for France, as for England and for the whole world, it will be true, for generations to come, yea even as long as his dust shall await the resurrection call, that he 'being dead, yet speaketh.'

"We mourn with you, dear English brethren, and yet we would not grudge to our departed brother the rest which he now enjoys. His life has been wholly to the glory of God—must we not believe also, however difficult it may be to do so, that the glory of God is magnified in his death?

"Our Saviour lives still. The cause which Spurgeon defended is imperishable. The Lord never took up an Elijah to heaven, without leaving an Elisha behind, on whose shoulders fell the mantle of the departed. May we all take courage, and, receiving a new baptism of the Spirit, take up, with a strong grip, the weapons which these valiant hands have for ever laid aside, in order to receive the crown of victory!

"On behalf of the Baptist Churches of France,
"R. SAILLENS."

Mr. C. RUSSELL HURDITCH, the last speaker of the evening, took the two texts Mr. Spurgeon heard the day in which he found rest in Christ, and grouped all his life around them. His preaching to unconverted men was ever "Look unto Me," and his teaching for the people of God was constantly of the privileges and power which became ours when "Accepted in the Beloved."

Rev. A. T. PIERSON, D.D., announced the hymn, "Give me the wings of faith to rise," which being sung, the meeting closed with the Benediction.

Memorial Meeting

FOR THE GENERAL PUBLIC.

On Wednesday night, February 10th, 1892, the service arranged for the general public, and announced to commence at 10.30 p.m., began about ten o'clock, the building then being entirely filled, a great proportion of the audience being men.

Rev. J. GRAINGER, of Christ Church, announced the well-known hymn, "There is a fountain filled with blood," a great favourite of Mr. Spurgeon's, and it was sung with zest.

Rev. H. O. MACKEY, of Peckham Park Road, led in prayer, entreating a manifest blessing at the close of the day so memorable.

Rev. J. MANTON SMITH, having first pathetically sung "Rock of Ages," the congregation joining in the last verse, then said: "Thousands of people with weary hearts have gathered in this place from time to time, to listen to him whose body is now lying in that coffin, and he, with a faithful finger, like the mariner's compass, always pointed those burdened ones to where alone they could find true rest. That rest is in Jesus; and 'Jesus' was the sum and substance of his life. Some years ago I saw, in Southampton, a notice on a certain house. The occupier of it lived and carried on his business in the same premises, and this signboard said, '*Workshop below; residence above.*' Our dear Pastor knew what it was to work below; his study was his workshop; and now he has gone to his rest, after his life of toil. How well he did his work, God knew, and God will reward him for it. But even in the midst of his labours on earth, he knew that rest which comes to those who trust in Christ. There is no rest to the soul apart from Christ; and if there are any here to-night who are weary and heavy laden, we invite you by the memory of the blessed ministry just closed to come where you may find sweet rest.

"Our Pastor has gone to his long rest; his service is over, but his works are permanent. They will remain and speak, thought he speaketh not. Oh, what vigour he had! what singleness of eye. 'He walked with God,' like Enoch, and he had this blessed testimony that he pleased God. He did not always satisfy other people, but he did not live to please any but his Lord and Master.

"I heard of a man who was taking tickets at a railway station, from an impatient crowd. He would only let them pass one at a time, and someone said, 'My man, you are not very popular with these people.' He answered, 'I do not care about that as long as I am popular with the man up there,' pointing to the station-master who was looking out of the window. Our Pastor acted upon this plan. As long as he had the testimony that he pleased God, he cared not who was offended. For him to live was Christ. Methinks that if it were possible for him to rise up out of that coffin to-night and stand before this congregation, he would crave no higher privilege, nor covet any higher joy, than just once more to ring out the old, old gospel, which it was the joy of his life to proclaim. It was the one passion of his being to invite sinners to the Saviour. How sweet the name of Jesus sounded when with his clear bell-like voice it was uttered in the ear of the believer, or sounded in the sinner's ear, many here remember right well.

"But we need not speak so much of him, who has left us,

as of his God, who is still with us. Our Pastor's God is our God. How it would rejoice his spirit if he knew to-night that over his dead body you yielded your broken heart to his Lord! It would add to his joy in glory. Those who have listened to his word on earth, but have not obeyed it, will perhaps hear the silent voice, which now speaks to them; for there is a silence that is better than speech: even the dumbness of that coffin is eloquence to us.

"I think I can hear a voice from it, which seems to say to me, 'Tell the people about Jesus.' I knew a man in this city, who preached Jesus Christ with all his heart. I heard him preaching his last sermon, as he stood in the pulpit supported by two of his deacons, because he was so weak. Turning round to me afterwards, he said, 'Here are my pulpit notes, brother; if they are any use to you, you can have them.'

"The next day he was carried to the London Hospital, and put in a little bed in a room set apart for him, over the clock in the Whitechapel Road. The doctor came and after he examined him, said, 'If you will consent to undergo an operation, I think we may save your life; if not, cancer will do its deadly work in a fortnight.'

"My friend answered, 'I will consent to the operation, for the sake of the church; I should like to preach again.'

"They came to chloroform him, but he said,

"'No, not yet. Let me go to the operator's room first.'

"Then they took off his clothes, and dressed him in a scarlet robe. That seemed to strengthen him, he thought it was like following his Master, Jesus: they clothed *him* in scarlet. He was supported into the operator's room, he mounted the table, and knelt down. Then looking at the doctors in the gallery, who were waiting to see the operation, he put his hands together and said,

"'Gentlemen, if I live I live unto the Lord; if I die I

die unto the Lord; living or dying I am the Lord's. I am ready.'

"They chloroformed him, and the operation took place. I went round the same night to his little room, and tapped on the door, which was ajar.

"The nurse said, 'You cannot come in; mortification has set in; your friend is dying.'

"He heard my voice, and said, 'Yes, you can let him come.'

"When I went in, his wife said, 'Do not speak, he is past that,' but he replied,

"'No, I am not,' he said, 'Come to my bedside,' and he put out his hand to grip mine. I almost fancy I feel the chilly sweat now.

"'Oh, brother,' he said, 'I want to tell you how precious Jesus has been to me through all my suffering. Take my dying message, tell the people about Jesus! Wherever you go, tell the people about Jesus! As long as blood shall flow through your veins, as long as the breath is in your body, tell the people—tell the people about Jesus!' And he fell back to be with Jesus.

"Sometimes when I am weary in the work, though, thank God, I am never weary of it, I seem to hear the echo of the old man's voice, saying to me, 'Tell the people about Jesus!' *There* lies one who did it constantly; all through his life, that was his theme. As long as he had breath left, it was used in speaking about his Master. Methinks he would say to-night, to every student here, to every church member, to every Christian, 'Tell the people about Jesus!' God help us who know the message to tell it, and those who hear to receive it. Amen."

Mr. IRA D. SANKEY then said: "About eight months ago there passed across the Atlantic ocean the intelligence that Mr. Charles Haddon Spurgeon was exceedingly ill. I was in the city of Minneapolis, in the Western States, attending a convention of over 12,000 delegates, and when that despatch was read by the Chairman of the meeting, a great hush fell upon that audience. Then it flashed upon my mind, I will sing a hymn—'*Only remembered by what I have done,*'—and I asked that great congregation to bow their heads in silent prayer for your Pastor here, while I sang those words. As an indication of the hold that this man of God had upon the people there, the whole congregation bowed like one man, and an earnest petition was sent up to God that he might spare his servant. Little did I think then that it would be my privilege in eight months to come and sing the same song here on this consecrated spot. May I ask the friends here to bow their heads, and pray that God may bless the message which has been delivered, and which is to be delivered, and the message of this song, so that souls may be won for Christ; and that from this hour many may consecrate their lives to him whom Mr. Spurgeon so faithfully served, and whom he declared to the multitudes throughout this land, and throughout all lands."

Mr. SANKEY then sang the new arrangement of the hymn, "Only remembered by what I have done."

Rev. W. Y. FULLERTON said: "Ten nights ago, a thousand miles from here, in a small room on the first floor, there lay upon his bed our beloved pastor. Around him stood a little group of loving friends. Ten nights ago, almost at this very hour, the drowsy eyes were closed in sleep, and the racked body was stilled for ever. That precious body is here to-day, having been, by the good care of God, brought safely over the sea; but Charles Haddon Spurgeon is gone. He has left behind him millions of bleeding hearts. There are many of you here who feel, as I do, that this is our greatest earthly loss.

"Mrs. Browning once asked Charles Kingsley the secret of his beautiful character, of his fortitude, of his nobility. With great tenderness, he answered: 'I had a friend.' Looking down at that coffin to-night, nothing more appropriate can come from my lips, 'I had a friend.' Any little usefulness in my life has been principally owing, on the human side, to that friend whose body lies before us. Perhaps I ought not to speak all I feel, but I cannot refrain from saying that I would willingly have gone to the grave to-morrow instead of him, if only he could have stood here in my vigour again to preach the glorious Gospel of the blessed God.

"Many of us are so very sorry that we have not yet adequately grasped our loss; we can scarcely bear to think of it, it is so overwhelming. Yet, why should we be sorry? When you come to argue with yourself, why should you so greatly mourn? Three months ago when our dear friend went to the sunny South, after that terrible illness of his, we were glad—glad, though he was going to a strange country, because he was going from fog to sunshine. We were content to bear the exile, because it was not to be for ever; we thought he would soon be better, and then we should see him again.

"Let us be more content to-night, for he has gone, not to a strange country, but to the Home-land, and he is WELL. He is nearer to us now than he was at Menton; it would have taken two days of quick travelling to have reached him there; but if God willed it, we might now reach him in five minutes. Why, then, should we be sorry? Let us lift up our hearts to-night, as we come to the very hour when his spirit passed away to be with his God.

> "It is not exile, rest on high;
> It is not sadness, free from strife.
> To fall asleep is not to die;
> To dwell with Christ is better life!"

There is a text which was very dear to him, whose mortal remains rest in that coffin—the text that brought light to his soul. It will be the motto of my discourse: 'Look unto me, and be ye saved, all the ends of the earth: for I am God, and there is none else.'—Isaiah xlv. 22.

"You know the story, how on a wintry morning, in a little chapel, from the lips of an unknown preacher, that text came with power to the heart of C. H. Spurgeon; you know how the preacher picked out the stranger, and looking to him said, 'Young man, you seem to be in trouble: look unto Jesus.' Now we are all in trouble, and I would repeat that word, 'Look unto Jesus.'

"This text in Isaiah is not only the message that brought life to Mr. Spurgeon, it is the history of his life. In that light let us view it.

I. "I would say, to begin with, that pre-eminently HE WAS A MAN OF GOD. 'I am God, and there is none else,' was the central truth of his being. He learned that there was one God, and he knew him. Not only was he a godly man, for there is many a godly man who is not a man of God in this sense. Many a man who lives a godly life, who does not realize the presence of God about him as Charles Haddon Spurgeon did. Oh, how near God came to him! Once when he came back from his rest in France, he came down these steps like a very lion, and standing in his pulpit, he preached a sermon that will never fade from the memory of those who heard it: 'I have yet to speak on God's behalf.' God was his Alpha and Omega. Almost the last letter that he wrote to us, urging us to pray that the scourge of influenza might be taken away, bore as its burden that the people seemed to have forgotten God.

He dwelt in the presence of God. He knew him; he had communion with him; his whole life was spent in the preaching of God to the people. I have had some heart-to-heart talk with him when he was here, but he has had closer heart-to-heart talk with God than ever I had with him. I remember once, when I asked him about his method of prayer, he told me it was on this platform, here in the presence of the people, that he had his nearest approaches to the throne of the Eternal. He was lifted up, even to the very presence of the great God, as he stood here praying with his people, whom he loved so well.

"Moreover, *he rested upon God's covenant.* The next verse to the text says, 'I have sworn by myself, the word is gone out of my mouth in righteousness, and shall not return, that unto me every knee shall bow, every tongue shall swear.' That is the covenant that God has made with his people, that he will save them, and that he will give their world to Christ. There are some of you who think that Mr. Spurgeon imagined that things were always going wrong. He saw the wrong, but he knew that through wrong, and in spite or it, God worked out his own purposes, and that the earth should yet 'be filled with the knowledge of the glory of God, as the waters cover the sea.' It shall be so. He was like Oliver Cromwell, whose last words were, 'The covenant is one. Faith in the covenant is my only support, and if we believe not, he abideth faithful.' He was like Cromwell in his faith in the omnipotent Jehovah, and in the boldness which springs from such faith. He knew that God would reign.

"Dwelling in God's presence, and resting upon God's covenant, *he feared none else.* 'I am God, and there is none else.' He did not seek to please men, but to witness to them of the verities of our faith. He keenly felt adverse criticism, but he did not fear it. His vision of God made him strong to do and to suffer. God was so much to him that there was practically to him 'none else.'

"For such a man, a man who lived with God here, to go and live with God there, is no very great change. It is only a higher development of the same life. It is only as if God, shutting the book of this life, said to him, 'Here endeth the first lesson.' The second lesson, a brighter and more glorious one, has been begun, where now he knows, even as he is known.

II. "In the second place, I will say of dear Mr. Spurgeon, that HE WAS A MAN OF THE PEOPLE. His sympathy went out to 'all the ends of the earth.' *He lived on the earth*. He did not live in the clouds. He was a man amongst men; he was absolutely the most common-sense minister of the gospel I have ever met; and I have met a good many. He was a true man. I am glad to see so many men at this service. Brothers! if you want to be true men, look unto Spurgeon's Saviour. You cannot say there was anything mawkish or sentimental about him, any unmanly weakness. None! He was a man, a man in Christ, a whole man! Would you be a real man? Look unto Christ, to whom that man of God looked, and you, too, will be every inch a man.

"*He helped the people.* The man who has most sympathy with Christ can best aid those around him! It was the glory of C. H. Spurgeon, that, like the Saviour, 'the common people heard him gladly.' He did not cater to reach the ear of the superfine few: he wanted to speak to the people. His heart was with the people, and he had experience of men such as very few have. In their temptations and their trials, he could give them a brother's hand. Many of you, when you came to hear him, found he put himself alongside you, and brought life and healing to you.

"*He girded the world with his influence.* 'All the ends of the earth' heard from him the truth of God. Very few men have helped to accomplish the text more than the dear friend whom we have lost. Little did that Methodist preacher think that day, when that young man looked to

Christ, that all the ends of the earth were, through him, to hear the gospel; but so it is—in every civilized land his message has been heard. He might have used Augustine's words more truly than Augustine: 'I have a whole Christ for my salvation; a whole Bible for my staff; a whole church for my fellowship; a whole world for my parish.' The whole earth is in his debt. Many a man at the ends of the earth, many a man in the backwoods of America, many a man in the bush of Australia, many a man in the islands of the sea, has, through his words, looked to the Saviour and begun to live the life of God.

III. "He was a man of God; he was a man of the people; and, in the third place, HE DESIRED TO BRING THE PEOPLE TO GOD. This the text hints at, and it was true of him. He knew the people need to 'be saved.'

"*He did not flatter men*, nor say soft things to please them. The crowds did not come to hear him because he made much of the dignity of human nature. He told the people the absolute truth about themselves, and never blinked the fact that they needed to be saved. His message was that sin was ruin; that sin was hell; but the people came to hear notwithstanding. They came because the truth he preached found an echo in their own heart, that is the only echo that has ever been in this building. God grant that the echo may be heard in the hearts of not a few to-night!

"*He entreated men to be saved.* Why, I have heard him stand here and speak more like a mother than a preacher, as with his whole soul he implored people to turn to God. His faith in the purposes of God did not, as some say, make him 'heartless' in his doctrine. He yearned over the souls of men. Oh, how Christ, his Master, yearns over you! 'Be saved!' Now, here, to-night, at this memorial service, the last night this precious body will ever rest in this Tabernacle; by the memory of the earnest words you have heard from those sealed lips, 'Be saved.' O men, O women, be saved!

"*He commanded people to be saved.* His was the voice of authority. He did not speak as the scribes, but in God's name, and as an ambassador of Christ, he commanded his hearers to believe, even as we would command you to-night. I think that is what he would have us do.

"Moreover, *he expected his hearers to be saved;* he looked for it as a natural result of his ministry, and in like manner, we expect that in this meeting, many of you, who have hitherto rejected the message, shall be led by the solemn circumstances of our gathering, to receive it and live. When on Monday I saw that beautiful olive-wood coffin, with the two black seals, which had been placed upon it at Menton, still intact, I could not help thinking of another great earnest servant of Christ. He was a Silesian shoemaker, but he knew God, and many were blessed through his word. On the marble cross, which marks his grave to-day, there is the inscription, 'Here rests Jacob Böhme, born of God, died in Christ, sealed with the Holy Spirit.' That would be a fitting inscription for the tomb where this body shall rest. Of God his servant was truly begotten; in Christ he has sweetly fallen asleep; and not only with this black seal on the coffin, but with the seal of the Spirit of God on his forehead he rests, claimed by the God of heaven, safe for evermore!

IV. "The last thing suggested by the text is this. Because Mr. Spurgeon desired to bring the people to God, HE THEREFORE POINTED THEM TO THE CHRIST OF GOD. The pith of all his message was 'Look unto Christ.'

He never pointed men to himself. I have heard him many times, but never yet have I heard him directing men to himself as the source of any blessing. Priestism he hated with a perfect hatred. Never was man more humble than he. He thought nothing of himself; when the work was done he gave all the credit to God, who worked in him both to will and to do of his good pleasure.

> "He blew the trumpet soft and clear,
>   That trembling sinners need not fear;
> And then with louder note and bold,
>   To raze the walls of Satan's hold;
> The trumpet coming thus between,
>   The hand that held it scarce was seen."

We thought of the message, and not of the messenger, when we listened to his voice. He preached not himself, but Christ Jesus as Lord.

"*He had as his theme the just God and the Saviour.* Even as it is written, 'A just God and a Saviour, there is none beside me, look unto me!' He preached no new gospel; he preached that God was a just God, and would punish sin; that he was a Saviour and would receive the sinner. He had marvellous facility of illustration, great freshness of view, and unexhausted fertility of mind, yet it was ever the same old truth which he declared, 'A just God and a Saviour. Look unto me.' Like King James, who always called for his old shoes, because they fitted him the best, he kept to the same grand gospel that he preached when he began his ministry. Yet Christ was more to him than his preaching. Christ was everything. He has left it on record, in one of his latest reviews of books, that he considered Samuel Rutherford's writings the nearest to the inspired Word. One of Rutherford's sentences well expresses the heart of our dear pastor: 'What astonishment shall be mine,' said that saintly man, 'when I first behold that fairest and most lovely face! It would be heaven to me just to look through a hole of heaven's door to see Christ's countenance!' Now he has seen him; it is at this moment almost midnight with us, but midnight is over for him; ten full days he has been in the light of that beautiful countenance! How can we sorrow for him? No! we are glad. We praise God on his behalf. He is in heaven. We are in the midst of sorrow, not for him, but for ourselves; but Christ is with us.

> 'And only heaven is better than to walk
> With Christ at midnight over moonless sea!'

The night may be dark, but if Christ is with us, over the billows we will go. Beneath this shadow we are almost sacred.

The last thing I will say concerning this man of God is that *he declared with all his might that salvation was by faith*. He told men constantly that it was by looking to the Crucified One they would be saved. Not by looking to self. God grant that self may die within us, as truly as Spurgeon's body has died! Not by looking to Spurgeon: he never preached that. He ever said while he was with us, 'Look to Christ.' To-night the Lord Jesus himself is speaking to some of you, and his word is, 'You have looked long to my servant for strength and comfort; I have taken away my servant, now look unto me.' And some of you are not saved! You have come and hung upon his lips, and have looked often to the preacher. The Lord says to you now, 'Look unto me. In life and death, look unto me.'

"Let me give you one of Mr. Spurgeon's own illustrations. He told how the Duke of Marlborough, when he was dying, was carried by some friends to see a picture of some great battle that he had fought. When he saw it he began to weep, and said, 'Ah! the Duke of Marlborough was something then, but now he is a dying man,' upon which Mr. Spurgeon beautifully says that the Christian *is* something when he comes to die. It is then he *is* something. Why! when we come to die we are only beginning to live! He whom we mourn is yet alive.

"Soon the day will come when we shall all look upon Christ, whether we have looked *to* him or not; we shall see him as he sits on the great throne. The coming of the Lord draweth nigh. The second advent of Christ was, in his later years especially, a great hope to the departed Pastor of this Tabernacle. He looked for the coming of the Saviour, but I have heard him say many times that, if he might have his choice, he would rather experience the bliss of the spirits who are now with their Master, than escape death by being permitted to tarry till Christ should come. The Lord has given him his wish. He is yonder with the enraptured throng before the throne of God, while his body rests until the first resurrection. On the very night in which 'our beloved Pastor entered heaven' an unknown astronomer discovered a new star. On the Monday morning on which we read in the newspapers the terrible news which almost paralyzed us, an anonymous postcard arrived at Edinburgh Observatory saying there was a new star in the heavens, near the Milky Way, almost at the zenith, a star of the fifth magnitude. But in the heavens yonder there was another star that night, another star that shall shine for ever, not of the fifth, but of the first magnitude. The astronomers have been observing their star, and I think the angels have learnt something more of the grace of God from those lips through which we learned so much of it. He turned many to righteousness here; there his theme will be still the same.

"Ten nights ago, just about this hour, from the margin of the tideless blue sea, his happy spirit went up to stand on the sea of glass mingled with fire! From the midst of the palm-trees, he went up to wave the palm-branch in the presence of the Throne. From amid the olive-trees, he, through faith in him who once poured out his soul under the olives, went up to rest beneath the Tree of Life, whose leaves are for the healing of the nations. From that sunny land, he went up to be in that other land where they have no need of the sun, neither of the moon to shine in it, for the glory of God does lighten it, the Lamb is the Light thereof. The last day of the month was the last day of his earthly course; the first day of the week was the first day of his glory.

"'After this, it was noised abroad that Mr. Valiant-for-Truth was taken with a summons,' said John Bunyan, and his words are almost prophetic; 'he had this for a token that the summons was true, that the pitcher was broken at the fountain. When he understood it, he called for his friends and told them of it. Then said he, 'I am going to my Father's, and though with great difficulty I am got hither, yet now I do not repent me of all the trouble I have been at to get where I am. My sword I give to him who shall succeed me in my pilgrimage; my courage and skill to him that can get it. My marks and scars I carry with me, to be a witness for me, that I have fought his battles, who now will be my rewarder.' When the day that he must go home was come, many accompanied him to the river side, into which, as he went, he said, ' Death, where is thy sting?' And as he went down deeper he said, 'Grave, where is thy victory?' So he passed over—and all the trumpeters sounded for him on the other side."

> "Servant of God, well done!
> Rest from thy loved employ,
> The battle fought, the victory won,
> Enter thy Master's joy."

This hymn, quoted in full on page 109, having been heartily sung, with special emphasis on the line, "The voice at midnight came;" the meeting was concluded by prayer, after which many lingered behind to have a last look at the olive-casket.

Funeral Service.

On Thursday morning, February 11th, 1892, commencing at 11 o'clock, the funeral service was held in the Tabernacle. Rev. A. T. PIERSON, D.D., presided. The centre of the area was filled with the mourners and delegates, the other places being occupied by seat-holders.

Rev. WILLIAM WILLIAMS, of Upton Chapel, announced the opening hymn: "Servant of God, well done," which, from its peculiar appropriateness, has been sung several times during the memorial services.

Mr. HARRALD then offered a most tender and comprehensive prayer, in which, having given thanks for the rest and reward which had been given to " our beloved and Thy beloved ", he very earnestly entreated, amid the fervent 'amens" of the congregation, that consolation and strength might be given to the bereaved wife, the aged father, the beloved brother, the dear sons, the sorrowing sisters, and all other relatives of the glorified Pastor. For the youthful grandchildren he besought a blessing, asking especially for the infant grandsons that, as they were descended from a long line of preachers, they, too, might, by the grace of God, be called to the ministry of the Word. The stricken Church, College, and Orphanage shared in the intercession, which included a request that, through the memorial services, many might be turned to the Lord; and that, by means of the printed sermons already published, and the others which shall yet be issued, a great multitude might be led to the feet of Christ. "Amen and amen" was the response from every heart, and from many lips, as Mr. Harrald closed with a devout ascription of praise to the triune Jehovah—"Unto the Father and the Son and the Spirit, the three-one God, be praises in the church above and the church below, thoughout all ages, by Christ Jesus. Amen."

Rev. ARCHIBALD G. BROWN, introduced by Dr. Pierson as "one of the early students of the College, one of the devoted Christian workers in this great city, and a personal friend of the pastor," in rising to read the Scriptures, said : " How cheerfully many of us would have died if, by our death, that life could have been spared, God knows. It is willed otherwise. He has gone, and the unworthy are left. Let us now read from the word of God a few passages which we have been led to select as appropriate. May the Spirit of God own his own truth!

" ' *So Moses the servant of the Lord died there in the land of Moab, according to the word of the Lord.*'

" The Holy Ghost evidently counted that to be Jehovah's servant is a higher honour than to be king of Jeshurun. Moses died there where his God took him ; in his God's presence, in his God's arms, ' according to the word of the Lord,' or, as it may be rendered, ' at the mouth of the Lord.' The Jews have a saying that Moses died with a kiss from God's mouth.

" '*And he buried him in a valley in the land of Moab, over against Beth-peor, but no man knoweth of his sepulchre unto this day. And Moses was an hundred and twenty years old when he died. His eye was not dim nor his natural force abated. And the children of Israel wept for Moses in the plains of Moab thirty days ; so the days of weeping and* mourning for Moses were ended. And Joshua the son of Nun was full of the spirit of wisdom, for Moses had laid his hands upon him; and the children of Israel hearkened unto him and did as the Lord commanded Moses. And there arose not a prophet since in Israel like unto Moses, whom the Lord knew face to face.'

"There is the high honour of this man of God; there the secret of his power. It was in this that Moses stood unapproached and unrivalled. The Holy Ghost has declared that the grand distinction in his character was that he knew God intimately, and that God knew him face to face.

"'*Behold this day I am going the way of all the earth,*' Joshua said. '*Now, therefore, fear the Lord, and serve him in sincerity and truth; and put away the gods which your fathers served on the other side of the flood, and in Egypt; and serve ye the Lord. And if it seem evil unto you to serve the Lord, choose you this day whom ye will serve; whether the gods which your fathers served that were on the other side of the flood, or the gods of the Amorites, in whose land ye dwell; but as for me and my house we will serve the Lord. And the people answered and said, God forbid that we should forsake the Lord.*'

"If it were possible for our departed Joshua to speak, I believe the words would be these: 'Serve my God, and your God in all sincerity.' Oh, that there might break from this assembled company of mourners, the same response that followed the word of Joshua, when the people said, 'God forbid that we should forsake the Lord'! As he, our President and Pastor, followed God, so may we follow hard after.

"'*Now Elisha was fallen sick of his sickness whereof he died. And Joash the king of Israel came down unto him and wept over his face.*'

"It is well when royalty acknowledges the worth of a faithful prophet in the land.

"'And said, O my father, my father! the chariot of Israel, and the horsemen thereof! And Elisha said unto him, Take bow and arrows: and he took unto him bow and arrows. And he said to the king of Israel, Put thine hand upon the bow, and he put his hand upon it; and Elisha put his hands upon the king's hands. And he said, Open the window eastward; and he opened it. Then Elisha said, Shoot; and he shot. And he said, The arrow of the Lord's deliverance.'

"The ruling passion with this man of God was strong in death

"'And Elisha died and they buried him. And the bands of the Moabites invaded the land at the coming in of the year. And it came to pass, as they were burying a man, that, behold, they spied a band of men; and they cast the man into the sepulchre of Elisha; and when the man was let down, and touched the bones of Elisha, he revived and stood up on his feet.'

"The influence of a prophet is not ended with his death. When good men die they yet speak, and life springs even from the sepulchre of the consecrated.

"'And they chose Stephen, a man full of faith and of the Holy Ghost,' and others, 'And the word of God increased; and the number of the disciples multiplied in Jerusalem greatly; and a great company of the priests were obedient to the faith.' But he died. 'And devout men carried Stephen to his burial, and made great lamentation over him.'

"Has the Book of God no word for those who are left? It may be said that it is the survivor who dies. Our leader, Moses, has gone into his rest. Our warrior, Joshua, has ended his fight. Our prophet has shot his last arrow.

"'God is our refuge and strength, a very present help in trouble. Therefore will not we fear, though the earth be removed, and though the mountains be carried into the midst of the sea. Though the waters thereof roar and be troubled, though the mountains shake with the swelling thereof.'

"Our Pastor's word to us is, 'Let the worst come to the

worst, the children of God should never give way to mistrust.'

"'*Shall we receive good at the hand of God, and shall we not receive evil?*'

"'*I was dumb: I opened not my mouth because thou didst it.*'

"A saintly silence. Sometimes it is impossible to say anything that can do good, and one would not, for all the world, say a word which could do harm; we honour God best at these times by silence. Happy the experience which leads the soul to say, even looking at that coffin,

"'*It is the Lord: let him do what seemeth him good.*'

"'*For we know, that if our earthly house of this tabernacle were dissolved, we have a building of God, an house not made with hands, eternal in the heavens. For in this we groan, earnestly desiring to be clothed upon with our house which is from heaven; If so be that being clothed we shall not be found naked. For we that are in this tabernacle do groan, being burdened, not for that we would be unclothed, but clothed upon, that mortality might be swallowed up of life. Now he that has wrought us for the selfsame thing is God, who also hath given unto us the earnest of the Spirit. Therefore we are always confident, knowing that, whilst we are at home in the body, we are absent from the Lord: (For we walk by faith, not by sight:) we are confident, I say, and willing rather to be absent from the body, and to be present with the Lord. Wherefore we labour that, whether present or absent, we may be well pleasing unto him.*'

"The brightest light that can be thrown upon a scene of sorrow, is the light which comes from the promised return of our Lord and Master. Let us read concerning his glorious advent.

"'*For if we believe that Jesus Christ died and rose again, even so them also which sleep in Jesus will God bring with him. For this we say unto you by the word of the Lord, that we which are alive and remain unto the coming of the Lord, shall not prevent,'* or take precedence of '*them which are asleep. For the Lord himself shall descend from heaven with a shout, with the voice of the archangel, and with the trump of God; and the dead in Christ shall rise first; then we which are alive and remain shall be caught up together with them in the clouds, to meet the Lord in the air; and so shall we ever be with the Lord.*'

"'*And John's disciples came and took up the body and buried it, and went and told Jesus.*'

"That is all we can do."

Rev. ROBERT TAYLOR, of Upper Norwood, announced the hymn, "which was the last our beloved friend gave out." We began to sing at the second verse—

> "The King above in beauty,
> Without a veil is seen;
> It were a well-spent journey
> Though ten deaths lay between."

Rev. A. T. PIERSON, D.D., then made the funeral address before the assembly, as follows:—

The giant cedar of Lebanon has fallen, and the crash of the downfall shakes the whole land, and echoes round the world. No vacancy so vast has been left in the church for, at least, a hundred years. The roots that held this cedar to the soil have spread so far and wide, that the desolation is incalculable. For a hundred years no such event as the death of Charles Haddon Spurgeon has startled and bereaved the Christian church.

I think it was 101 years ago when John Wesley died; in the year 1791. There is a very curious correspondence in the lives of the two brothers, John and Charles Wesley, and the lives of the two brothers, Charles and James Spurgeon; and they lie apart in history by this century. In each case the two brothers wrought together as right hand and left hand work together in mechanic arts. And it is but due to the surviving brother to say, that the general public has not altogether appreciated, as yet, the contribution that he made, in a very unselfish spirit, to the usefulness and the wide-reaching work of his departed brother. Standing in the background, while his brother stood in the foreground, he was an inspiration to his faith, an encouragement to his activity, and a constant co-operator in everything which he undertook. God bless him, and long may he survive to give his wisdom, his counsel, and his energy to the work which they jointly carried forward!

The posthumous work of John Wesley was greater than the work he did during his life; as we look back over the century, we surround Mr. Wesley's name with much of the glory of the work carried on after his decease. The posthumous work of Charles Haddon Spurgeon no man can, at this day, estimate or conjecture.

We must, moreover, remember that Mr. Wesley, who was born in 1703, and converted in 1738, at the age of thirty-five, was privileged to live until the age of eighty-eight, dying in 1791; whereas Mr. Spurgeon, born in 1834, and converted at the age of sixteen, in the year 1850, has fallen asleep in Jesus before his fifty-eighth birthday had been reached. What that life would have wrought if thirty years more had been added to it, we can only imagine. And am I not, at least, justified in saying, especially in view of the comparatively brief term of this marvellous life, that there has been no life like it, in the church of God, in the century, and that, therefore, no vacancy so vast has been created by the withdrawal of any one of God's servants during that time?

Men, generally, concede to Mr. Spurgeon *genius in the intellectual sphere;* but genius is a very vague and indefinite term. It usually stands for the creative faculty; but what is the creative faculty but the combination of observation, accumulation, classification, and application? In other words, is it not the using of all our powers, the gathering of facts and truths, their orderly, methodical arrangement, and their practical utilization in matters of personal, social, and public life?

I trust that we shall not, being dazzled by his genius, forget that he set us a glorious example of the power of systematic activity. It was no mere genius that produced three thousand sermons in the course of these years, and gave to the world thirty-seven annual volumes of weekly discourses. It was no mere genius that sent twenty-seven volumes of *The Sword and the Trowel* forth month by month. It was no mere genius that gave some one hundred volumes, larger and smaller, to the world, on all variety of topics connected with the gospel, the gospel ministry, and the Christian life. *The Treasury of David*, which itself might have stood, with its seven volumes, as the one colossal work of one man's life, and which is the most popular and useful commentary ever written on a single book of the Bible, attaining already a sale of 125,000 volumes, a larger sale than has ever been known for any commentary on a single book,—this work cost, I understand, twenty years of labour in the leisure hours of a most laborious pastorate. All this meant hard, constant, and conscientious work.

Some of us have wondered at the marvellous accumulations of Mr. Spurgeon's life-time. I trow that all this came not of any inherent endowment of genius. 'If the iron be blunt,' says Solomon, in the tenth chapter of Ecclesiastes and the tenth verse, 'If the iron be blunt and he do not whet the edge, then must he put to more strength,'—a profound proverb. 'A whet is no let,' says the old maxim. The time that the mower occupies in giving edge and keenness to his scythe, is no lost time in his work. One needs less strength if he has a sharp weapon. Mr. Spurgeon so sharpened his mental faculty by diligent culture, that, if he lacked anything in native strength, he certainly lacked nothing in the efficiency of the weapons and the implements that he used.

We have all marvelled at the peculiar freshness, fulness, and forcefulness of the stream that he perpetually poured forth, in public utterances by pen as well as by tongue. If he himself should explain it, I am sure that he would tell us that the secret lay in two things. First, he kept filling up the cask ; and, in the second place, he tapped the barrel, not at the top, but at the bottom ; so that we always got from him a full and forceful stream. Nothing more surprised me in his intellectual life than the lavishness with which he bestowed it. He never seemed to fear self-exhaustion ; he gave with the same lavishness to one poor soul from among the least and lowest, as to the throng of the greatest and noblest on the grandest occasion. The reason was, not simply that he was endowed with transcendent intellectual genius, but that he knew where the fountain of the best thought, and the noblest emotions and affections, was evermore to be found ; putting himself beneath that fountain, he was filled with the unsearchable riches of the Word of God, of the Spirit of God, and of the life of God.

But though, perhaps, it is not quite so obvious, I believe that Mr. Spurgeon represented *genius in the moral sphere*, which is even more rare than genius in the intellectual sphere. I mean by genius in the moral sphere, just what our blessed Lord said when the disciples were contending who should be greatest in the kingdom of heaven. Taking a little child, and placing him in their midst, he said, 'Whosoever therefore shall humble himself as this little child, the same is greatest in the kingdom of heaven.' Genius in the moral sphere, is the carrying forward of the characteristics of childhood into the period of manhood, and even of mature age. That is precisely what Charles Haddon Spurgeon did. He was always a little child in his own eyes and in his own spirit. In the last prayer I heard him offer, when I made a private visit to Beulah Hill, to see him once more before he left for Menton, he reminded me of young Zinzendorf, when, at five years of age, he used to toss his love-letters out of the window directed to his ' Dear Jesus.' Yes, he was a little child.

What is a child-like spirit? Did you ever undertake to analyze it? When we think of little children we think of three groups of graces. One group centres in *truth*, and embraces simplicity and sincerity; one group centres in *love*, and embraces gentleness and generosity; and one group centres in *faith*, and embraces confidence and compliance. Was he not in every one of those respects a man of a child-like spirit?

What rare simplicity! *sine plicâ*, without a fold : opened up like the Bible on his coffin ; opened up so that all might read what was in his soul. What rare sincerity! *sine cerâ*, without wax: a possible reference to the Roman potters' habit of thrusting wax into the cavities of the vessel that they might conceal the flaws. Sincerity means that there is no attempt to conceal the flaws. The vessel can stand the searching and melting ray of the sunlight.

What rare love was his! what unspeakable gentleness! such as we think of in a wife or a mother. He seemed to me to represent all the masculine virtues and most of the feminine virtues too. He was as brave and courageous and aggressive as the most heroic man, but he was as gentle and tender, as sympathetic and compassionate, as the most beautiful womanly character. What generosity he displayed! The unique story of that generosity never has been written, and it never will be fully written, for the data are unknown except to the omniscient God. It was a life perpetually imparting, and one reason it closed so early was because the giving out was more rapid than the taking in. Let us not deceive ourselves: he gave himself for humanity, and that is perhaps the reason why we have him not to-day. He lost his life in serving.

How beautiful was his faith! What simple and sublime

confidence in his Lord! unwavering, unaltering, unfaltering faith. I never saw such trust in any other human soul. It rebuked my own unbelief, and made my own scepticism seem a crime. More than anything else about him, it seemed to illustrate to me what a disciple could be who was in constant touch with God, and the circuit of whose invisible telegraphy with God never knew an interruption. Then what compliance, what obedience, there was with him! I remember that, on one great occasion, when the most tempting offers of a popular character were put before him, his simple and sublime answer was, "Gentlemen, these things do not affect me. The only thing of any consequence to me in this world is to do the will of God."

I want now to add a word about *genius in the spiritual sphere;* for there is such a thing, and he illustrated it. I mean, by genius in the spiritual sphere, what Paul speaks of in the sixth chapter of the 1st Epistle to the Corinthians: 'He that joined unto the Lord is one spirit.' That is genius in the spiritual sphere—the absolute oneness with God that comes from the merging of spiritual life, on the part of the believer, into the spiritual life of his Lord. I call the attention of my brethren here present, especially those in the ministry, to the fact that this is the last and grandest of all representations of the unity between a believer and Christ. That unity is illustrated from every department. It is illustrated from the material realm, in the building, the lively stones of which are built into one symmetrical structure. It is illustrated from the vegetable realm, in the vine and the branches that interwrap their fibres. It is illustrated from the animal realm, in the sheep and the shepherd that are associated closely in flock and fold. It is illustrated from the human realm, in the body and its members which constitute one organism; and in the bride and the bridegroom, which form the closest union known among men. It is also illustrated from the family, with one father, one home, and one household; and from the state, community, or commonwealth, under one supreme head or sovereign. But all these are defective, though they are given to us in their entireness and combination, so that what one lacks the other may make up. We turn, therefore, to this last and grandest of all: 'He that is joined unto the Lord is one spirit.' You may disintegrate a building. You may separate branches from the vine. You may part sheep and shepherd. You may take members off the body. A bride may be divorced from her bridegroom; a family may be broken into fragments; and a state may be shattered by rebellion. But the spirit is indivisible, and he that is joined unto the Lord forms with the Lord one indivisible and immortal spirit. That is genius in the spiritual sphere, and that was the genius of Charles Haddon Spurgeon. From that indivisible unity sprang his faith. From that indivisible unity sprang his zeal. From that indivisible unity sprang his obedience. From that indivisible unity sprang his adherence to the gospel of our Lord Jesus Christ. From that indivisible unity came his sympathy with souls as such, so that the soul of the least and lowest was in his eyes as valuable as the soul of a king on the throne.

My friends, though there was much that was inimitable in this marvellous man, nevertheless there was much that he did and said, believed and lived, which challenges not only our admiration but our holy imitation.

And now, as time forbids me to speak longer on this august occasion, I can only add that we have come together to bury the dead. Glad we are that those precious remains were not left to rest among the palms and olives by the shores of the Mediterranean; then only the noble and the affluent might have made their pilgrimage to his tomb. But we thank God that we are to lay these sacred ashes in our Norwood, where the common people who heard him gladly may wend their way to the place of his burial. You have no occasion to build him a monument, for his monument, more enduring than brass, is in the hearts of millions of the human race. You have no need to employ a gardener to keep his grave green, for the tears of widows and of orphans will moisten the sod. You have no occasion to see that flowers are planted round his sepulchre, for there will be fragrant blooms from all parts of the earth, which will be brought by pilgrim hands in the remembrance of untold blessings that came through his lips and pen; flowers that will be borne from all quarters to be set beside his place of rest.

My brother, we shall never see another like unto thee. The eyes now closed in death, that twinkled like two stars in a dark firmament, and brought light and joy to many bereaved and saddened hearts, have lost their light for ever. The voice that spoke in tones so convincing and persuasive is hushed in death. The hand whose grasp uplifted many a fallen one, and gave new strength and encouragement to many a stricken one, will never again take our hands within its holy embrace. We bless God for thee, my brother. We are glad that heaven is made richer though we be made poorer; and by this bier we solemnly pledge ourselves that we will undertake, by God's grace, to follow thy blessed footsteps, even as thou didst follow thy blessed Lord!

Rev. NEWMAN HALL, LL.B., at this point of the service, offered a most beautiful and touching prayer, in which adoration mingled with thanksgiving; and intercession with grief. "We mourn that the gift has been withdrawn, because we bless thee that the gift was ever bestowed," was a sentence which drew forth the hearts of the congregation; and a sobbing assent was given to this other, "We bless thee that his death is not premature, for thou knowest when thy servants are mature and fit for glory."

The people now joined in singing a verse of a hymn which was a great favourite with the departed Pastor:—

> "Knowing as I am known,
> How shall I love that word;
> And oft repeat before the throne,
> For ever with the Lord!"

Then the coffin was reverently carried by eight bearers to the hearse. As it slowly moved down the aisle, followed by the mourners, many of them choking down their sobs, a few of the boys from the Stockwell Orphanage sang the *chorale*.

> "Thou art gone to the grave,
> But we will not deplore thee,
> Though sorrows and darkness
> Encompass the tomb;
> The Saviour has passed
> Through its portal before thee,
> And the lamp of his love
> Is thy guide through the gloom.
>
> "Thou art gone to the grave;
> We no longer behold thee,
> Nor tread the rough path
> Of the world by thy side;
> But the wide arms of mercy
> Are spread to enfold thee,
> And sinners may hope,
> Since the Sinless has died.
>
> "Thou art gone to the grave,
> But 'twere wrong to deplore thee,
> For God was thy ransom,
> Thy guardian and guide;
> He gave thee, he took thee,
> And he will restore thee;
> And death has no sting,
> Since the Saviour has died."

Thousands of handkerchiefs were raised to tearful eyes, that took a last loving look at the beautiful casket that contained all that was mortal of him to whom all owed so much. Thus the dear body left the Tabernacle for the last time.

From the Tabernacle to the Tomb.

The open hearse which conveyed the olive-casket to its resting-place at Norwood Cemetery, had, on both sides of it, the appropriate text which was also on the coffin, "I have fought a good fight, I have finished my course, I have kept the faith." By this means, a sermon, five miles long, was preached as the procession slowly passed through the streets. On the coffin itself was placed Mr. Spurgeon's pulpit Bible, wide open, with a marker pointing to that precious passage which long ago brought salvation to the beloved man of God: "Look unto me, and be ye saved, all the ends of the earth: for I am God, and there is none else." As a warrior has his helmet and sword placed on his bier, the warrior of God had the Sword of the Spirit, which he so valiantly wielded for so many years, carried with his body to the grave. His death, as well as his life, was a continuous testimony for God.

It is not necessary to chronicle the progress of the funeral procession along the roads crowded on either side with silent, awe-struck people, many of whom were in mourning and in tears; nor to praise the arrangements and courtesy of the police force, though no praise, however high, would be more than they deserve. But we must notice that as the *cortège* moved along the route, the bells of St. Mary's, Newington, and St. Mark's, Kennington, were tolled, all the shops were shut, many of them draped, and some with portraits and mottoes upon them. The very public-houses were closed, and flags floated half-mast high. Thus the procession passed on, the hearse headed by mounted police, and immediately followed by *the empty brougham* of the departed preacher. After this came the carriage bearing his son, Pastor Charles Spurgeon, who ventured from a sick chamber to pay this last homage to his beloved father : Mrs. Charles Spurgeon accompanied him, and Pastor Archibald G. Brown rode in the same carriage. Pastor James A. Spurgeon shared his carriage with the Bishop of Rochester, who desired to pay the parting tribute to Mr. Spurgeon of being present at the grave. Other relatives were followed by Secretaries, Deacons, Elders, Representatives, Delegates, and Friends, and so the long line of vehicles passed on between the living throng.

At the Stockwell Orphanage, a covered platform had been erected ; and, in deep mourning the children sat there, supposed to be singing, but most of them weeping, now doubly orphaned as they were; for Mr. Spurgeon had taken them all to his heart, and a child's instinct for a true friend is seldom at fault.

When the procession started from the Tabernacle, a meeting of ministers and students of the Pastors' College Evangelical Association began at Chatsworth Road Chapel, close to Norwood Cemetery. Those present at this service joined those who came in the procession, and a most striking sight it was to stand at the cemetery gate, and watch the long curving line of men reaching right up to the grave, all of them in black.

The near relatives of the departed Pastor gathered first around the tomb, which was beautifully decked with foliage and flowers, then over a thousand mourners assembled within the barriers, and many thousands crowded beyond.

While we stood there a little patch of blue sky appeared, just over our heads, as if to remind us of the glory-land above ; and while Mr. Brown was speaking, a dove flew from

THE FUNERAL CORTÈGE ENTERING NORWOOD CEMETERY.

the direction of the Tabernacle towards the tomb, and wheeling in its flight over the crowd, almost seemed to pause. In ancient days it would have been an augury: to us it spoke only peace. As the service proceeded, a little redbreast poured forth its liquid note all the while from a neighbouring tombstone; it was appropriate music, for the redbreast is fabled to have had its crimson coat ever since it picked a thorn from the Saviour's bleeding brow. Well, we do not believe that; but we believe what we sang at the grave, the truth that the beloved Pastor lived to preach, and died to defend:—

> "Dear dying Lamb, Thy precious blood
>   Shall never lose its power
> Till all the ransomed Church of God
>   Be saved to sin no more.

And we joined heartily in the confession and resolve.

> E'er since by faith I saw the stream
>   Thy flowing wounds supply,
> Redeeming love has been my theme,
>   And shall be till I die.
> Then in a nobler, sweeter song,
>   I'll sing Thy power to save,
> When this poor lisping, stammering tongue
>   Lies silent in the grave."

When the olive-wood coffin, with the open Bible still upon it, was lowered into the midst of the palms and lilies,

Rev. ARCHIBALD G. BROWN said: "It has pleased our heavenly Father, the sovereign Lord of life and death, to call away from this world the soul of our departed brother. We therefore commit his body to the grave—earth to earth, ashes to ashes, and dust to dust, surely expecting the coming of the day in which all that are in the grave shall hear the voice of the Son of God, and come forth."

Nothing could have been more beautiful, nor more suitable, than Mr. Brown's closing words. They were delivered from

PASTOR A. G. BROWN DELIVERING HIS ADDRESS AT THE GRAVE.

the heart: they will lodge in thousands more. With great pathos and many pauses, he said:—

"Beloved President, Faithful Pastor, Prince of Preachers, Brother Beloved, Dear Spurgeon—we bid thee not 'Farewell,' but only for a little while 'Good-night.' Thou shalt rise soon at the first dawn of the Resurrection-day of the redeemed. Yet is not the good-night ours to bid, but thine; it is we who linger in the darkness; thou art in God's holy light. Our night shall soon be passed, and with it all our weeping. Then, with thine, our songs shall greet the morning of a day that knows no cloud nor close; for there is no night there.

"Hard-worker in the field! thy toil is ended. Straight has been the furrow thou hast ploughed. No looking back has marred thy course. Harvests have followed thy patient sowing, and heaven is already rich with thine ingathered sheaves, and shall be still enriched through years yet lying in eternity.

"Champion of God! thy battle, long and nobly fought, is over; the sword which clave to thy hand, has dropped at last; a palm-branch takes its place. No longer does the helmet press thy brow, oft weary with its surging thoughts of battle; a victor's wreath from the great Commander's hand has already proved thy full reward.

"Here for a little while shall rest thy precious dust. Then shall thy Well-Beloved come; and at his voice thou shalt spring from thy couch of earth, fashioned like unto his body, into glory. Then spirit, soul, and body, shall magnify thy Lord's redemption. Until then, beloved, sleep. We praise God for thee, and by the blood of the everlasting covenant, hope and expect to praise God with thee. Amen."

Rev. A. T. PIERSON, D.D., led in solemn prayer, in which he besought that comfort in sorrow, and stimulus in service, might come to all those who were standing by the grave.

The BISHOP OF ROCHESTER (DR. RANDALL DAVIDSON), then pronounced the Benediction.

Many remarked that the whole of the Memorial Services, unique as they were, were characterized by a simplicity and heartiness entirely in harmony with the whole life of the beloved Pastor; and it was most significant that, when the olive-casket was lowered into the vault, not even the glorified preacher's name was visible—it was just as he would have wished it—there was nothing to be seen but the text at the foot of the coffin, and the open Bible. Of course, the Bible was not buried; it is not dead, it "liveth and abideth for ever"; and who knows whether it may not prove, more than ever, the means of quickening the dead, now that he, who loved it dearer than his life, can no longer proclaim its blessed truths with the living voice? God grant it!

Memorial Service

FOR CHILDREN.

On the afternoon of Lord's-day, February 14th, 1892, the children of the various Sunday-schools connected with the Metropolitan Tabernacle; the boys and girls of the Stockwell Orphanage; and the orphans from Mrs. Sharman's Homes, which are situated in the immediate neighbourhood, were gathered together, almost ten thousand of the little people being crowded into the building.

Rev. V. J. CHARLESWORTH, head-master of the Stockwell Orphanage, conducted a selected choir of the boys of the Institution, who sang, "Servant of God, well done!" and "The Homeland," being accompanied by Mr. F. G. LADDS, the secretary.

Deacon WILLIAM OLNEY, president of Haddon Hall, led in a brief and impressive prayer between these two hymns, the children repeating sentence by sentence after him.

Deacon S. R. PEARCE, superintendent of the Tabernacle Sunday-school, gave a short address, in which he contrasted previous gatherings of the children in the Tabernacle with the meeting now held under such sad circumstances. Pointing to the mourning draperies which surrounded the platform, he said:—" Most of the young friends present know why these were placed here, and what they mean. This memorial service is one of a series, occasioned by the death of our beloved Pastor, C. H. Spurgeon. After forty years of faithful service, he has gone to be with Jesus. From this sacred spot, where I am now standing, the gospel has been preached in all its fulness and simplicity, so that the youngest amongst them might understand.

"Mr. Spurgeon was once a little boy like some of you, and on one occasion, when he was engaged in making 'mud pies' at his father's door, a visitor drew near, and asked his father who that little fellow was he had just seen outside. Yet that little boy grew up to be a great preacher, and the beloved of all our hearts. His lips were now silent, and his dear hands were cold in death; but let us remember what he had said, and let us love the God whom he had loved, and serve the dear Saviour whom he had served so faithfully.

"If the Pastor could speak to us now, he would say, 'Sorrow not for me: trust Jesus whom I have trusted, and be ready in season and out of season to serve him.'

In conclusion, Mr. Pearce told the simple and touching story of an officer wounded in the fight, who, when a soldier came to comfort him, said, "Never mind me, keep the flag flying." "So," he said, "the beloved one would have us not to sorrow as those without hope, but he would desire us to keep the gospel flag flying, that others might become true soldiers of the cross, and more than conquerers, through him who loved us and gave himself for us."

Mr. J. MANTON SMITH, whose cornet had a bow of crape upon it, after leading the children in the singing of two hymns, "There is a land of pure delight," and "Anywhere with Jesus," asked them to repeat his text word for word. With great gusto, the children thundered:—

"Samuel one—chapter three—verse nineteen: 'The Lord was with him, and did let none of his words fall to the ground.'"

He then said:—" Dear children,—On several occasions it has been my happy privilege to speak to united Sunday-schools from this platform. I have always found it to be an easy and delightful task. But to-day I have a somewhat more difficult duty to perform, for all our hearts have been made sad by the death of our beloved Pastor. He has gone from our midst, but his noble deeds and loving message will never die, for the Lord was with him, and he will not let his words fall to the ground. Some of you may remember that a little over a year ago, in a somewhat similar gathering to this, I told about a little shepherd boy in Scotland, named Jamie, who was very ill. His master loved him and was very kind to him, but felt sad because he did not know how to help him to die. So he asked a nobleman, who was a Christian, if he would go to the shepherd's cottage with him, and speak to the dying boy. The nobleman spoke to him about sheep and lambs in such a way, that Jamie became quite interested. Then he said, 'I know a shepherd, Jamie, who has a great many sheep and a great many lambs. He knows them all and loves them dearly, and he laid down his life for his sheep. Jamie, I am one of his sheep, and he wants you to be one of his lambs. If you will, from your heart, say to him, 'Lord Jesus, I will accept thee as my Saviour just now,' then you will be able to say truly, with me, 'The Lord is my Shepherd.'

"Jamie said, 'I should like to say that.'

"'Well, Jamie,' said the nobleman, 'I will tell you how you can remember it; repeat it, after me, on your knuckles. There are five words, and you have five knuckles. So with a finger on one knuckle after the other, they said several times, 'The Lord is my Shepherd.'

"The next day, when the nobleman called at the

shepherd's cottage to see Jamie, Jamie's mother was weeping bitterly.

"He said to her, 'How is Jamie this morning?'

"She sobbed out of her broken heart, 'Jamie's gone. Jamie's gone.'

"'Well,' said the nobleman, 'And how did he die?'

"'He died with his finger on the fourth knuckle,' said the mother.

"What word does that stand for, children?" asked Mr. Smith, and the children all shouted, "MY, sir."

"At our last gathering, when I told this story, there was a little fellow three years old here, named Stanley Smith, who sometimes calls me father. He evidently remembered it, for last Monday week, when his mother told him that dear Mr. Spurgeon was dead, little Stanley looked up, and said—

"'Is he? Which finger did he die on?'

"And when I arrived home from Dover, he met me in the hall, and said—

"'Father, Mr. Spurgeon has died, and gone to heaven on the fourth knuckle.' I took the little fellow up and kissed him. 'God bless you, my child,' I said, what Jesus said is true, 'Out of the mouth of babes and sucklings thou hast perfected praise.'

"Our beloved Mr. Spurgeon was the shepherd of the sheep who worship in this Tabernacle, he was also himself a sheep of the Shepherd who is in heaven; and now he has gone to the great Shepherd's fold.

"When Mr. Spurgeon was a little boy, a gentleman, visiting his grandfather, took him on his knee and gave him a new sixpence, and said, 'Charley, my boy, when you become a preacher remember this sixpence, and let the first hymn you give out be—

"God moves in a mysterious way,
His wonders to perform."

"And Mr. Spurgeon did so. During the last week we have been learning the truth of this hymn, but we know God always does right.

"What the people said about John the Baptist can be truly said about our dear departed Pastor. 'Spurgeon did no miracles, but all things that Spurgeon spake of Jesus were true.' Like the child Samuel, who is referred to in our text, he began early in life to serve the Lord."

Mr. SMITH here told, in his own graphic way, the story of Samuel and Eli, and then showed the children how Mr. Spurgeon, like Samuel, early heard God's voice, and answered to his call.

"Those who hear the call of God," he continued, "and obey it, are safe, trustful, useful, and happy. Would you not all wish to be like that? What is it to be safe? When Mr. Spurgeon was a little boy, he used to live with his grandfather. On his grandfather's shelf there stood a large bottle with a small neck, and inside this bottle there was a large apple. This was a standing puzzle to Mr. Spurgeon when he was a little boy.

"'How did the apple get inside the bottle,' he asked his grandfather.

"The reply he received was, 'Find out.'

"He then asked his grandmother, who gave him the same kind of answer. He examined the bottle to see if there were any joins and marks where it had been put together, but could not see any, and so he asked his grandfather again.

"His grandfather still said, 'Find out.'

"When quite alone, he put on his grandmother's spectacles, and looked carefully into the bottle to see if the apple had been put in in sections, but no, it was quite whole.

"One day he walked down his grandfather's garden, and saw a bottle tied on to one of the branches of an apple tree, and a little tiny apple growing at the end of the branch inside the bottle. He had now discovered the secret, and ran into the house, saying, 'Now I know how that big apple got into that bottle on the shelf: it grew inside.' The cold frost might come, and nip some of the other apples, but this one was safe, because it was inside the bottle. Now the Sunday-school and the Church are like this bottle: they shield many who enter it while they are young from a cruel, cold world, and many blasts of temptation."

Several other interesting illustrations followed, showing what it was to be trustful and useful, the children paying eager attention. To make the last point clear, the speaker said:—"Some years ago I visited a little boy, at the point of death, in Scotland. Seeing how weak he was, I told him I would not weary him with a long talk, so sang to him a verse which ran as follows:—

> "Oh! you must be a lover of the Lord,
> Or you can't go to heaven when you die."

He looked at me smiling, and said—

"'I like that, I should like to sing it myself.'

"It pleased him much, and he said—

"'I should like Mr. Fullerton to hear me sing that.' As he was in the next room, I called him in, and we both listened to his feeble effort to sing the verse, which, in his pretty Scotch accent, sounded very sweet. The next morning I called to see him before leaving for London, and he said—

"'I have learnt another verse.'

"'What is it?' I said; and he at once began to sing—

> "Yes! I am a lover of the Lord,
> So I shall go to heaven when I die."

Then he looked up into my face, and said—

"'Shall I go to heaven?'

"'Yes, indeed,' I said, 'you will if you are a lover of the Lord.'

"'Ah, sir!' he said, 'I do love him, and I know he loves me.'"

Rev. A. T. PIERSON, D.D., led the children in prayer, which, as at the beginning, they repeated clause by clause; and after singing—

"Oh! that will be joyful,
When we meet to part no more,"

the large company of little people dispersed.

An Example of Service.

A SERMON DELIVERED BY

REV. ARTHUR T. PIERSON, D.D.,

AT THE METROPOLITAN TABERNACLE,

On Lord's-day Morning, February 14th, 1892.

"David, after he had served his own generation by the will of God, fell on sleep."—ACTS xiii. 36.

"After he had served his own generation by the will of God!" One of the most beautiful things about the Word of God is the brevity of its biographies—the short sentences in which, by the Holy Ghost, the entire story of a consecrated and useful life is often told. In this thirteenth chapter of the Acts of the Apostles, we have two verses which give God's estimate of David. One is the twenty-second verse: "I have found David the son of Jesse, a man after mine own heart, which shall fulfil all my will." And the other is the thirty-sixth verse: "David, after he had served his own generation by the will of God, fell on sleep." Now let us be as brief and as pointed as possible. Take these three thoughts that are suggested at a moment's glance:—service, service to one's own generation, service to one's own generation by the will of God. In other words, the thought of service first; the sphere of service second—one's own generation; the spirit of service third—"by the will of God."

First, as to service itself, we are accustomed to say that the Christian life in its completeness, consists: first, of salvation;

second, of sanctification; and third, of service. But this is narrowing down the conception of salvation to very small limits. Salvation is not simply deliverance from the penalty of sin, which is justification; but from the power of sin which is sanctification, and from the dominion of selfishness: and what is *that* but service? When you forget yourself and begin to live for others, that is serving God and serving man. And surely no salvation is complete that does not include service as well as sanctification; and to show you that the saints of all ages have felt this, notice the last verse that we sung—

> "Take, my soul, thy full salvation;
> Rise o'er sin, and fear, and care;"

what is that but sanctification?

> "Joy to find in every station,
> Something still to do or bear."

That is service. So that there is no "full salvation" which does not include deliverance from the power of sin, and deliverance from the sway of all selfishness that confines our thought and our endeavour to our person, to ourselves.

We look quite too far for the sphere of our service. It is in our own generation, and not only so, it is in the very place where God has already put us that we are to find the sphere of our service. We look too far off. Doing the next duty, according to the will of God, is serving God—taking up the burdens of life and bearing them in the fear of God, and in the spirit of contentment, and for the glory of God: that is service. It is service in the house-maid to sweep the corners that she has neglected, to wash the pots and kettles and not fret about it. It is service in the carpenter to do good work, and furnish good material; it is service in the mason to build the wall, and put his piety and his conscience into brick and mortar. It is service in any man or woman or child to do the very next thing, and do it as one that loves God and wants to please him. There was a little girl in America who at the age of eight years found Jesus Christ. She lived in a district where, as yet, there was no church; it was a little hamlet in the West; she had a drunken, blasphemous, profligate father, and she began to ask God to bless her father. One Sunday morning she took her father's hand with caressing tenderness, and said, "Father, would you go to Sunday-school with me to-day?" Her father could not resist the omnipotence of that little hand, and he said, "Oh, yes, yes, I will go with you." He went, and he found Jesus Christ that afternoon. Not long since he died, having himself established 1,180 Sunday-schools in destitute districts. How little did that child understand what significance hung on her simply doing the next thing that was before her—the simplest thing that she could do, and the most natural thing that she could do! She never thought of doing a great thing. Is it not true that most servants of God that accomplish great things have not meditated great things to begin with? The Lord had a great plan, but his servant knew very little of it, and he simply began to do the next thing that was at his hand; and the Lord expanded his sphere and greatened his soul, and increased his faith, and crowned him with abundant success.

It is a blessed lesson to learn that I can stay right where I am, not change my sphere at all, but only change the spirit in which I do God's work, and ask my blessed Saviour to become a partner with me in my daily toils, and sweeten my cup, and use my life, and so make it a blessing to my soul and other souls. I am tempted to tell this great congregation an incident that happened in my own pastoral life; though it is scarcely of so dignified a character as to justify appearing in print, it is a most helpful story. I preached one Sunday morning on the text, "Let every man, in that calling wherein he is found, therein abide with God." There was a woman in my church who, having a husband, but no family, used to do all her own work; and there was a part of that work over which she used every day to fret, and that was washing the dinner dishes after the dinner was done. She went home that Sunday noon, and after dinner was over she came to the usual drudgery of washing the smudged pots and kettles. "Oh!" she said to herself, "it is the same old drudgery!" Then she thought of the text of my sermon, "Let every man abide in that calling wherein he is found," and "therein abide with God"; and she just stood there right at the kitchen table, lifted up her heart and said, "Jesus, come into this kitchen with me, and help me to wash these pots and kettles, that I may never again fret at any lot that God gives me." And she told me before I left America, that from that day she had never known what it was to fret at her kitchen work. That woman grew so much in grace, in knowledge of God, and in knowledge of the Holy Scripture, that she is to-day the head of the women's missionary society in a State of millions of people. Who can tell what a blessing might come to the men and women of this congregation, if, coming out of this house of God this morning, they should say to Jesus, "Come with me into my poor daily drudgery, and sanctify it; and help me never again to fret or worry at my lot." What a peace of God might come into your souls, and what a confidence in God into your daily toil! How Christ might sweeten even your bitter cup for you!

And I desire to add, moreover, that service can only be done when we are living a life of faith. There is a notion in some peoples' minds that, when Jesus Christ said to his disciples in Matthew vi. 33, "Seek ye first the kingdom of God, and his righteousness; and all these things shall be added unto you," it was meant only for apostolic days. Believe me, we should cut about nine-tenths of the sweetest promises out of the Word of God if we treat them in that fashion. There is just as much occasion to live a life of faith to-day as there was in the days of the apostles; and that promise is just as much for you and for me as it was for them. And what does it mean? Take as the first object of your life, the extension of the kingdom of God, and the incorporation into your own life of his righteousness, and he will give you everything that he sees to be necessary for you. That is the promise! The fact is, we need a single eye and a single aim. No man can see double and see correctly and safely. And God wants his children to be single-eyed in his service, to aim at the extension of his kingdom, to aim at the development of righteousness in the human character, to keep the eye on the glory of God. You cannot serve God and Mammon; you cannot be careful and troubled about many things, and yet have your central and concentrated affection fixed on the one thing needful. And so our blessed Lord bids you no more to worry even about your daily support; and he says, if you will first of all live for him, he will see that, as no sparrow falls to the ground without his notice, and even the hairs of your head are numbered, you shall have just what is necessary for you. That is a great promise, is it not?

I hold that worry is calculated, not only to hinder the work of God, but absolutely to encourage sin in our hearts; and that worry is therefore not only needless, since we have the promise, but it is sinful—sinful. If you are doing God's work, what are you worrying about? Is not God able to take care of his own work? And are you so impertinent as to suppose that he cannot get along without your solicitude and anxiety concerning his work? And if it is something that demands worry, then it is not God's work but yours. That is very short logic, but, to my mind, very conclusive. If you are doing God's work, leave responsible issues with him; if you are doing work that is not God's work, get out of it just as soon as possible, and take your proper stand at the side of God, and let all you do be service for him.

There are some secrets of service that I must touch upon; and may I not first of all mention obedience? I am satisfied that very few people understand what obedience is — absolute obedience to God. To hear his Word and follow it; to hear the suggestions of his Spirit by the "still, small voice," and at once yield compliance; to mind instantly what conscience enjoins, and never to continue in a course when you are even doubtful with regard to its propriety — that is absolute obedience. And it would not be possible to express, in any fitting language, what God could do with his Church if there were absolute obedience even in one half of the members of Protestant communions. In the 277th Hegira, as it is called, there was a rebel sect known as Carmathians, led by Abu Said and Abu Taher. They were able to command in the field only about five hundred horse at the time I am speaking of, but they swept down the coasts of Persia, and approached the city of Bagdad, the capital. The caliph trembled before their onset, for there was a blind vow of absolute submission to their leader, on the part of these soldiers. As these five hundred horsemen approached the city, the caliph sent out his soldiers and burned the bridges, so that they could not retreat. Then he sent his own lieutenant to say to Abu Taher, who was leading this body of cavalry, "If you do not surrender, all of your company will be destroyed." Abu Taher said to the lieutenant, "Your master has thirty thousand soldiers at his command, but he has not three that are as loyal to him as all these five hundred horsemen of mine are to me.' He beckoned to one. Said he, "Plunge the dagger into your breast," and he instantly drove the dagger into his heart. He said to another, "Leap from that precipice," and immediately he sprang from the precipice and was dashed in pieces. He said to another, "Fling yourself into the waters of the Tigris," and, without murmur or hesitation, he threw himself into the waters and was drowned. "Now," said he, "you may go and tell the caliph that I have five hundred horsemen mounted, anyone of whom will do just what these men have done at my command, and tell him that before night I will have his generals chained with my dogs." And before night the generals of the caliph were thus chained with those dogs. Five hundred horsemen overcoming thirty thousand soldiers! How? By absolute obedience to their leader. If God had in his church to-day one-tenth of its membership that were absolutely surrendered to his will, never hesitating, never murmuring, content to follow where he leads, and do exactly what he commands— with that one-tenth of his followers Jesus Christ could conquer this whole world to himself.

Let each one of you, as a child of God, ask yourself, "Am I serving God? Am I serving him? and if not, how may I serve him?" Look at the Greek word here: it is a word that means to be an under-rower. You know that the ancient war galleys had banks of oars arranged along the sides of the vessel in tiers, one, two, three, four, and sometimes five. At each one of these openings in the vessel's side, an oarsman presided at his oar, sometimes so limited in his range of vision that he could not even see the oarsman that sat in front of him on account of the partitions between. The oarsmen were all regulated by one superior will—the voice and beck of the pilot, and the word used here is the very word applied to an under-rower. "David, after he had under-rowed in his own generation." He just took his place at the oars that God gave him, and he pulled away at those oars, and the vessel was propelled forward under the will of the pilot. That is all you have to do, just take your place where God puts you, and do the work he gives you. Never envy your companions in labour, their spheres, their activities, their services; but look at your own sphere, activity, and service; and yield absolutely to the will and command of the divine pilot.

Let this great church consider what could be done if all the disciples in this membership were to work and live in the spirit of service. Here are, at least, five thousand members in active communion. Suppose that every one of these five thousand members should resolve, by the grace of God, to take one soul until the 1st of January next as the object of prayer and devout labour, seeking to lead, at least, one soul to Christ during the coming ten months; there would be five thousand converts as the reward of that work, for can you doubt for a moment that God would bless such a consecrated effort as that? There would be double the membership of this church within one year if each soul here led one other soul to Jesus Christ. I was yesterday making some slight computation as to what could be done if there were consecrated giving here, even in small sums. Suppose each member of this church, for example, should steadfastly set apart a single penny a day as an average; in one year we should have the princely sum of £7,600, or more than twice as much as was necessary to pay all the running expenses of this great church during the last twelve months, irrespective of benevolent institutions. But since the ability to give is unequal in this great congregation, suppose there should be two thousand five hundred persons who would give a penny a day; one thousand five hundred, twopence; five hundred, threepence; two hundred and fifty, sixpence; one hundred and fifty, a shilling; and one hundred who would give two shillings a day (which is only about £36 a year), it would amount to £19,000 at the close of the year. Some people talk about these great institutions connected with the Tabernacle going down into decline because the head Pastor has been withdrawn. I hold that it would be the greatest reproach, not only to the name of the Pastor, but to the Lord Jesus Christ and to this church itself, if any paralysis should come upon one of the institutions connected with this great congregation. This large Christian membership, by a small average of daily consecrated giving, could support not only this church, but all its institutions, and, instead of declining, every form of work for Christ would go forward.

Then consider what people can do in serving God by simply praying. If you are bed-ridden, if you are too poor to give a penny a day, if you cannot go to a single public service, is there anything that shall hinder you from praying to Almighty God for every interest connected with his kingdom and the progress of his cause here?

We turn for a moment to reflect on the second and third clauses, upon which I will be brief. "David served his own generation by the will of God;" that is, he found the sphere of his service in the generation in which he lived. Our benevolence is sometimes too far sighted, it overlooks immediate wants for more remote wants. I cannot myself understand how any man to whom God has given large means, can accumulate those means with reference to their distribution by legacy. It seems to me a great instance of folly, to say nothing more, that a man should risk the final appropriation of great gifts which God has entrusted to him in the way of accumulations of money—that he should risk their finally reaching their destination by leaving those gifts to be distributed by will. I have known in America, a princely fortune of two millions sterling absolutely wasted in legal processes in the court, devoured by those vultures, called lawyers, instead of being distributed through the channels for which it was designed. A man who gives while he lives has the satisfaction of seeing his gifts reach their destination; and has the satisfaction of seeing that the work of God is advancing under his benefactions. We talk about "generous legacies," and "munificent bequests." I do not see how there can be such a thing as a generous legacy or a munificent bequest. How can a man be generous when he has no longer any other opportunity of using the money for himself? What munificence can there be on the part of a man whose dying hand relaxes its grasp on every earthly possession, and out of which even the gold he had accumulated and coveted drops? There may be munificent gifts to God and glorious benefactions while a man lives, but it is very doubtful to me whether we ought to call any legacy or bequest generous or munificent. What a blessed thing for a man while he lives so to bestow his goods as that widows and orphans are made glad, as that the greatest institutions are permanently founded on a firm basis, as that the gospel is spread abroad in all parts of the earth! William E. Dodge, in New York, was so beneficent a giver that when he died no less than two hundred and fifty institutions in America, Europe, Asia, and Africa owed either their existence, or their extension, to what he had done on their behalf. "David served his own generation." He served his own generation when he was feeding his flocks, when he learned to use the sling that hurled the stone that smote Goliath in the forehead, when he learned to play the harp and prepared himself to become the great psalmist and psalmodist of Israel. He served his own generation when he carried on the wars of the Lord, and made preparation for building the temple of the Lord; and there is no reason to believe that he did not serve God as much in the faithful care of his flocks as when he was gathering together gold, silver, and precious stones for the erection of the stately temple of ancient times. We need only to see that all is according to the will of God. If it is not in obedience to the voice of your Divine Pilot that you take your place at the oars and do your work, if the plan of your life is not embraced in the plan of God, if your heart does not by its love and its loyalty take God's pleasure as your pleasure, how can there be any real service unto God or unto humanity?

I leave all this to say one word in application on the

life of the beloved departed Pastor of this church. Let me instance one example of his service to his own generation by the will of God. I will not say a word about the Orphanage, or the Pastors' College, or the Almshouses, but will simply speak of him as a preacher of the gospel—a simple, earnest, gospel preacher. I was making a computation, and I found that he must have preached the gospel, during the time of his public ministry, to no less than ten millions of people; that during his pastorate he must have received into communion between ten and twelve thousand converts; that his sermons must have reached a total of between twenty and forty millions of readers during the last thirty years; and that, probably, to-day there are over fifty millions of people that are reading the account of his life, and his labours, and his decease and burial. Here then was one man gathering into the Church of God, through his ministry, not less than twelve thousands converts, preaching the gospel to not less than ten millions of people with the living voice, and reaching from twenty to forty millions of people with his printed sermons during thirty years! Then all of you must know how those sermons have gone round the world, translated into twenty languages and dialects, at least, of which we know—Danish, Swedish, Russian, Dutch, German, French, Swiss, Spanish, Portuguese, Italian, Hindustani, Chinese, Japanese, Syriac, Arabic, Gaelic, the languages of Africa and of the South Sea Islands; on the continent of Asia; on the continent of Europe; going into South America, North America, Canada; penetrating into every part of the earth, so that it is impossible for us to form a correct and exact estimate to-day, of the marvellous influence of that one voice and that one pen. And I have made no reference whatever to the multitude of works, aside from sermons and volumes of sermons, that he produced by his laborious pen. The testimony has been given throughout this memorial service, and given by men of all denominations from all quarters, that he was the princely preacher of this century, and that no doubt his messages of the gospel had more rapidly and more distantly permeated the world than those of any other man, living or dead, in the century.

Would it not be a privilege to serve the same God that Charles H. Spurgeon served? Are there none of you this morning that will look unto Jesus and be saved as he was, and find the secret of pardon and acceptance in those blessed words, "He hath made us accepted in the beloved"? What a marvellous change will take place in your life this morning, if, as you go out of this house, you should say to God, "Henceforth thy will shall be the guiding star of my whole existence; I will undertake to serve God with holy living, to serve God with holy giving, to serve God with devout praying, to serve God by instant and constant obedience, to serve God by taking my place wherever God puts me, doing whatever work he gives me to do, and with all my heart seeking to glorify my Master." Then, my beloved friends, it may be your joy and mine, by-and-by, to stand where he stands in the presence of the Lord of Glory, and receive from our Master, the divine words of commendation that have already fallen upon his ears, "Well done, good and faithful servant."

Remember your Leader.

A SERMON DELIVERED BY
REV. ARTHUR T. PIERSON, D.D.,
AT THE METROPOLITAN TABERNACLE,
On Lord's-day Evening, February 14th, 1892.

"Remember them which have the rule over you, who have spoken unto you the word of God, whose faith follow, considering the end their conversation."—HEBREWS xiii. 7.

Along this upper railing you may all read that significant motto: "Remember the word that I said unto you; being yet present with you;" and to amplify the meaning of that motto will be my special object now.

Those who were present at the Memorial Service for the church members, will recall how Dr. Angus made this text the staple of his remarks, venturing to give a new rendering of it, which is rather more literal: "Bear in mind your leaders, since they have spoken unto you the Word of God; observing the end of their life-course, imitate their faith."

Spiritual leaders are of the highest importance to the human race. Few of us are capable of leadership, and so we need to have leaders to follow; and in all ages of the world God has given to men leaders—leaders in education, leaders in politics, leaders in philanthropy, and leaders in great religious movements; and inasmuch as the well-being of souls is of supreme importance, leadership in spiritual things is a supreme want and need of the human family.

It is of great importance that we should recognize such leaders, when God gives them to us. If it be needful that we should have leaders, it is equally so that we should not be misled by false guides, and therefore it is of such high importance that we should be able to determine what are the marks of a true, God-sent teacher. This text, whatever may be its other value, is mainly of importance, because it indicates three tests of a genuine, God-sent leader. In the first place he speaks the word of God, in the second place his faith is fixed on a personal Saviour; and, in the third place, his life conforms to the Word of God and to the faith in Christ, and ends in a glorious immortality. Wherever we find those three indications meeting in any man or woman, we may recognize the heaven-sent leader, and it is at our peril if we do not follow such leadership. There may, apparently, be one of these signs without the other two, or there may even appear to be two of those signs without the other, and third. In such cases doubt is justified: but, when the three are united, there can be no more reasonable question that such a man is one of God's anointed kings.

As there are three indications of God's heaven-sent leaders here noted, so there are three corresponding duties that pertain to the common mass of mankind. The first is that we should bear in mind the heaven-sent leader for the sake of his message. The second is that we should watch and observe his heavenly course of life, and especially its glorious end; and the third is that we should copy or imitate his faith in a personal Christ; and I am sure you will agree with me, that no text could be more appropriate to the closing portion of these memorial services, that have extended through a fortnight, than this text. Bear in mind your great departed leader, because he spoke to you faithfully the Word of God; look back over the course of his life, and especially mark its glorious end; and from henceforth become imitators of his personal faith in a personal Saviour.

Let us, then, for a few moments, reflect upon these signs of a heaven-sent leader, and then apply them to the beloved and departed Pastor.

In the first place, A HEAVEN-SENT LEADER SPEAKS THE WORD OF GOD. God has communicated his messages to men; and I believe, personally, that in a grand sense the prophetic office always has been in the world, and always will be in the world, till the end of time. What is a prophet? A prophet is not necessarily one who predicts future events. Prediction was but one mark of a prophet, and did not mark all prophets, either. A prophet is one who stands before men, to speak in behalf of God. Most of the Old Testament prophets predicted, because it was pleasing to God that those who spoke in his name should indicate to men the great events of the future, and especially the coming events that had to do with the Messiah; but, as was said before, it is no necessary mark of the prophetic office or person, that he predicts future events.

The difference between the Old Testament prophets and New Testament prophets lies mainly in this: Old Testament prophets spoke in behalf of God when, as yet, there were no written Scriptures, or when those written Scriptures were being gradually accumulated to make the complete book. Therefore, it was essential that prophets should be guarded by divine inspiration from any false or even fallible utterances. It was needful that there should be a compact body of revelation known as the Word of God, and they were chosen as the vehicles for creating or producing this Word of God, and therefore the great requisite was infallible inspiration. The character of the man speaking was of no particular consequence, in comparison to the character of his message. And so it pleased God sometimes to speak through men that were not what they ought to be, as in the case of Balaam and as in the case of Saul, because He thus magnified the office and function of the prophet above the person or character of the man. The message of God was the main thing, and if God chose to give that message through lips that were estranged from Him by wicked works, He might follow His own pleasure. But in these New Testament times the Word of God has been given, and given in final completeness. Hence there is no longer a necessity that any should help to produce the written Word of God. We have that in its entirety, its inspiration, its infallibility, and now, what we need prophets for is to *interpret* the word that God has given and apply it to human hearts. Hence arises a necessity that the character and life of the man who is to interpret the Scriptures shall be in accordance with the Scriptures. I think that we may safely say that, in modern times, God never chooses an unconverted or an unholy man to be the true vehicle of His message to his fellow-men. Character is of prime importance, as we shall see before we get through with this investigation; but what I would just now impress upon your minds is that a prophet is essentially a divine teacher and that, although the gift of predicting future events may no longer be a part of the qualification of a prophet, the prophetic office continues in the Church of God. Every man who preaches, and teaches, and testifies the Gospel of the grace of God, in accordance with the conditions here laid down, backing his gospel message by his personal faith in a personal Christ, and living such a life of godliness as shows that the message has taken root in his own heart—such a man is one of God's prophets, one of God's anointed ones, and it is at the peril of men that they do not receive the testimony of his lips and of his life. That I take to be the solemn sentiment of the text; and the meaning of that august and solemn admonition is, "Bear ye in mind your spiritual leaders, seeing that they have spoken unto you the very message of God. Keep your eye on their lives, and especially mark their glorious end, and become ye imitators of their faith in a personal Christ, who is the same yesterday, to-day and for ever, and therefore as ready to be your Saviour as he was to be theirs."

With regard to the application of the test, whether a prophet speaks the Word of God or not, how shall we know that the message which God's spiritual leader brings to us has the authority of the Most High? Even this is not left without criteria or means of forming a judgment. For instance, we are told in the eighth chapter of the prophecy of Isaiah, one of the great marks that shall always distinguish the utterances of a true spiritual leader. In the twentieth verse of that chapter we read "To the law and to the testimony: if they speak not according to this word it is because there is no light in them." That is the first test. Does the preaching or teaching of a spiritual leader correspond with the written Word of God? There is to be found the infallible standard of doctrine and duty. There is the great court of final appeal; beyond this no appeal can be carried, even to the throne of God, because the authority of God is in that book: and therefore he says, "Test every spiritual leader by the law and by the testimony of Holy Scripture, and if he speaks not according to this word, there is no light in him, and therefore he can shed no light on your spiritual darkness and duty." That criterion would unseat from their thrones hundreds of so-called spiritual leaders, who, in this day, to the astonishment of those of us who thoroughly believe this Word of God, seem to consider that their office is rather to cast doubt on the Holy Scripture than to confirm the confidence of men in this blessed Word; men who seem to use the pulpit as the place from which to spread rather their own misgivings and negations than their own convictions and affirmations, and who employ both tongue and pen rather to destroy than to construct faith in other souls. For one, I say, away with all these leaders! They are not God-given men. Again, let it be put on record, that the first test that a man is God's leader and speaks God's message, is that, accepting this Word of God as his guide, as the source from which he derives the authority of his message, the substance of his message and the spirit of his message, he preaches and teaches nothing new—old truths in new lights, it may be, but no new truths, for there are none. That which is new and not old is not true. All spiritual truth is as old as God is, and even the revelation of spiritual truth is as old as the Bible is. Men may talk about "progressive theology," but such a progressive theology only goes backwards, progressing only in the wrong direction. There is no addition to be made to the law and testimony. The only addition possible is in the spiritual interpretation and understanding of the law and testimony by the increase of spiritual insight and life in the teacher and the believer. That is the only true progress; and if people would pay more attention to their capacity for progress in that direction, leaving the Word of God unmutilated, and seeking simply to open their own minds and hearts to its testimony and to the incoming of the Holy Ghost, we should find, instead of a progressive theology, progressive theologians and progressive disciples.

A second test that the spiritual leader is delivering God's message is to be found in the fact that he considers his own thoughts and conceptions as insignificant in comparison with those of God. They are mere "chaff." If they include and embrace the Word of God, and are the means of setting forth that Word, they are, like the husk, valuable for the sake of the kernel within; but if it be only their own dreams and visions that these teachers are giving to men, there is nothing but chaff without a kernel, to be borne away by the first wind that blows. And so Jeremiah says concerning the preaching of the Word: "What is the chaff to the wheat?" We have long insisted, and again emphatically repeat, that what the people need on matters of doctrine and duty, is not what "I think" or another man "thinks" (for all have equally a right to "think,") but WHAT GOD THINKS. Man's "opinion" changes; God's opinion never changes; man's "conceptions" of truth differ; God's idea of truth is eternally the same.

A third evidence is given to us in the second Epistle to the Corinthians, in the first chapter, and it is especially necessary to emphasize this in our day. Paul says, in the seventeenth verse, "The things that I purpose, do I purpose according to the flesh, that with me there should be yea, yea, and nay, nay? But as God is true, our word toward you was not yea and nay. For the Son of God, Jesus Christ, who was preached among you by us, even by me and Silvanus and Timotheus, was not yea and nay, but in him was yea." That passage seems by many hard to be understood, but it is very simple. "Yea" is the word of affirmation—"It is so." "Nay" is the word of denial—"It is not so." Paul says, "Our preaching among you was not yea and nay." It did not consist of alternate positive and negative statements, of affirmations here and denials there; but it was one great, emphatic "YEA," that is, the utterance of positive truth backed by positive conviction. There are some professed teachers who, as I said before, seem to feel themselves called upon to tell others what they doubt. Goethe, the sceptic, says, "Give us your convictions; as for doubts, we have quite enough of our own." Men have no need to have their faith destroyed; they rather want to have it built up. They have no need to have doubts implanted in their minds; doubts spring up like weeds. What we want is faith, and, in order to faith, we want men of positive conviction, speaking positive truths. And here is another sign of a God-sent leader. He comes before men with truths and facts that he doubts not, to speak what he knows, and so he speaks with the positiveness and authority of absolute certainty. "We *know* that if our earthly house of this tabernacle were dissolved," etc. "We *know* that we have passed from death unto life." "We *know* him that is true." "We *know* that we have eternal life." "We *know* that we are of God." Who would not rather hear a preacher of the gospel say with confident certainty of conviction, "One thing I know," than to have him tell you ten thousand things that he did not know, or of which he was uncertain?

A fourth sign that one is speaking according to the Word of God, is that the true teacher of Christ speaks by the testimony of the Holy Ghost. In the first Epistle to the Corinthians, the second chapter, we read these words: "I brethren, when I came to you, came not with excellency of speech or of wisdom, declaring unto you the testimony of God. For I determined not to know anything among you, save Jesus Christ, and him crucified. And I was with you in weakness, and in fear, and much trembling. And my speech and my preaching was not with enticing words of man's wisdom, but in demonstration of the Spirit and of power; that your faith should not stand in the wisdom of men, but in the power of God." A true spiritual leader will be known by the fact that, when he speaks to men, his utterance is attended with the demonstration of the Holy Ghost—not simply the demonstration of logic, but the demonstration of the Holy Spirit; that is to say, God will acknowledge and own his appointed leader by accompanying his teaching with his own power. There will be conversions among the unsaved; there will be edification and sanctification among believers; there will be a stirring up in the church of God and in the world when God's anointed king wields God's sceptre, and delivers God's message. It is a sign of spiritual leadership that spiritual power, in some form, attends the utterance of God's message.

Here, then, are God's great marks of a spiritual teacher: he will speak according to the written Word of God; he will not deliver himself of mere human opinions; he will speak the language of personal conviction and positive statement; and he will speak with the demonstration of the Holy Spirit. When you find those four things united, you need have no more doubt that the spiritual teacher is one who is delivering to you the message of God.

Another test is hinted by Jeremiah, in the twenty-third chapter, where he writes about the false prophets, who delude and deceive Israel "*by their lies and by their lightness.*" Notice the collocation of those two words, "*lies* and *lightness,*" *i.e.*, falsehood and frivolity! In proportion to the soundness of a gospel preacher, his attachment to the Word of God, the depth of his experience, and the consistency of his life, will be the solemnity with which he preaches. On the other hand, when a man cuts loose from the Word of God, and begins to lead an inconsistent life, and loses hold on a personal Saviour, he begins to talk frivolity. For myself, although I have the keenest sense of the humorous and the ridiculous, and doubt not that humour has its part to play in a man's service, and has its lawful place in his utterance, I have always avoided conscientiously all invasions of the solemnity of the house of God by any jesting or trifling. And why? Suppose you go to a physician, believing yourself to have a cancer on the breast that is eating away at your vitals, and so close to your heart that it imperils your very existence. You go to one who is accustomed to deal with cancer as his specialty. You open your mind to him, and show him the cancerous sore. With a smile and a joke, he says, "Oh, just go home and put on a bread and milk poultice." What would you think? You would come to the conclusion either that the man does not know anything about cancers, or else that you have *nothing serious to worry about*—would you not? You come to the house of God; the man in the pulpit professes to deal with the realities and verities of eternity, and to speak in the name of God to men; he professes to believe that you are a lost sinner, that perdition is before you, and that there is no hope for you except in the blood of Jesus Christ. And yet he gets up and begins to trifle, to talk lightly and deal in frivolities; and you come to the conclusion either that he does not believe his own message, or else that you are in no danger. I therefore protest that, for the preacher of the gospel, no attitude of mind is proper, except *the solemnity of deep earnestness;* and that lies are scarcely more delusive than lightness on the part of a gospel preacher. And so God would have his appointed leaders manifest and exhibit the fact that they are his appointed leaders, not only by their clinging to the Word of God, by their assertion of positive conviction in positive statement, by the abundant power of the Spirit of God in their ministry, but also by the solemn and awful earnestness with which they press the truths of God upon the consciences of men.

Let us now consider briefly the other two great marks of an anointed king of God—the PERSONAL FAITH in a personal Christ, and the HOLY COURSE OF LIFE that ends in a glorious immortality. Do not you see a "progress of doctrine" here?—a development of truth? How can a child of God become God's anointed teacher and preacher to men, if the Word of God has not first taken hold of himself and made a new man of him? How can he preach the Christ of God, who is the centre of the gospel revelation, unless he personally believes in that Christ, and believes on that Christ, and is one with him by faith? Is not the preaching of the gospel *experimental?* Men do not want a mere intellectual display of learning, even though that learning be the mastery of the contents of the Word of God. You all like to hear a man speak whose heart speaks to your heart, instead of his head speaking to your head? That man preaches the gospel most powerfully on whose soul that gospel has first wrought the very results that he seeks to work in the souls of others. If I am not enamoured of Christ, I cannot make Christ appear as the Sun of righteousness, in whose presence all the stars fade. If he is not to me as precious ointment poured forth, that fills every apartment of my being with its glorious savour, how can I make him appear precious and fragrant to you? If he has not redeemed me from my sin, with what force can I assure you that he will redeem you from yours? If he has not satisfied my soul, how can I assure you that you will find in him the living bread and water that make hunger and thirst impossible? God's anointed king, who shall melt a million wills into the will of God, must be the man who comes with God's message, that has set his soul afire, and has set his own tongue ablaze. He must feel its melting power who would make others feel it. The man who preached in this Tabernacle, was a living sermon on this text. Let us look at this magnificent example of these principles, which was thus, for thirty years, furnished in this very pulpit, and for nearly forty years in his ministry in the city of London. God's word to this congregation to-night is, " Remember your great spiritual leader, who spoke to you the word of God. Mark his life, and its end, and copy his faith."

Charles H. Spurgeon was the most notable example that modern times have furnished of the union of these three elements to which I have adverted. There has been perhaps, no preacher of the age or century who has so rigidly confined his message to the Word of God as did that man. I call this congregation to witness, that they have heard from no other living preacher, messages so saturated with the thought and very *dialect* of the Holy Scriptures. It has been my privilege to hear most of the greatest preachers of the world, and I say, without depreciating any other man, living or dead, that I never heard such a gospel preacher as Charles H. Spurgeon. Nearly twenty-six years ago I was in this

Tabernacle, in the month of August, 1866. I remember just where I sat, and the whole scene is indelibly impressed on my memory. I had then myself been preaching the gospel of Jesus Christ for more than six years, as an ordained minister, but on that morning I was convicted of sin. Such preaching I never had heard; such praying I never had heard; such praising I never had heard; and I went home to be a different man. That morning's experience revolutionized my ministry. It created in me a divine dissatisfaction with everything that I had been or done before, for I saw how mighty the simple gospel might be made, backed by deep heart-conviction and preached with a positiveness of statement; and I said, "If Christ Jesus, and he alone, can be made so gloriously attractive as that, and draw the people in such multitudes, God forbid that I should attempt any other method of making my life serviceable to men, or of drawing the people within the sound of my voice!" And if there is any power in my preaching of the simple gospel I owe it, under God, to what I heard from Charles Haddon Spurgeon in 1866. I challenge you to find any man living who exalts Christ more than he did, whose personal conviction of the truth was more positive, or who lived out, to the end, more consistently, the faith he preached.

Some say that he was so positive in his beliefs, that he had no compassion upon people who doubted. Would that we had many more like him! He would not encourage doubt where doubt concerned the infallible Word of God. He was not the man to countenance the notion that doubt is something meritorious, the sign of a higher order of intellect and culture, a notion which is one of the subtlest snares of the day in which we are living. Doubt is so in the fashion, that the "first families" in the intellectual world have adopted a new escutcheon, or shield, to signalize their intellectual greatness, and on that shield they have had engraved a huge question mark, an interrogation point (?), as though the mark of a great mind and superb culture is to question all things that have been undoubted, and put a doubt upon all the verities of God.

Dr. C. F. Deems says, "believe your beliefs, and doubt your doubts." Never make the mistake of believing your doubts and doubting your beliefs, for that temptation is in the very atmosphere of this sceptical age. Men and women are prone to doubt the things that have always been believed, and to believe the things that at least have been always doubted, and so to transfer their confidence to the wrong side of the scale. I bless God for the man that stood in this pulpit. He knew whom he believed, and knew the truth, for all his testimony was the result of experience and experiment. There must be an awful condemnation in store for those who, in this place, have heard this greatest of gospel preachers, and have not yet believed. I would to God that I had the tongue of the archangel to plead with and persuade you. Suppose that God should say to you, in eternity, only this one word: "*Remember*, REMEMBER, REMEMBER"! What if, hereafter, your mind is compelled to turn back to the sermons that you have heard delivered with such transcendent power from this platform, by that departed saint, and you must "remember" how he never preached a sermon in which he did not plead with sinners.

When he was a lad he wandered through the place in which he lived seeking to find some comfort for his awakened soul, and could not, until at last he heard a plain sermon, whose message was: "*Look unto me and be ye saved, all the ends of the earth.*" Then, the same day, he heard another sermon about being "accepted in the beloved," and he came home and told his father that he learned the way of salvation in the morning, but that he found the secret of pardon, peace and conscious acceptance in the evening. What a day that was for him! "And now" he said, "*I will never preach a gospel sermon in which a sinner may not find the way to Jesus Christ.*" I do not think that there has been another man in the century who could say that. For myself, while I have tried to be a gospel preacher, I am sure I have preached many sermons in the course of my life, in which a sinner would have found it very difficult to discover the message of grace, or the way of salvation. Yet I bless God that, when I came to preach in this pulpit, I resolved, God helping me, that I would never henceforth preach a sermon in which I did not, in some form or other, uphold the crucified Christ. Well may less faithful preachers envy that blessed man, who could thus look back over forty-two years of his preaching of the gospel, and could never recall a sermon through which a sinner could not have found Christ! I pray God that you, who have sat under such a ministry, may not be lost, else you will be dreadfully lost. I pray you do not persist in going down to perdition, for every sermon that you have heard from Charles H. Spurgeon will be an additional weight on you to sink you down to the lowest depths. Remember him. He has been taken from you, but remember him. Remember his message. Follow his faith. Mark the consistency and beauty of his life, and even at this late day be turned to the Saviour that he served, and follow him.

I will read to you, as I close, a passage from one of Mr. Spurgeon's sermons, which he preached at Park Street Chapel, Southwark, in 1858. It was on the subject of "Death a Sleep"; and in the course of it he used these words—let us think of him as saying them to us to-night:—

"And now, beloved, we shall soon all of us die. I shall have a gravestone in a few years planted over my grave in memory of me. Some of you I hope may say, 'There lies our minister, who once gathered us together in the house of God, led us to the mercy seat and joined us in our song. There lies one who was often despised and rejected of men, but whom God did nevertheless bless to the salvation of our souls, and whose testimony he sealed in our hearts and consciences by the operation of the Holy Ghost.' Perhaps some of you will visit my tomb and bring a few flowers to scatter upon it in glad and grateful remembrance of the happy hours that we spent together in the house of God."

It almost seems to me that, absent, he is still present and pleading with souls here to come to Christ. If there be any such thing in heaven as a knowledge of what is going on, on earth, Charles Haddon Spurgeon is assuredly looking down on this great congregation to-night. If there is such a thing as prayer in heaven, he is praying now for souls in this assembly. We know nothing about the communication between this world and the other; but communication will be opened by-and-by, and with each one of you in turn. While the Lord tarries, let us hope that Charles Haddon Spurgeon's reward will go on accumulating even now in multiplied conversions. But, best of all, we would have the jewels in the Saviour's crown made complete, and Christ see of the travail of his soul and be satisfied.

Here stood, for all these years, one of God's anointed kings. He preached the gospel with royal authority and spiritual power; he preached it with positive conviction; with personal faith in a personal Saviour, for I never knew a man whose heart bounded toward a personal Christ with intenser love than his. He preached it by the demonstration of the Holy Ghost. Multitudes were converted and saved and rejoice in God to-day; and I say to you now, solemnly, that if any of you have ever been doubtful that this is the Word of God, ever been doubtful that there is such a person as the Holy Ghost, ever been doubtful that there is such a thing as a transforming power in the Christian life, that departed Pastor ought to be the sufficient evidence of Christianity to you all; for there is no possibility of accounting for that one man if there is not a God;

if this Bible is not his Word; if Christ is not a real Saviour; and if the Holy Ghost does not give the new heart and transform the life into the image of God. In the face of all infidels of all ages, and of the abounding infidelity of the present age, I boldly affirm that that one man, who has recently gone from us into the eternal glory, is the standing refutation of infidelity. He can be accounted for in no way, except by God the Father, God the Son, and God the Holy Ghost. The only philosophy sufficient to explain him is that this Bible contains, and is, the very Word of God, and that the message faithfully proclaimed, embedded and embodied in the heart and expanded in the life, is the essential divine message of reconciliation and salvation.

I can say no more. May God the Holy Spirit seal to your mind and heart the message of life and salvation that Mr. Spurgeon preached in this pulpit; and make it impossible for you to do otherwise than "REMEMBER THE WORD THAT HE SPAKE UNTO YOU, — BEING YET PRESENT WITH YOU"! Amen.

A Thoroughly Furnished Life.

A SERMON DELIVERED BY
REV. ARTHUR T. PIERSON, D.D.,
IN THE METROPOLITAN TABERNACLE,
On Thursday Evening, February 25th, 1892.

"I call to remembrance the unfeigned faith that is in thee, which dwelt first in thy grandmother Lois, and thy mother Eunice; and I am persuaded that in thee also."—2 Timothy i. 5.

"Continue thou in the things which thou hast learned and hast been assured of, knowing of whom thou hast learned them; and that from a child thou hast known the Holy Scriptures, which are able to make thee wise unto salvation through faith which is in Christ Jesus. All scripture is given by inspiration of God, and is profitable for doctrine, for reproof, for correction, for instruction in righteousness: that the man of God may be perfect, thoroughly furnished unto all good works."—2 Timothy iii. 14-17.

You will all expect me not only preach the gospel, but also to speak of that departed saint and pastor, preacher and organizer, who for so long a time, stood in this pulpit as God's ambassador. Happily, it is quite easy and natural to combine these two things. It is not every man of whom we might discourse, and at the same time, preach the gospel; but as Charles Haddon Spurgeon was a kind of living gospel, to talk about him is to talk about the blessed Master himself, whose he was, and whom he served. So I shall endeavour, by God's help, in some measure to meet your expectation, by combining gospel truth, with an illustration and example of it, in the beloved and departed Spurgeon.

No question absorbs more of the thought, especially of the young, than the question, What are the secrets of success in life? Every one of us desires success. Failure is humiliating, disappointing, disastrous. Success is inspiring, encouraging, rewarding.

What, then, are the secrets of the highest success? Not a success that is temporary and transient; not a success which is deceptive and superficial; not a success which, as God interprets it, is itself failure; but a success which God counts such, and which in God's book of remembrance has an honourable record; for there is a scroll on which stands no unworthy name, and where no deed done for Christ and for humanity, fails of an honourable, illustrious, and enduring record. And the question is, "How may my name stand on that scroll, emblazoned in letters of light, with a record as imperishable as the life of God?" That is an aspiration which may well put to shame any inferior and worldly ambition. Such an aspiration is not unworthy of the Lord Jesus Christ himself, "who, for the joy that was set before him, endured the cross, despising the shame."

These verses from the second Epistle of Paul to Timothy, as we shall see, if we closely and carefully examine them, suggest to us certain great secrets of a successful life; and for convenience sake, I will select first the foundation; second, familiarity with the Scriptures; third, faith in a personal Saviour; and fourth, furnishing for good works. All these four are suggested in these verses, and constitute, in fact, the leading thoughts of this passage.

The foundation of Timothy's successful life was laid in a holy ancestry; the source of his knowledge and wisdom was found in familiarity with the entire Word of God; the bond of faith in the personal Saviour supplied the personal element and inspiration; and last of all, there was a thorough furnishing or complete equipment for the work of life. Of course there may be other secrets of power;

and yet I question whether, within these four, there may not lie the germ of every possible secret of the highest success, I shall first advert to these very briefly, and then show how they were illustrated in the marvellous career of that servant of God, whose work of faith and whose voice of witness we shall henceforth know only in remembrance.

I. First, let us look at THOSE FOUNDATIONS OF SUCCESS, WHICH ARE LAID IN A GODLY PARENTAGE AND ANCESTRY.

When a distinguished philosopher and wise man of these modern times was asked the question, "When should the character of a child begin to be formed?" he answered, "At least, one hundred years before the child is born." And this was no jest: he indulged in no trifling. He meant that in parental character—nay, even farther back than that —in ancestral character—there were found the formative influences that determine largely what the child or the grandchild shall be. We do not sufficiently appreciate the far-reaching influence of what is called, in these days, "heredity," or the influence that flows down through the channels of our ancestry and affects our character, our conduct, and, largely, our destiny. In the recent criminal investigations in the United States of America, there was found a family, known as the Jukes family, that was traced through all the branches back to one godless, profane stock. To one vile man were traced, directly, 709 descendants, and indirectly, 1,200. The most of these were criminals, vagabonds, outcasts and paupers. At least, 76 of the number had been habitual criminals, guilty of 115 different offences; and there were 52 per cent. of all the women in that large family that were abandoned, living by the price of their own shame. Most of these descendants had been for some time, greater or less, in prison. There were not more than 20 of the entire 709 that had ever learned a skilled trade, and 10 out of the 20 had learned that trade in jail. Now here were from 700 to 1200 characters, mostly criminal, all of whom could be traced to one ancestral fountain. Those who have been familiar with such slums in great cities as the Five Points in New York, and the Seven Dials in London—those who have seen the successive crops of generation after generation of iniquity, will know how the product deteriorates, and by how fearfully rapid a descent children sink to lower and lower depths of degradation and depravity. If this is the case where vice and crime are regnant, who shall dare to tell us that there may not be a corresponding ascent to higher levels, when godly parents, holding body, mind, and will in subjection to conscience and the Spirit of God, beget, conceive, and rear their children in the fear of God? We have no reason to hope that children will ever be regenerated before birth, though many have, doubtless, like John the Baptist, been full of the Holy Ghost *from* their mothers' womb; but I have no doubt that godly parents, by self-sacrifice and self-control in the grace of God, may transmit to children *aptitudes*, to say the least, for a higher mental, moral, and spiritual condition than would have been possible under other circumstances; and these *aptitudes* may, at least, prepare the way for *altitudes*—higher elevations, nobler and purer and hoiler attainments, characters and lives. Paul called to remembrance the unfeigned faith which was in Timothy, which dwelt first in his grandmother Lois and his mother Eunice. That is to say, there was a sort of heredity to his faith; it bore the parental complexion and feature, and there was a connection between the faith of the mother and the faith of the child, and even that of the grandmother and the grandchild. Here, then, the foundations of a successful life were laid in parental consecration. I speak of this first, not only because it is first in the text, but because I am addressing largely those who are, or in the future are likely to be, parents. I beseech you, sanctify your bodies, your minds, your hearts. Sanctify wedlock and marriage.

Let children be begotten, conceived, born, reared, in the fear of God, and let it be felt to be the most solemn responsibility that any human being can assume in the eyes of God, to bring a child into this world. These are delicate subjects, for the most parts forbidden to the pulpit; but the time is coming when this mock-modesty will no longer be countenanced, and when ministers of Christ shall feel free to speak in the name of God concerning the springs of human life in parental character and personal self-dedication, and how those springs may be purified with the salt of the gospel.

II. The second secret of a successful life, here unveiled to us, is FAMILIARITY WITH THE HOLY SCRIPTURES. It is said of Hengstenberg, the famous scholar, that on one occasion in the presence of his students, he took up a Greek New Testament and said, "Young gentlemen, within the covers of this book, all the wisdom of the ages is concentrated." If I might contribute my little word of witness on this great subject, I have found in the patient study of the Word of God, in the original tongues, which began when I was twelve years of age, the fountain of the highest knowledge and wisdom—knowledge is only the accumulation of information, but wisdom is skill and sagacity in the use of knowledge. That one book imparts both, and is itself a library as well as an encyclopædia. To the fervent, devout, and careful student that one book brings the advantages of a university education. All the treasures of divine wisdom and knowledge that can be communicated to man, are hid in this Thesaurus or treasury of God. And those who, from beginning to end, revere it as the Word of God, those who study it daily, systematically, and prayerfully, those who believe it to be the utterance of the Holy Ghost, and therefore to be illumined properly to our understanding and heart only by the Holy Ghost, and who both expect and receive divine guidance in searching into these wonders, will find in the Bible everything that stimulates the noblest thought, the purest love, the most correct conscientious judgment, and the holiest and firmest resolve.

Begin therefore with children, and teach them the Holy Scripture. Let children commit the Scriptures to memory, even before they are able to understand the words which they commit, for, be assured, while such commission to memory of the Holy Scriptures in childhood, may, for the time being, oftentimes be a form, without a proper and intelligent apprehension, that form will abide in the memory, to be filled out by increasing intelligence and growing appreciation of what the words contain and express.

I am thankful to God, in every fibre of my being, that for thirty years I have been accustomed to commit to memory, day by day, texts of Scripture; and, as the Malagasy, during the great persecution of twenty-five years in Madagascar, found that the Scriptures which they had put in memory's keeping, could neither be torn to pieces, nor burned to ashes, but were their permanent and perpetual possession, so I bless God that, however men might destroy the written Word of God as printed in various languages, upon the unseen tablets of my own intellectual and moral being, much of the Word of God is permanently engrossed, and only the annihilation of my memory could remove it. From a child let your little ones learn the Holy Scriptures, and commit their sacred words to memory; and then, so far and so fast as the understanding enlarges by experience and observation, the form of sacred words will become more pregnant with the spirit, and what was, in the child, the mere shell of knowledge, shall be found to hold a precious kernel for his intellectual and spiritual apprehension and appreciation.

III. The third element in success suggested here is FAITH IN A PERSONAL SAVIOUR. Whenever we stop short of the Christ of God, we have not found the centre even of gospel truth. The Word of God, to those who carefully study it, seems, the more they search it, only a firmament for the glorious display of the Sun of Righteousness, or a garden for the setting forth of the beauty of the Rose of Sharon, and the diffusing of his sacred fragrance. To those who love the Christ of the Scriptures, the Church itself in its best estate is only a telescope, through which to look at the Star of Bethlehem; to separate it from all surrounding objects, and limit the field of vision so that one may gaze upon it with the more satisfaction and the more enlargement of soul; and every fellowship of disciples becomes the more precious, because in the resemblance of the children of God to the eternal Son of God, his image is made more vivid and visible. We must magnify the personal bond of faith! Suspect any creed that either leaves out the Christ or obscures him. Suspect any church that teaches you to look at its machinery of ordinances and sacraments, rather than through and past them all, to the eternal Redeemer himself. Suspect any work, even of mercy and charity and philanthropy, that leaves out of view the glory of Jesus Christ. The personal bond is that which determines the Christian, for Christianity is not a creed without a life, any more than it is a life without a creed. Christianity is CHRIST-ianity. It makes Christ central in its doctrine, central in its duty, central in the destiny of believers; and whoever has not gotten hold of Christ, has not gotten hold of Christianity. Humboldt, the great German, wrote five volumes of "The Cosmos," or description of the material universe; but in those five volumes I have never yet found the word "God." Some people discuss Christianity in volumes, and do not see that the King of the Christian system, who, from his throne, sways his sceptre over all Christian doctrine, and life, and history, is the eternal Son of God,

Moreover, no man understands the Bible who does not understand Christ, for Christ is the key of the Bible. He interprets types; he fulfils prophecies; he unlocks even historic characters and historic events. Adam and Abraham and Joseph, Moses and Joshua, David and Solomon, Daniel and Isaiah, are enigmas if you do not understand Christ. He unlocks the mysteries of the word, and the blood that he shed unlooses the seven-sealed book of the Apocalypse.

IV. One other secret of success suggested by the text demands notice, before I apply and illustrate these truths by that remarkable life that has faded out from before our eyes; and that secret is THE THOROUGH FURNISHING FOR GOOD WORKS.

"Thoroughly furnished unto all good works." It is not to be overlooked that this furnishing, like the learning, the wisdom, the knowledge, to which we have referred, is here traced to the Holy Scriptures. "All scripture is given by inspiration of God, and is profitable for doctrine,"—that is teaching; "for reproof,"—that is the rebuking of evil and the stirring up of the conscience; "for correction,"—that is the reinstatement of the man after he has fallen, putting him upon his feet; "and instruction in righteousness,"—that is the full training of the man in the knowledge and performance of all that which is righteous in God's sight; "that the man of God may be made perfect," or complete, "thoroughly furnished," or equipped, "unto all good works."

The Bible is, then, not only the source and foundation of the highest knowledge and wisdom, it is the House Beautiful, such as Bunyan saw in his vision of the pilgrim; within it there is everything that a pilgrim can ask: the Dormitory, where he can rest after the weariness of the labour and toil of his march, the Refectory where he will find living bread and living water, the milk for the babe, the strong meat for the man, and the delicious honey out of the rock. There is the Picture Gallery, where he shall look on the characters of olden times portrayed for warning, on the one side, for imitation on the other. In that

House Beautiful is the Armoury, where he can equip himself from head to foot with the complete panoply of God.

There is also the Lavatory where the fountains of water and of blood give him perfect cleansing from the penalty and power of sin. Not only so, but the Observatory through whose windows he can look out on celestial scenes, and even into the very face of God. There is nothing that cannot be found in that House Beautiful for him who goes forth as God's pilgrim-saint to God's work and war in this wicked world.

Let us now spend a little while in ILLUSTRATING THESE FOUR SECRETS OF SUCCESS by this most remarkable man.

I need not tell you that Charles Haddon Spurgeon had a godly ancestry reaching back to the times of the martyrs. He belonged not only to godly parentage and grand parentage, but to a line of ministers of the Word of God, who held fast to the old truths which he so gloriously preached, and for which he so laboriously strove, so that he was but the last result of a series of generations of Christian fathers and mothers who had feared God and served him, who had studied the Holy Scriptures, and had been linked by faith to a personal Christ; and in himself he represented aptitudes that had been created or fostered in them, and so rose to altitudes seldom attained by any of the men of his generation. As was eloquently said here by Dr. Evans, on the day of the commemorative services, some people have tried to depreciate Mr. Spurgeon by saying that he was "without early advantages of birth and training," but, with Dr. Evans, we affirm that no man of his generation, perhaps, was more blessed by early advantages of birth and training. Give me a godly father and mother, and godly grandparents, and I will forego social position and rank and honourable titles, and the wealth and the fame of this world. Give me this, and I will forego, if it please God, all the schools of man for the sake of training in this school of God.

He who owed so much under God to a godly ancestry was, from a child, trained in the Holy Scriptures; and everybody who knew him knows how wise they made him unto salvation. Even as a boy he knew his Bible; and at an age when most of us were but boys, he began to preach the gospel, and, from the first, with such remarkable knowledge of the Word of God, and facility and felicity in its presentation as turned the eyes of all men to the boy-preacher of London. Surely this was no accident. We may talk about his "genius," but it was not genius that gave command of the Holy Scriptures, and made him mighty in them; that made him familiar with the events narrated in the Old and New Testaments, and filled his mind with those grand illustrations of truth that are scattered all the way through the Word of God. All this meant painstaking industry, research, prayer for divine guidance, and the opening of mind and heart to the instruction of God's Spirit through the Word. Mastery comes not by genius, but by effort. A man may be born with fine faculties, but acquisitions come by painstaking endeavour. And when that boy-preacher startled all London by the marvel of his preaching, and still more by the marvel of his praying; it was the result of early and long study of the Word on the one hand, and communion with God in the closet on the other. From a child he knew the Scriptures. What a blessed thing to have a child who is precocious in godliness. I do not care for intellectually precocious children, but I like a precocious child spiritually—a child that has in him the heart of a man, and the conscience of a man, and the will of a man, and the experience of a man. If you call such a child "abnormal" he is not half as abnormal as those Christian disciples of sixty years that have not outgrown their babyhood yet! Think of people threescore years of age singing—

> "Where is the blessedness I knew,
> When first I saw the Lord?"

to the Palm-Branch.

when they ought to have grown past that blessedness, as the dawn of the day moves on to its zenith splendour.

> "Where is the soul-refreshing view
> Of Jesus and His word?"

whereas those first views of the Word and of Jesus should have been but as the dim glance of the man who saw men as trees walking, but who needed another touch to give the clearness and the vividness of perfect vision!

> "What peaceful hours I once enjoyed!"
> How sweet their memory still!"

think of it, sighing for the peace that was felt fifty years ago!

> "But they have left an aching void,
> The world can never fill."

How any "void" can ache is a mystery to me anyway, but if any of you are troubled with an "aching void" I think that you would better get the void filled up! Oh, give us stalwart Christian disciples! How often the little child puts the oldest of us to shame by the simplicity of his faith and the fervour of his prayers, and the unfaltering nature of his trust. May God give us a generation of children that from their childhood know the Holy Scriptures! And do you, as parents and teachers, be more anxious that your child shall get a knowledge of the Word of God than a smattering of French and German and other languages that the inhabitants of these countries scarcely recognize when they hear them! Why should we be so jealous to have our children get some little acquaintance with foreign tongues and modern philosophies, and all manner of worldly learning, while the Bible is to them a shut and sealed book? Oh, for the university training of the Word of God! Oh, for a generation of young men and young women like Apollos, "mighty in the Scriptures," though they may have none of the "learning and wisdom of the Chaldeans."

One never wearies of speaking of the personal faith of

Mr. Spurgeon in a personal Saviour. Nothing has melted my heart in the remembrance of him more than this, that he always seemed to think of Christ as one that was immediately in his presence. To a great many people Christ is a being of eighteen hundred years ago, and they strain their eyes looking back through these long centuries to get a glimpse of the crucified and risen Jesus. Mr. Spurgeon went into his closet, handled Christ, and saw that it was he himself. When he prayed it was a personal prayer into a personal ear. His daily walk of faith and hope and humility, was a daily fellowship with the Lamb of God. He got his inspiration for work from studying Christ. Hope found its foundation in the promises Christ affirmed and confirmed. He got his courage in suffering from the supporting power of those everlasting arms. Christ was to him, not a flower in a garden, but a living, present, almighty Saviour. Christ was to him not a vision of the past, but a vivid reality of the present, and when he communed with Jesus Christ it was as a man talks with his friend; and because Christ was to him inseparably associated with the Holy Scriptures,—because those Scriptures everywhere testified of him, because they foretold him and he fulfilled them, he had no patience with those who, in the name of scholarship and learning, disintegrate the Rock of Ages, so that a man has no firm footing for his feet!

If I pause to consider how he was thoroughly furnished for all good works, it will be gathering up and braiding together all the other thoughts I have presented. Nothing is more wonderful about him than how he was furnished for everything he did by the study of the Word of God, and contact with a personal Redeemer. That is what I have specially sought to emphasize, because all the rest largely goes without saying. His furnishing unto all good works was derived from the Scriptures of Christ, and the Christ of the Scriptures. It was a singular providential diversion of plan, which led him away from university training and caused him to enter the gospel ministry without what men call in these days, "a thorough classical education." Why did God ordain that, but to give you and me encouragement? Had Charles Haddon Spurgeon been a university trained man, a prize scholar in Oxford or Cambridge, men would have attributed his success very largely to what he had learned and acquired in those great schools of human learning. But God decreed that that mighty man should come before the people without a university to back him, that he might prove to men that it was "not by might, nor by power," but by the Spirit of the living God, and that his success might say, in all future years, to young men like you, and the young men of other generations after you, that thoroughly to know Christ in the Word of God, and to know the Word of God as interpreted by the Christ and the Holy Spirit, is the grandest qualification for a Christian minister, and a Christian worker, that can possibly be bestowed. I wish that I had a thousand times the power of emphasis to proclaim and enforce this truth.

Look at his kaleidoscopic preaching. I can think of nothing to represent it but a kaleidoscope, which, at every turn, reveals new beauties, new combinations, new glories of form and colour out of a few small pieces of coloured glass! He took these few great initial truths of the Holy Scripture: atonement by blood, substitutionary sacrifice, justification by faith, the work of the Holy Ghost in regeneration and sanctification, and kindred truths to these; he put them within the kaleidoscope of his preaching, and at every new turn men saw, from the combination of those simple elements, forms of symmetry and colours that had all the variety of the rainbow, and they wondered that out of the old word of God alone such ever new attractions should be revealed. There is the secret of his furnishings for all good works. No man will dare to affirm that his furnishing came essentially from any source but the Word of God and the personal experience of the Christ.

What did Mr. Spurgeon mean when he said that, if at any time he lost his track of thought, he put himself into his gun and fired himself at the people? What did he mean but that from the depths of an experience of the communion of his soul with Christ, he drew that impulsive and propulsive force that, like the gunpowder in the gun, drives the ball to its mark? Even a mastery of Holy Scripture without an experience of grace, is only like the finest ordnance without gunpowder or spark of fire. But give us first the knowledge of God as here revealed, and then the knowledge of God as confirmed by personal contact of faith: and you have a mighty piece of ordnance provided with an explosive force, that can shake the very walls of the fortress of the devil!

Here was found his furnishing for all good works. Take those two thousand sermons of his, preached in this pulpit, printed at a penny a piece, and then scattered in twenty-five languages over the entire world, read by thousands and millions of readers. Whence came the furnishing for these sermons? From that blessed Word. I read with greatest interest that address which he delivered before the Conference, and which is now published under the name of *The Greatest Fight in the World*. I have no hesitation in saying that I think that to be the greatest single utterance that Mr. Spurgeon ever gave to the church. It is, I suppose, the last one that he prepared with careful and painstaking elaboration before he left this world. If you will read that you will find that, in the first place, it is full of the most glorious gospel truths. In the second place, it fairly bristles with Biblical illustrations and figures of speech. And, in the third place, which is more wonderful, it runs in the mould of a Scriptural dialect, as though the man were himself first of all saturated with the phraseology of Scripture, and when he came to express himself on that critical occasion, his thoughts fell into the forms of Scriptural expression as naturally as water runs in the channel scooped out for it by the brook. That is a marvellous address. I wish it might be published in the cheapest form and given away to every living soul that can read the English tongue, and then translated into every language on earth, that every man that is open to convictions of truth might read it. And I would to God that the men that have learned the art of preaching a sermon and leaving out the Christ, or of preaching the Christ in the language and after the fashion of the schools, and so shooting their arrows over the heads of the common people, could, from that single address, learn the secret of telling the truths of the Word of God, "not in words which man's wisdom teacheth, but which the Holy Ghost teacheth," expressing spiritual things in spiritual terms. I never have met, in all my own experience, a discourse that made a deeper impression on my mind as to reproducing the prophetical style of utterance in the modern pulpit, and so stamping a preacher as one of God's prophets. Here is another example of his furnishing unto all good works, and its source.

Whence came those twenty-seven volumes of *The Sword and the Trowel?* What are they? Those volumes are full of exposition of the Word, and the practical application of the Scriptures to the experience of the godly life. That is the soul and substance of twenty-seven years of that monthly issue. Take his hundred books: commentaries, tracts, leaflets, collections of proverbs. What are they? They are historical, and biographical, and expository, and exegetical; but the foundation of them is this: Scripture, on the one hand; experience of God's life in the soul, on the other. So again, for all this wonderful work of an author, he got his furnishing in the Word of God, and in the contact with a personal Christ. The *Treasury of David*, that seven-volumed commentary on that single book of the Bible, the Psalms,—which some "higher critics" would make us believe is not worthy, after all, of very much study,—has sold more largely than any other single commentary in the English tongue on one book of the Bible. What are those volumes, again, but the evidence that the furnishing for his work was a furnishing in Bible knowledge, and in the interpreting power of the Christian experience.

Whence came these institutions? First of all, where did he get the model for this church of Christ? There is nothing else like it, that I know of, anywhere in the world. It is a Baptist church in this, that believers' baptism is here emphasized, and that immersion in water is the form of baptism. It is a Methodist church in the ardent zeal, and the fervent prayer, and the aggressive work, manifested here, and in the audible "amens" and responses that you hear in prayer and preaching. It is a Congregational church in this, that it is independent of all outside ecclesiastical authority, and the people are the ultimate rulers. It is a Presbyterian church in this, that the bench of elders is the centre of its authority and its life, only that these are more consistent Presbyterians than most others, because when they choose a man as an elder, that choice carries with it the authority to preach, and teach, and administer the sacraments, if circumstances require, and if the brother exhibits the fitness for these duties; whereas, in other Presbyterian churches, if a man is set apart for the eldership, and afterwards shows fitness for preaching and teaching, and is called to the pastorate of a church, he must be ordained over again to make a minister of the gospel of him, which I have consistently held for many years to be utterly opposed to all New Testament precedent. Mr. Spurgeon, when he completed the organization of this church, looked to the Holy Scriptures for his model, and because he found, or believed that he found, in the New Testament, a bench of elders that, being once consecrated to the eldership, had right and authority to fulfil any function of teaching, preaching, ruling, or oversight, he modelled his church on that New Testament basis; and I say again in your hearing, and venture my reputation upon it, that it is the purest and most apostolic specimen of Scriptural Presbyterianism in the world.

And then I like, again, the Scriptural sentiment here, that if any man has or develops the gift of preaching, he has the right to preach. These deacons and elders are preachers, all of them who have the gift, and I wish that they all felt that they had the gift and would go to work; but what I seek to impress is, that, according to his perception and understanding of the Word of God, Mr. Spurgeon sought to model this greatest church in Christendom; here, then, is another good work which found its furnishing in this blessed Book.

Whence came the Pastors' College? Whence came the Orphanage? Whence came the Almshouses? Their suggestion was found in the Word of God. He looked upon those orphans as fatherless ones of whom Christ said, "Suffer them to come to me and lead them to my sheltering arms." He looked upon the Pastors' College, as a school to train those who were dear to Christ, to perpetuate the true apostolic succession in the preaching of an apostolic gospel. And when these Almshouse were built, or enlarged and provided with inmates, was it not for the sake of Jesus and the charity commended in the thirteenth chapter of first Corinthians, that all this colossal work was done?

I have not attempted anything like a eulogium of this wonderful man. His works are his encomium; but I yearn to say—especially to young men before me—that you are verily guilty before God if your life does not attain a high degree of success, for in the midst of the metropolis of the world you have a living illustration of how a child, trained in the Scriptures, may begin at sixteen years of age to preach a mighty gospel, may keep up that preaching without interruption, except as his health and strength forbade, until he is nearly fifty-eight years of age, and then die in the midst of the prime of his life, and at his bier draw forth the tears of more disciples of Christ, and I venture to add, of more men of the world, than any one man that has departed during the present century. Young men, you may not have a chance for scholarly learning, but the Bible is in your hands, and you can study that. You may not have a chance for wealth and worldly honour, but you can be rich in the experience of a saint, and be honoured as a chosen vessel of God, to bear his name before the Gentiles and kings and the children of Israel. You may not have opportunities for gratifying a secular ambition, but you can gratify in God the aspiration after the highest attainments in holiness and the largest spheres of service to God and man. I pray you look back to-night through the years to the time when the little boy knelt in the arbour of his home, and Mr. Knill put his hands together on his head in benediction and prayer, beseeching God that that little boy might be taken up by the power of the Holy Spirit, anointed to be a preacher of the gospel, and made a distinguished instrument by whom that gospel should pervade the world. We shall not perhaps find very much of Mr. Knill on the records of history, any more than we hear much of Ananias in Damascus in the period of church history in which the apostles lived; but Mr. Knill's prayer over that little boy in the arbour, like Ananias's uplifted hands on the head of the converted Saul, inseparably links him with the glory of Spurgeon's future, as Ananias is linked with the glory of Paul the evangelist.

If you cannot preach like Spurgeon, cannot you pray like Knill? If you cannot claim the genius of Spurgeon, cannot you claim the spiritual contact with God that sets apart a child under your hand as a chosen vessel for the Lord? If you can do nothing more, parents, cannot you take your children, and, Sunday-school teacher, cannot you take your pupils, and lead them to Christ? You can come down to a level with them, make them feel at home in your society, and induct them into the mysteries of God and a holy life. You cannot possibly tell what God may do with the little child that you, as a mother, nourish at your breast, or as a teacher seek to lead into the knowledge of God.

There was a little waif picked up by a Sunday-school teacher who gave him a sixpence to induce him to go to a Sunday-school, and to that converted man in after years we owe the greatest triumphs of Christ in the vast empire of India. There was a bishop in the church in the United States who was found in a sugar barrel on the Pacific coast, and who was as a poor, homeless little orphan taken up in loving arms, led to the Sunday-school, and taught the things of God. We look too far for the spheres of service. They lie at hand and close by us; and he that has the spirit of his Master, and like him, can take little children in his arms, and put his hands upon them and bless them, may be setting apart a Samuel, or a John, the Baptist, or a Paul, for the work of the modern prophet, preacher, and evangelist.

My closing word is one of appeal. You sometimes hear the gospel preached where only the tongue does the preaching, and where there seems to be no heart and no spiritual experience at the back of the utterance. Charles Spurgeon was a man whose heart answered to the heart of man, as in water face answereth to face.

Once more, in the presence of God and this assembly, let it be said, as on a previous occasion, that Charles Spurgeon was the perpetual and all-convincing evidence of Christianity. The gospel that he preached can never be a falsehood while it makes such a man. One such disciple in these days is an answer to all infidelity and all irreligion the world over—a triumphant vindication of the existence of a God, of the truth of these holy Scriptures, of the reality of a crucified and risen Christ, and of the verity of a present Spirit abiding in the church, and working in the world. We, at least, have no excuse for our infidelity. The sceptic that knows the story of Spurgeon will stand speechless before the bar of God when called to account. In the early days of the apostles, when the Sanhedrim accused them, and forbade them to preach any longer in the name of Christ, we are significantly told that the man who was healed by Peter and John stood beside them, and they "could say nothing against it"; and when they went aside to confer about this new religion, this concession they were compelled to make—"that a notable miracle hath been done by these men we cannot deny."

So I say to you, that the man who stood here, spiritually healed of God, was a sufficient answer to all the attacks of modern doubt, and so long as the memory of Charles Haddon Spurgeon survives, and the savour of his presence is shed abroad in the fragrance of that memory, you, that hear me now, if you perish, will go down to perdition with a weight that will sink the soul to the lowest depths, in that you have seen such a visible and living proof of the truth of God, and have turned your ears to fables.

List of Deputations,

FROM VARIOUS SOCIETIES REPRESENTED AT MR. SPURGEON'S FUNERAL.

Baptist Union.
Baptist Missionary Society.
Particular Baptist Fund.
Baptist Building Fund.
Baptist Total Abstinence Association.
Irish Baptist Mission.
Home Counties' Baptist Association.
Metropolitan Association of Strict Baptist Churches.
Strict Baptist Mission.
Suffolk and Norfolk Baptist Union.
East London Baptist Ministers' Fraternal.
Essex Baptist Union.
Strict Baptist Pastors' Conference.
North-West Kent Baptist Association.
Manchester District Baptist Union.
Northern Association of Baptist Churches.
Regent's Park College.
Bristol Baptist College.
Nottingham Baptist College.
Leicestershire Association of Baptist Churches.
Congregational Union of England and Wales.
Congregational Union of Wales.
Congregational Total Abstinence Association.
Cheshunt College.
London Missionary Society.
Wesleyan Methodist Conference.
Wesleyan Missionary Society.
Primitive Methodist Conference.
United Methodist Free Churches.
Bible Christian Conference.
West London Mission.
London Nonconformist Union.
Protestant Dissenting Ministers' Association.
The Moravian Church.
Evangelists' Fraternal.
Oldham Nonconformist Ministers' Association.
Chesham District Ministers' Fraternal.
China Inland Mission.
Young Men's Christian Association.
Young Women's Christian Association.
Religious Tract Society.
Sunday School Union.
Ragged School Union.
British and Foreign Bible Society.
Evangelical Alliance.
Evangelistic Mission.
Evangelization Society.
National Temperance League.
Open-Air Mission.
City of London Total Abstainers' Union.
Liberation Society.
Hebrew Christians' Prayer Union.
Aged Pilgrims' Friend Society.
Salvation Army.
Monthly Tract Society.
Hospital Saturday Fund.
Society for the Rescue of Young Women and Children.
The Corporation of Croydon.
Legation of the United States, London.

List of Churches, Societies, and Public Bodies,

FROM WHICH LETTERS OF CONDOLENCE AND SYMPATHY WERE RECEIVED BY THE CHURCH AT THE METROPOLITAN TABERNACLE, OR MRS. C. H. SPURGEON. [*See Page* 17.]

BAPTIST CHURCHES.

Abbey Road, St. John's Wood.
Abercarn (English).
Aberdare (Welsh).
Abertillery, "Ebenezer."
Acton.
Aldershot.
Appledore, North Devon.
Ashford, Kent.
Ashton-under-Lyne, Welbeck Street.
Ayr, N.B.

Bacup, "Ebenezer."
Barnsley.
Bath, Manvers Street.
Barrow-in-Furness, Abbey Road.
Barnoldwick, near Colne.
Barnstaple, Boutport Street.
Battersea Park Road.
Battersea, York Road.
Barking, Queen's Road.
Beccles, Martyrs' Memorial.
Bedford Row, John Street Chapel.
Belfast, Regent Street.
Belfast Great Victoria Street.
Birmingham, Stratford Road.
Birmingham, Graham Street.
Birmingham, Great King Street.
Birmingham, Longmore Street.
Birmingham, Spring Hill.
Birmingham, Sparkbrook (Union).
Birkdale, Lancashire.

Bishop Burton, Yorkshire.
Bilston.
Blackburn.
Blaenavon, "Horeb."
Blaenavon, "Ebenezer."
Bloomsbury Chapel.
Bombay (India).
Borough Road.
Bow, East London Tabernacle.
Bow Common, Blackthorn Street.
Bowdon, Cheshire.
Bournemouth, Lansdown.
Brompton, Onslow Chapel.
Bristol, Philip Street.
Bristol, City Road.
Bristol, Buckingham Hall.
Bristol, Tyndale Chapel.
Bristol, Hillsley.
Bristol, Broadmead.
Bristol Tabernacle.
Bristol, Counterslip.
Bristol, Kensington.
Bristol, "Bethesda," Alma Road, Stokes Croft, and Totterdown.
Brixton, Gresham Chapel.
Brixton, Kenyon Chapel.
Brixton, Wynne Road.
Bradford, Westgate.
Bradford, "Bethel."
Brentford, Park Chapel.
Bures, Suffolk.
Burton-on-Trent, Derby Street.

Burnley.
Burwell, Cambridgeshire.
Buckley, "Bethel."
Brockley Road (Church and School).
Bromley, Kent.
Bromley Road, Burnt Ash Hill, Lee.

Caersalem, Glamorganshire.
Calstock and Metherill, Cornwall.
Camberwell, Cottage Green.
Camberwell, Denmark Place.
Camberwell, Clarendon Chapel.
Cambridge, "Zion."
Camden Road.
Canning Town, Barking Road.
Cardiff, Longcross Street.
Cardiff, Maindy Place.
Cardiff, Woodville Road.
Cardigan, Bethania (Welsh).
Caversham, New Zealand.
Chatham, "Zion."
Chester, Grosvenor Park (Church and School).
Chelsea, Lower Sloane Street.
Cheltenham, Cambray Chapel.
Christchurch, New Zealand.
Church, near Accrington.
Chiswick, Annandale Road.
Cinderford, Gloucestershire.
Cirencester.
Clapham, Courland Grove.
Clapham, Victoria Chapel.
Clapton Downs.
Coatbridge, N.B.
Coseley, Darkhouse.
Coventry, Gosford Street.
Coventry, Queen's Road.
Coventry, St. Michael's.
Colne, East Parade.
Combmartin, Devonshire.
Corwen, North Wales.
Coxall, Shropshire.
Croydon (Strict and Particular).
Croydon, West (Church and School).
Crewe.
Cross Keys, Monmouthshire.

Dalston Junction.
Darlington, Grange Road.

Dartmouth.
Dartford.
Deal, Victoria Chapel.
Desborough, Market Harborough.
Devonshire Square.
Devonport, Hope Chapel.
Dewsbury.
Dorchester, Dorford.
Dulwich, East, Barry Road.
Dulwich, East, Lordship Lane.
Duluth, Minnesota, U.S.A. Endion.
Durban, Natal (Church and School).

Ealing, Haven Green.
East Dereham, High Street.
East Finchley.
East Plumstead.
Eastbourne, Ceylon Place.
Edinburgh, Charlotte Square.
Edinburgh, Dublin Street.
Elgin, N.B.
Epworth.
Erith.

Falmouth, "Emmanuel."
Faringdon, Berkshire.
Farnworth, Lancashire.
Farsley, Yorkshire.
Faversham.
Forest Gate, Wood Grange.
Forfar, N.B.

Gillingham.
Glasgow, Queen's Park.
Gosport Tabernacle.
Gravesend, Windmill Street.
Greenwich, South Street.

Hackney, Shoreditch Tabernacle.
Hackney, Mare Street.
Hackleton, Carey Memorial.
Halifax, "United Meeting."
Hampstead, Heath Street.
Hamburg.
Harlesden (Church and School).
Harpole, Northamptonshire.
Harrow Road, Queen's Park.
Hastings, Wellington Square.
Hartlepool, East.
Hereford.

Hebden Bridge and Birchcliffe, Yorkshire.
Helensburgh, N.B.
Heywood, Lancashire.
Highgate.
Highgate Road.
Hitchin, Walsworth Road.
Hitchin, Tilehouse Street.
Honor Oak.
Holyhead, New Park Street.
Huddersfield, Salendine Nook.
Huddersfield, New North Road.
Hull, George Street.
Hull, South Street.

Ilfracombe.
Ipswich.
Islington, Salters' Hall Chapel.

Jarrow-on-Tyne.

Kansas City, Third Baptist Church.
King's Cross Road, Vernon Chapel.
Kingstanley, Gloucestershire.
Kingston.
Knighton, Radnorshire.

Lancaster, White Cross Street.
Lee.
Leeds, Hunslet Tabernacle.
Leeds, York Road.
Leeds, South Parade.
Leicester, Carley Street.
Leicester, Melbourne Hall.
Leigh, Lancashire.
Leith, N.B.
Leyton, Vicarage Road.
Leytonstone, Cann Hall Road.
Leytonstone, Fillebrook.
Leighton Buzzard, Hockliffe Road.
Liverpool, Waterloo.
Liverpool, Myrtle Street.
Long Preston, Yorkshire.
Louth, Lincolnshire, Northgate.
Lower Tooting.
Llangollen, Penybryn.
Llangollen, "Ebenezer."
Luton, Park Street.
Lydbrook.

Macclesfield, St. George's Street (Church and School).
Maidenhead, Marlow Road.
Mason, Michigan, U.S.A.
Maryport, Cumberland.
Manchester, Haline.
Manchester, Wakefield Road.
Manchester, Oxford Road, Union Church.
Manchester, Moss Side.
Margate, "Ebenezer."
Merthyr Tydvil.
Middlesbrough, Newport Road.
Milnsbridge, Yorkshire.
Minneapolis, First Baptist Church.
Morley, Yorkshire.
Morriston Tabernacle.
Mount Eden, New Zealand (Church and School).

Netherton and Dudley.
New Brompton.
New Malden.
New Southgate.
Newbridge, Monmouthshire (English).
Newbury.
Newport, Castlehold.
Newport, Commercial Street.
Newport, Stow Hill.
Newport, Summer Hill.
Newport, Usk Road.
Newcastle-on-Tyne, Jesmond Road.
Newcastle-on-Tyne, Westgate Road.
Notting Hill, Ladbroke Grove.
Notting Hill, Talbot Tabernacle.
Northampton, College Street.
Northampton, Grafton Street.
Northampton, Mount Pleasant.
Northampton, Princes Street.
Norwich, St. Clement's.
Norwich, Sayer Street.
Norwich, Unthank's Road.
Nottingham, Hyson Green.
Nottingham, Woodborough Road.
Norbiton, Bunyan Chapel.
Nuneaton and Attleborough.
Nupend, Gloucestershire.

Old Brentford, North Road.

Old Kent Road, Maze Pond (Church and School).
Oldham, King Street.
Oxford, Commercial Road (Church and Bible-class for Young Women).

Paignton, Devonshire.
Paisley, Victoria Place.
Peckham Park Road.
Peckham, Rye Lane.
Penarth.
Penarth, Stanwell Road.
Penzance.
Penge Tabernacle.
Peterhead, N.B., King Street.
Plumstead, Conduit Road.
Plymouth, George Street.
Portsea, Kent Street.
Portslade-by-Sea, Sussex.
Portsmouth, Lake Road.
Pontypridd, "Carmel."
Pontypridd (Welsh).
Poplar, Cotton Street.
Presteign, Radnorshire.
Preston, Pole Street.
Putney, Werter Road.

Radcliffe, Lancashire.
Ramsgate, Cavendish Chapel.
Raunds, Northamptonshire.
Reading, Providence Chapel.
Redditch.
Regent's Park.
Rhondda Valley, Pentre.
Rhondda Valley, Porth.
Rhondda Valley, Tonypandy.
Rickmansworth.
Rickmansworth, Mill End.
Rochdale, "Ebenezer."
Ross, Herefordshire.
Roseberg, Oregon, U.S.A.
Rowley and Blackhill.
Ryde, Isle of Wight.

Sandown, Isle of Wight.
Scarborough, Albermarle and "Ebenezer."
Sheerness Tabernacle.
Sheffield, Cemetery Road.

Sheffield, Townhead Street.
Shepherd's Bush Tabernacle.
Shipley, Yorkshire, "Bethel."
Shrewsbury, Claremont Street.
Skipton-in-Craven, Yorkshire.
Southend-on-Sea, Clarence Road.
Southend-on-Sea Tabernacle.
Southsea.
Southsea, Elm Grove.
Southwell, Nottinghamshire.
South Norwood.
Southport, Town Hall.
Streatham, Lewin Road.
Stockport.
Stockton-on-Tees.
Stamford Hill, Woodberry Down.
Stanningley, near Leeds.
Stow-on-the-Wold.
St. Helen's, Lancashire, Park Road.
Stafford.
Stratford New Town, Major Road.
Stoney Stratford.
Sunderland, "Bethesda."
Sunderland, "Enon."
Surbiton Hill, Oakland's Chapel.
Swansea, "Mount Pleasant."
Swindon Tabernacle.

Talysarn, Carnarvonshire, "Salem."
Taunton, Silver Street.
Teignmouth.
Teddington.
Tenterden.
Tenby.
Thornton Heath, "Beulah" Chapel.
Tonbridge.
Trowbridge, Back Street.
Tredegar, Church Street (English).
Treharris, Glamorganshire, "Bethel" and Brynhyfryd.
Transvaal, Pretoria.
Twickenham Green.

Upton Chapel, South Lambeth Road.

Ventnor, Isle of Wight.

Waltham Abbey, Paradise Row.

Waltham Cross.
Walthamstow, Boundary Row.
Walworth Road.
Walworth, Arthur Street.
Walworth, Wansey Street.
Walsall, Stafford Street.
Walsall, Vicarage Walk.
Wandsworth Road, Victoria Chapel.
Wandsworth, East Hill.
Waterbeach.
Watford, Chalk Hill.
Watchet and Willirgton.
Waterford.
Warminster.
Wellington, Somerset.
West Malling, Kent.
West Norwood, Chatsworth Road.
Westbourne Grove.

Westbury Leigh, Wiltshire.
Westbury, "Providence."
Weston-super-Mare, Wadham Street.
Whitestone.
Willingham Tabernacle.
Wimbledon, Queen's Road.
Wisbech, Hill Street.
Windsor, Victoria Street.
Wick, N.B.
Willesden Green.
Wigan.
Woolwich, Parson's Hill.
Woolwich, Queen Street.
Wolverhampton, Waterloo Road.
Worcester, Sansome Walk.

York, Priory Street.

BAPTIST SOCIETIES, ASSOCIATIONS, &c.

Anglesea Baptist Association.

Baptist Mission Camp (14 miles from Agra), India.
Baptist Union of South Africa.
Baptist Total Abstinence Association.
Baptist Churches of Leicester.
Baptist Churches of Belfast.
Baptist and Congregational Fraternal, Burnley.
Baptist Ministers' Conference of Boston, U.S.A.
Baptist Association of Bucks.
Baptist Building Fund Committee.
Baptist Union of Great Britain and Ireland.
Baptist Union of Scotland.
Baptist Union of New Zealand.
Baptist Tract and Book Society.
Baptist Missionary Society.
Baptist Home Missionary Society for Scotland.
Baptist Tract Society.
Breconshire Baptist Association.
Bristol Baptist College.
Burnley Baptist and Congregational Ministers' Fraternal.

Cambridge Baptist Association.
Cardiff, Brunel Street, Baptist Church Young People's Improvement Class.
Cleveland, Ohio, U.S.A., Baptist Ministerial Conference.
Coventry District of the West Midland Baptist Association.

Dacca, Eastern Bengal Mission.
Delhi, Baptist Zenana Mission.
Devon Baptist Association (Northern Division).
Devonport, Three Towns Ministers' Fraternal (Baptists and Congregationalists).

East London Baptist Ministers' Fraternal.
Essex Baptist Union.

Farsley and District Baptist Union.

General Baptist Committee.
German Union of Baptist Churches.

Home Counties' Baptist Association.

Irish Baptist Association.

Ladies' Association for Zenana Work in India.
Leeds, Meanwood Road, Baptist Friendly Society.
Leicester Representative Baptist Ministers' Meeting, held in Belvoir Street Chapel Vestry.
Liverpool Baptist Association Committee.
Liverpool Baptist Union.
London Baptist Association Committee.
London Baptist Board of Ministers.
London Strict Baptist Ministers' Association.

Manchester Baptist Ministers' Fraternal.
Manchester District Baptist Union.
Metropolitan Association of Strict Baptist Churches.
Metropolitan Tabernacle Men's Bible-class.
Metropolitan Tabernacle Women's Bible-class.
Metropolitan Tabernacle Poor Ministers' Clothing Society.
Metropolitan Tabernacle Sunday-school.
Metropolitan Tabernacle Almshouses' Sunday-school.
Midland Baptist Association.

New York and Ohio, U.S.A., Brethren of the Pastors' College.
Northern Baptist Association.
North-West Kent Baptist Association.
Norway, Trondhjem, Baptist Community.

Particular Baptist Fund.

Pastors' College, Tutors and Students.
Pastors' College Evangelical Association, the Emergency Committee, on behalf of the whole brotherhood.
Philadelphia, U.S.A., Conference of Baptist Ministers.
Pioneer Mission.
Pontrhydyrun, near Pontypridd, Fraternal Union Baptist Ministers.

Rawdon Baptist College.
Regent's Park Baptist College Committee.
Regent's Park Baptist College Students.
Rochester, New York, Baptist Social Union.

Secunderabad Baptist Mission House.
South Australian Baptist Association.
South Australia, Mount Barker, Furreedpore Mission.
Strict Baptist Mission, London.
Suffolk and Norfolk Baptist Union.

Tamworth Baptist Community.
Treherbert Hope Baptist Sunday-school.

Union des Églises Évangèliques Baptistes de France.

Washington City, U.S.A., Baptist Ministers' Conference.
Wallington Strict Baptist Mission.
Welsh Baptists' Association.

Yorkshire Association of Baptist Churches.

CONGREGATIONAL CHURCHES, SOCIETIES, &c.

Anerley.
Annan.
Ashton-under-Lyne.

Battersea.
Barnard Castle, Hall Street.
Bedworth, Old Meeting.

Beverley.
Birmingham, Carr's Lane.
Bishopsgate Chapel.
Borough (Welsh).
Borough Road.
Boston, Mass., U.S.A.
Brighton, Clifton Road.
Bromley, Kent.
Brixton.

Camberwell New Road.
Canonbury, Harecourt Chapel and Sunday-school.
Cardigan (United).
Cheshunt College.
Chishill.
Clayland's Road, Clapham.
Colchester, Lion Walk.
Commercial Street Congregational Young Men's Society.
Congregational Board, Memorial Hall.
Congregational Union of England and Wales.
Congregational Union of Wales.
Congregational Total Abstinence Association.
Cork.
Cork, George Street.

Dedham, Essex.
Doncaster.
Dulwich, "Emmanuel."

East Carmarthenshire Congregational Association.
East Dereham, Cowper.
Edinburgh, Charlotte Street.
Ely.
Enfield Highway.
Exeter.
Exeter, Southernhay.

Forest Gate.

Glamorganshire and Carmarthenshire English Congregational Union.

Haddington.

Hanham, near Bristol.
Heathfield.

Kentish Town.
Kidderminster, Dudley Street.
Kilburn, Greville Place.

Lambeth, York Road.
Lancashire Congregational Association.
Lancaster Road, W.
Leeds, Headingley Hill.
Leicester, Humberston Road.
Leominster.
Linton, Cambridgeshire.
Liverpool, Wavertree.
London Missionary Society.
Lower Edmonton.

Maidstone, West Street.
Manchester Congregational Board.
Millwall, West Ferry Road.

Needham Market.
Newport, Monmouthshire (Welsh).
Nottingham Congregational Institute.
Nottingham, Mansfield Road.

Old Kent Road, Marlborough Chapel.
Old Street, New Tabernacle.

Peckham, Hanover Chapel.
Peckham, Clifton Chapel.
Pontypridd and Rhondda Valley Welsh Congregational Association.

Radnorshire and Wye Side Congregational Association.
Ramsgate.

Scarborough, Peak.
Scarborough, "The Bar."
Sheffield, Attercliffe.
Sheffield, Broome Park.
Sheffield Tabernacle.
Sheffield and Doncaster District Congregational Union.

to the Palm-Branch. 275

Sherborne, Dorset.
Southampton, Albion Chapel.
Southampton Road, N.W., Gospel Oak.
South London Congregational Ministers' Association.
South-west Carnarvonshire Congregational Association.
Spalding.
Stamford Hill.
Stamford.
Stockwell Green.
Stratford.

Sunderland, Grange Chapel.
Swansea, St. Paul's.

Walworth, Sutherland Chapel.
Wanstead.
West Brompton.
West Kensington.
Westminster.
Westminster Bridge Road, Christ Church.
Wolverhampton, Snow Hill.
Wolverhampton, Queen Street.
Wolverhampton, Cleveland Street.

PRESBYTERIAN CHURCHES, &c.

Arbroath Presbytery of the Free Church of Scotland.
Armagh Presbyterian Church.
Athlone Presbytery.

Belfast Presbytery.
Birmingham Presbyterian Church of England.
Brechin Free Church Presbytery.
Bristol Presbytery.

Carlisle Presbyterian Church of England.
Carrickfergus Presbytery.
Cavan Presbytery of the Presbyterian Churches in Ireland.
Church of Scotland.
Clapham Road, Trinity Church: Presbytery of South London.
Cullybackey Presbyterian Church.

Dingwall Free Church of Scotland.
Dublin, Ministerial Meeting of Presbyterian Ministers.
Dumbarton Free Church of Scotland.
Duns, N.B., Free Church Presbytery of Duns and Chirnside.
Dundee Free Church of Scotland.

Elgin and Inverness Presbytery.

Forfar Presbytery of the Church of Scotland.

Forfar Presbytery of the Free Church of Scotland.

General Assembly of the Free Church of Scotland.
Glasgow Presbytery of the United Presbyterian Church.
Glasgow Free Church Presbytery.
Glasgow, Gorbals' Tabernacle Church.
Glasgow, Free Anderton Church.
Glasgow, London Road Church.
Greenock Free Church Presbytery.

Helensburgh, N.B., Presbyterian Court.

Irvine Free Church Presbytery.

Kilmarnock and Ayr Presbytery.
Kirkaldy United Presbyterian Presbytery.

Liverpool Presbytery.

Manchester Presbytery.

Nairn Free Church Presbytery.
Newcastle-on-Tyne, Walker Presbyterian Church.
North London Presbytery.

Perth and Aberdeen Presbytery of United Original Seceders.
Paisley Free Presbytery.

Saltcoats Free Presbyterian Church.
South London Presbytery.

Stafford, Presbytery of Birmingham.
Somers Town Presbytery.
Swansea, St. Andrew's Presbytery.
Stranraer Presbytery.
Synod of the Presbyterian Church of Eastern Australia.

WESLEYAN & OTHER METHODIST CHURCHES, &c.

Anglesea Calvinistic Methodists.
Ashton-under-Lyne Methodist New Connection.

Bala Calvinistic Methodist College.
Barnsley Wesleyan Reform Union.
Bristol Wesleyan Methodist Council.

Cable Street, St. George's Chapel.
Cardiff, Plas-Newydd, English Calvinistic Methodists.
Cardiff Wesleyan Methodist Council.
City Road, Wesleyan Methodist Chapel.
Combined Methodist Bodies of Manchester.

Demerara Wesleyan Mission.
Denmark, sixteen Pastors of the Methodist Episcopal Church.
Denmark, Svendborg Methodist Church.
Dublin Methodist Ministers.
Dublin, Rathmines Methodist Church.

Falmouth Road, Welsh Calvinistic Methodist Church.
Flintshire Wesleyan Council.

General Committee of the Primitive Methodist Connection.

Hayle, Copperhouse Wesleyan Church.
Huddersfield United Wesleyan Ministers.
Hyderabad, Wesleyan Mission House.

Ireland, Newtown Barry Methodist Church.

Liverpool Presbytery of the Calvinistic Methodist Church of Wales.
Liverpool Wesleyan Ministers.
London District, United Methodist Free Churches.
London Methodist Free Church, 7th Circuit.
London Wesleyan Methodist Council.
London Wesleyan Ministers.
Loughborough Methodist Free Church.

Manchester Methodist Bodies.
"Methodist Monthly Magazine" Staff.
Montgomeryshire Welsh Calvinistic Methodists.
Manchester Presbytery of the Welsh Calvinistic Methodists.

North Cardiganshire Monthly Meeting of the Welsh Calvinistic Methodists.
North Wales Calvinistic Methodist Association.
Nottingham Primitive Methodist Council.

Philadelphia Episcopal Methodist Church.
Pembroke Dock Welsh Calvinistic Methodist Presbytery.
Primitive Methodist Church, New Surrey Chapel, Blackfriars Road.

Primititive Methodist Church, Sumner Road, Peckham.
Primitive Methodist Church, Norbiton.
Primitive Methodist Connection, First District.
Primitive Methodist Sunday-school, Portsmouth.
Pontypridd Monthly Meeting of Methodist Churches.

Sheffield Wesleyan Methodist Council.
Sunderland United Methodist Free Church.
Sunderland Methodist Ministers' Association.
Sunderland Methodist Free Church, South Durham Street.

Sydenham Wesleyan Men's Sunday Afternoon Bible-class.
Wakefield United Methodist Free Church.
Wesleyan Missionary Society, Centenary Hall, Bishopsgate.
West Hartlepool Wesleyan Churches.
West Indian Wesleyan Methodist Church, Eastern Annual Conference.
West Kensington Methodist New Connection.
West London Mission, St. James's Hall.
West Merioneth Calvinistic Methodist Presbytery.
Woodford Wesleyan Church.
Welsh Calvinistic Methodists of London.

UNITED NONCONFORMIST CHURCHES, &c.

Abergele: All the Nonconformist Ministers.

Birmingham Meeting of Pastors of Baptist, Congregational, and Presbyterian Churches.
Buckley United Churches.
Burnley United Nonconformist Churches.
Colchester Evangelical Nonconformist Churches.
Deptford, New Cross, and Brockley Free Churches.
General Body of Protestant Dissenting Ministers of the three Denominations.

London Nonconformist Council.

Montgomeryshire, Meifod Nonconformists.

Norwich Nonconformist Ministers.

Ryde, Isle of Wight, Nonconformist Ministers' Monthly Meeting.

South-West Ham Nonconformist Council.

United Service of Evangelical Churches, held in the Reformed (Dutch) Church of St. Thomas, West Indies.

MINISTERS' ASSOCIATIONS, FRATERNALS, &c.

Aberdeen Evangelical Association.
Auckland (N. Z.) Ministers' Association.

Birmingham and West Midland Evangelical Association.

Brighton and Hove Association of Free Churches.
Brisbane, Ministers' Association of Queensland.
Broughton District Evangelists' Association.

Burnley Nonconformist Ministers' Association.

Cambridge Village Preachers' Association.
Canada Ministerial Association.
Cardiff Ministerial Union.
Carlisle Nonconformist Ministers' Association.
Chesham District Ministers' Fraternal.
Chester Nonconformist Association.
Coventry Preachers' Union.
Croydon Ministers' Association.

Duluth, Minnesota, U.S.A., Ministers' Association.
Dunstable and Luton Ministers' Fraternal Union.

Glasgow Congregational and Evangelical Union.

Hastings and St. Leonards Ministers' Fraternal.
Hinckley Nonconformist Ministers' Association.

King's Langley Ministers' Fraternal.

London Hospital Christian Association.

Medical Missionary Association.
Midlothian Evangelists' Association.
Montreal Protestant Ministerial Association.

Mountain Ash Nonconformist Ministers' Association.

Nelson, Colne, and District Nonconformist Ministers' Association.
Nottingham Nonconformist Ministers' Fraternal.

Oldham Nonconformist Ministers' Association.

Pastors' College Evangelical Association.
Penzance Nonconformist Ministerial Association.
Preston Nonconformist Ministerial Association.
Pontypridd Dissenting Ministers' Association.
Portsmouth Ministerial Union.

Reading Ministers' Fraternal.

Scarborough Nonconformist Ministerial Association.
Scotland Sabbath Protection Association.
Sheffield Ministers' Fraternal.
South-East London Nonconformist Ministers' Union.
South Shields Nonconformist Ministers' Association.
Stroud District United Ministers' Fraternal.
Swansea Nonconformist Ministers' Union.

SUNDAY SCHOOLS, &c.

Barsbridge Mission Sabbath School, Belfast.
Birmingham Sunday School Union.
Bristol Sunday School Union.
Brixton Auxiliary Sunday School Union.

Camberwell Mission and Ragged School Union.

India Sunday School Union.

Lambeth Auxiliary Sunday School Union.

Nottingham, Arnold, Pleasant Sunday Afternoons.
Spalding United Sunday School Teachers.
Stockwell Orphanage Sunday Schools.
Sunday School Union.
Wintown Street, Leeds, Women's Pleasant Sunday Afternoon.
Wolverhampton, Mount Zion, Pleasant Sunday Afternoon.
Wolverhampton, Wood Street, Pleasant Sunday Afternoon.

MISSION HALLS.

Birmingham, Vauxhall Railway Mission.
Borough, Arcadia Mission.

Costers' Mission Hall, Hackney.

Edgware Road, Metropolitan Mission Hall.

Morley Hall, Hackney.

Nottingham, Redoubt Street, Gospel Mission.

Pimlico, Ebury Mission.

Philippopolis, Bulgaria, Mission Hall.

Richmond Hall, Seven Sisters Road, Holloway.
Richmond Street, Walworth, Workers' Annual Meeting.

Southampton, Nichols Town Mission Maternal Society.
Surrey Gardens Memorial Hall, Young Men's Bible-class.

Working Men's Mission, New Cut, Lambeth.

YOUNG MEN'S CHRISTIAN ASSOCIATIONS.

Acton.
Adelaide.

Birmingham.
Bristol.

Cardiff.
Central.
City of London.
Cork.
Croydon.

Dublin.

Glasgow United.
Grays.

Halifax.
Hammersmith.

National Council.
Newcastle-on-Tyne.

TEMPERANCE SOCIETIES.

Bishop's Waltham Blue Ribbon Gospel Temperance Union.
Blue Ribbon Gospel Temperance Mission.
British Women's Temperance Association.

City of London Total Abstinence Union.

Derby Temperance Society.

Gosport, Union Chapel, Temperance Institute.

Independent Order of Good Templars, Happy Home Lodge, No. 269.
Independent Order of Good Templars, Ponder's End.
Independent Order of Good Templars, Gunnersbury Lodge, No. 1,292.
Independent Order of Good Templars, South-West Lancashire District.
Independent Order of Good Templars, Staffordshire District Lodge.

Independent Order of Good Templars, Battersea Advance Lodge, 3,036.
Independent Order of Good Templars, Sunningdale.
Independent Order of Good Templars, East and Mid Surrey District Lodge.
Independent Order of Good Templars, Star of Worcester Lodge.
Independent Order of Good Templars, Dublin Castle Lodge.

Moss Side, Manchester, Baptist Temperance Society.
National Temperance League.
Newcastle-on-Tyne, Abbott's Terrace, Gospel Temperance Society.
New Surrey Chapel Gospel Temperance Society.
North of England Temperance League.
United Kingdom Railway Temperance Union.

RESOLUTIONS FROM VARIOUS SOURCES.

Abergele, English Calvinistic Churches.
Aged Pilgrims' Friend Society.
Alford Scripture Reading and Prayer Union.

Bedminster Union.
Bible Christian Church, Crediton.
Bible Christian Conference.
Birmingham, Bloomsbury Institute.
Birmingham Police Institute.
Board of Delegates Hospital Saturday Fund.
British and Foreign Bible Society.
British and Foreign Bible Society, Bombay Auxiliary Committee.

Cabragh Society, Ballymena.
Camberwell, Albany Institute.
Cape General Mission.
Cardiff Town Mission.
Children's Home, Bonner Road.
China Inland Mission.
Church of England Zenana Mission.
Clapham Reform Club.
Committee, Free Church of England, Rockdale, New South Wales.
Constantinople, Churches in and around.
Croydon Protestant Alliance.

Dublin United Religious Services.

East London Mission to the Jews.
Ebenezer Young Men's Mutual Improvement Society.
Evangelical Alliance.
Evangelical Alliance, South London Branch.
Evangelistic Mission.
Evangelization Society.
Exeter Local Preachers' Union.

Festiniog Local Board, N. Wales.
Free Church of England, Cathay's Terrace, Cardiff.
French Reformed Evangelical Church.

Hackney Road Conservative Club.
Hamburg English Reformed Church.
Hanley Salvation Mission.
Hastings Calvinistic Protestant Union.
Hebrew Christians' Prayer Union.
Highland Orphanage, Inverness.
Holy Trinity Church, Gray's Inn Road.
Holywell School Board, Flintshire.

Kentish Town Adult School.

Lambeth Board of Guardians.
Lambeth Vestry, Kennington Road.

Legation of the United States.
"Lewiston Journal," Editorial Rooms.
Liberation Society.
London City Mission.
London United District of Ancient Order of Foresters.
Loyal Orange Institution of England.
Loyal Orange Lodge, No. 17, Portsmouth District.
Loyal Orange Lodge, No. 667, Hatcham.

Magistrates and Town Council of the Royal Burgh of Wick.
Margate, Emmanuel Church.
Mayor, Aldermen, and Burgesses of Great Torrington, Devon.
Metropolitan Hospital Sunday Fund Council.
Monthly Tract Society.
Moravian Churches.

Northampton, Commercial Street, Young Men's Society.
Nottingham Men's Sunday Morning Institute.

Open Air Mission.
Open Air Mission, South London Auxiliary.

People's Mission, Great Arthur Street, Golden Lane.
Plymouth Church, Brooklyn, New York, U.S.A.
Pontypridd Eisteddfod.
Preachers' Preparation Class, Bristol.

Ragged School Union.

Religious Tract Society.
Royal Hospital for Incurables.

Salvation Army.
Scottish Protestant Alliance.
Seamen's Institute, Rotterdam.
Society for the Propagation of Bibles and Religious Books, Port-au-Prince, Hayti.
Society for the Rescue of Young Women and Children.
Society for the Suppression of the Opium Trade.
Society of Friends in Great Britain.
South London Association for Assisting the Blind.
South London Early Closing Association.
South London Hospital Sunday Fund.
South Norwood Literary Societies.
St. Luke's Institute.
St. Mary's Vestry, Newington.
St. Winifred's Youths' Institute, 112, Lower Road.
Stepney Meeting.

The Christian League, St. Philips, Sydney, New South Wales.
Theological Seminary, Louisville, Kentucky, U.S.A.
Tremont Temple, Boston, U.S.A.
Trowbridge Local Board.

Upper Tooting Reformed Episcopal Church.

Women's Prayer Union, Christchurch, New Zealand.
Working Men's Lord's Day Rest Association.

APPENDIX

THE
FINAL SERMONS
OF
CHARLES H. SPURGEON

"Lo, I Come"
A Doctrinal Sermon

Delivered on Lord's-Day Morning, April 26th, 1891, by
C. H. SPURGEON,
At the Metropolitan Tabernacle, Newington

"Sacrifice and offering thou didst not desire, mine ears hast thou opened: burnt offering and sin offering hast thou not required. Then said I, 'Lo, I come: in the volume of the book it is written of me, I delight to do thy will, O my God: yea, thy law is within my heart'."—Psalm 40:6-8.

Explained to us by the apostle Paul in Hebrews 10:5-7:
"Wherefore when he cometh into the world, he saith, 'Sacrifice and offering thou wouldest not, but a body hast thou prepared me: in burnt offerings and sacrifices for sin thou hast had no pleasure.' Then said I, 'Lo, I come in (the volume of the book it is written of me,) to do thy will, O God.'"

WE HAVE, in the use made of the passage by the inspired apostle, sufficient authority for applying the quotation from the fortieth psalm to our divine Lord and Savior Jesus Christ. With such a commentary, we are sure of our way and our whereabouts. We might have been perplexed as to its meaning had it not have been for this; although, I think, even without the guidance of the New Testament passage, those who are familiar with Holy Writ would have felt that the words could not be fulfilled in David, but must belong to a greater than he, even to the divine Messiah, who in the fullness of time would come into the world. We rejoice that the Lord Jesus himself here speaks of himself. Who but he can declare his own generation? Here he is both the subject of the words and the speaker also. The word is from himself and of himself, and so we have double reason for devout attention. He tells us what he said long ago. He declares, "Then I said, Lo, I come."

Because he has come to us, we gladly come to him; and now we reverently wait upon him to hear what our Lord shall speak; for, doubtless, he will speak peace to us, and will cause us to learn, through his Spirit, the meaning of his words. O Savior, say to each of our hearts, "Lo, I come"!

I. Without further preface, I call upon you to notice, first, THE SWEEPING AWAY OF THE SHADOW. "Sacrifice and offering thou didst not desire...burnt offering and sin offering hast thou not required."

When the Son of God is born into the world, there is an end of all types by which he was formerly prefigured. The symbols end when the truth itself is made fully manifest. The sacrifices of the law had their times and place, their teaching and their influence. Blessed were those in Israel whose spiritual minds saw beneath the outward sign, and discerned the inward truth! To them the sacrifices of the holy place were a standing means of fellowship with God. Day after day they saw the Great Propitiation as they beheld the morning and the evening lamb: so often as they looked upon a sacrifice, they beheld the Lamb of God which taketh away the sin of the world. In the Paschal supper they were instructed by the slaying of the unblemished victim, the roasting with fire, the sprinkling of the blood upon the door without, and the feasting upon the sacrifice within. Spiritual men could have found in the rites and ceremonies of the old law a very library of gospel literature; but, alas! the people were carnal, sensual, and unbelieving, and therefore they often forgot even to celebrate the appointed sacrifices: the Passover itself ceased for long periods, and when the festivals were maintained, there was no life or reality in them. After they had been chastened for their neglect, and made to wander in exile because of the wandering of their hearts after their idols, they were restored from captivity, and were led to keep the ceremonial law; but they did it as a heartless, meaningless formality, and thus missed all spiritual benefit: with the unlighted candle in their hand they blindly groped in the dark. They slew the sacrifices, and presented their peace-offerings; but the soul had gone out of the service, and at last their God grew weary of their formal worship, and said, "Bring no more vain oblations; incense is an abomination unto me." We read, "To what purpose is the multitude of your sacrifices unto me? saith the Lord: I am full of the burns offerings of rams, and the fat of fed beasts; and I delight not in the blood of bullocks, or of lambs, or of he-goats. When ye come to appear before me, who hath required this at your hand, to tread my courts?" When once the life is gone out of the best symbolism, the Lord abhors the carcase; and even a divinely ordained ritual becomes a species of idolatry. When the heart is gone out of the externals of worship, they are as shells without the kernel. Habitations without living tenants soon become desolations, and so do forms and ceremonies without their spiritual meaning. Toward the time of our Lord's coming, the outward worship of Judaism became more and more dead: it was time that it was buried. It had decayed and waxed old, and was ready to vanish away, and vanish away it did; for our Lord set aside the first, or old, that he might establish the second, or new. The stars were no longer seen with their twinklings, for the sun had arisen.

The removal of these things was wholesale. We have four sorts of sacrifice mentioned here, but I need not go into details. Sacrifices in which blood was shed were abolished when the Son of God offered himself without spot unto God. Bloodless offerings, such as fine flour, and wine, and oil, and sweet cane bought with money, and precious incense—which were tokens of gratitude and consecration—these also were no longer laid upon the altar. Sacrifice and offering both were not desired; and burnt-offerings, which signified the delight of God in the great Sacrifice, were ended by the Lord's actual acceptance of that Sacrifice itself. Even the sin-offering, which was burned without the camp as a thing accursed, altogether ceased. It represented sin laid upon the victim, and the victim's being made a curse on that account. It might have seemed always useful as a reminder, for they were always sinning, and always needing a sin-offering; but even this was not required. Nothing of the old ceremonial law was spared. Now we have no ark of the covenant, with its Shekinah light between the wings of the cherubim. Now we have no brazen laver, no table of shewbread, no brazen altar, and no sacred veil: the holy of holies itself is gone. Tabernacle and temple are both removed. "Neither in this mountain, nor yet at Jerusalem, shall men worship the Father"; but the time is come when "they that worship him must worship him in spirit and in truth." A clean sweep has been made of all the ancient rites, from circumcision up to the garment with its fringe of blue. These were for the childhood of the church, the pictures of her first school-books; but we are no longer minors, and we have grace given us to read with opened eyes that everlasting classic of "the glory of God in the face of Jesus Christ." Now hath the brightness of the former dispensation been quite eclipsed by the glory which excelleth.

As these outward things vanish, they go away with God's mark of non-esteem upon them: *they are such things as he did not desire.* "Sacrifice and offering thou didst not desire." The Lord God had no desire for matters so trivial and unsatisfactory. They were good for the people, to instruct them, if they had been willing to learn; but they fulfilled no desire of the heart of God. He says, "Will I eat the flesh of bulls, or drink the blood of goats?" By the prophet Micah he asks, "Will the Lord be pleased with thousands of rams, or with ten thousands of rivers of oil." These furnish no delight for the great Spirit, and give no pleasure to the thrice holy Jehovah. The formal worshipper supposed that his offerings were, in and of themselves, pleasing to God, and therefore brought his "burnt offerings, with calves of a year old." So far as they believingly understood the meaning of a sacrifice, and presented it in faith, their offerings were acceptable; but in themselves considered these were far from being what the Lord desired. He that filleth heaven and earth saith, "I will not reprove thee for thy sacrifices or thy burnt offerings, to have been continually before me. I will take no bullock out of thy house, nor he goats out of thy folds. For every beast of the forest is mine, and the cattle upon a thousand hills. I know all the fowls of the mountains: and the wild beasts of the field are mine. If I were hungry, I would not tell thee: for the world is mine, and the fullness thereof." The spiritual, the infinite, the almighty Jehovah could not desire merely outward ritual, however it might appear glorious to men. The sweetest music is not for his ear, nor the most splendid roses of priests for his eye. He desired something infinitely more precious than these, and he puts them away with this note of dissatisfaction.

And more, these sacrifices passed away with the mark upon them that *they were not what God required.* "Burnt offering and sin offering hast thou not required." What did God require of man? Obedience. He said by Samuel, "To obey is better than sacrifice, and to hearken than the fat of rams." He saith in another place, "He hath shewed thee, O man, what is good; and what doth the Lord require of thee, but to do justly, and to love mercy, and to walk humbly with thy God?" The requirement of the law was love to God and love to men. This has always been God's great requirement. He seeks spiritual worship, obedient thought, holy living, grateful praise, devout prayer—these are the requirements of the Creator and Benefactor of men. Ritualistic matters were so far required as they might minister to the good of the people, and while they stood they could not neglect them without loss; but they were not the grand requirement of a just and holy God, and therefore men might fulfill these without stint or omission, and yet God would not have of them what he required. Yes, he asks, "Who hath required this at your hand, to tread my courts?" To see his law magnified, his justice vindicated, his sovereignty acknowledged, and his holiness imitated, is more to his mind. Absolute conformity to the standard of moral and spiritual rectitude which he has set up is his demand, and he can be content with nothing less. These things are not found in sacrifice and offering, neither do they always go therewith, and therefore the outward sacrifice was not what God required.

They were so to be put always as never to be followed by the same kind of things. Shadows are not replaced by other shadows. The ceremonials of Aaron are not to be followed by another set of carnal ordinances. There are some who seem to think that they are so to be. Instead of Aaron, whom God ordained, we have a so-called priesthood among us at this day, claiming an apostolic succession, which is impossible if they are priests, since no apostle was a priest. Instead of rites which God has ordained we have rites of man's invention. The blessed ordinances of our Lord Jesus Christ, such as baptism and the Lord's Supper, have been prostituted from their instructive and memorial intent into a kind of witchcraft; so that by what is called baptism children are said to be born again, and made members of Christ and children of God, while in the second, or what they call Holy Communion, the sacrifice of Christ is profanely said to be repeated or continued, even in the unbloody sacrifice of the mass. Ah, friends! our Lord did not put away that grand, magnificent system of Mosaic rites to introduce the masquerade in which Rome delights, which certain Anglicans would set up among us. No, no; we have done with the symbolic system, and have now but the two outward ordinances of baptism and the Lord's Supper, which are meant only for believers who know what it is to be buried with Christ, and to feed on him. You have no right to bring in your own forms and ceremonies, and place them in the church of Christ. Beyond what God has ordained we may not dare to go; and even in those things we may not rest as though there were anything in them of their own operation, apart from their sacred teaching. These are instructive to you if you have a mind to be instructed, and if you know the truths which they set forth; but do not imagine that men have come under another kind of ceremonialism, another system of ritual and rubric, for it is not so. The rites appropriate to priests are abolished with the Aaronic priesthood, and can never be restored: "He taketh away the first, that he may establish the second." When he cometh into the world these carnal ordinances must go out of the world. Sacrifice and offering, burnt offering and sin offering, and all other patterns of heavenly things, are swept away when the heavenly things themselves appear.

II. Thus much upon the shadows being swept away; and now, secondly, let us view THE REVELATION OF THE SUBSTANCE. We find the Son of God himself appearing. We read here, and we hear him say—"Mine ears hast thou opened." The Lord himself comes, even he who is all that these things foreshadowed.

When he comes he has a prepared ear. The margin hath it, "Mine ears hast thou digged." Our ears often need digging; for they are blocked up by sin. The passage to the heart seems to be sealed in the cave of fallen man. But when the Savior came, his ear was not as ours, but was attentive to the divine voice. He says, "He wakeneth mine ear to hear as they that are taught. The Lord God hath opened mine ear, and I was not rebellious." Our Lord was quick of understanding in the fear of the Lord: he knew what the will of the Lord was, and he could say, "I do always the thing that pleases him." As man, he had a divine instinct of holiness, which made him to know and love the Father's will, and caused him always to translate that will into his own life. You see he came with an opened ear, and some think that here we have an allusion to the boring of the ear in the case of the servant who had a right to liberty, but refused to quit his servitude, because he loved his master, and wished to remain with him for ever. It is not certain that there is any such reference; but it is certain that our Lord was bound for ever to the service which he had undertaken for his Father, and that he would not go back from it. He pledged himself to redeem us, and he set his face like a flint to do it. He loved his Father, and he loved his chosen so much that he vowed to execute the Father's work, even to what I might call "the bitter end," if I did not know that it was a sweet and blessed end to him. His ear was prepared for his service.

But *our Lord came also with a prepared body:* hence, the apostle Paul, when he quoted this passage, probably taking the words from the Septuagint translation, writes, "A body hast thou prepared me." You will wonder how, in one passage, it should speak of the ear, and the next should speak of the body; and yet there is small difference in the sense. We do not think of an ear without a body—that would be a sorry business. The reading in the Hebrews is involved in the text as it stands in the Psalm. If the ear is there, a body is there; you cannot even dream of an ear hearing if separate from the rest of the body. The apostle gives us the sense of the text rather than the words; and, at the same time, dealing as he was with Jews by whom the Septuagint was prized, he quoted from the version which they would be sure to acknowledge— and very properly and wisely so—because that version was perfectly accurate as to the meaning of the Hebrew. Any way, he was inspired to read it—"A body hast thou prepared me." There was fashioned by the Holy Ghost, in the womb of the blessed Virgin, a body fitted to embody the Son of God. Wrought mysteriously, by means into which we must not inquire—for what God hath veiled must remain covered—that body was suited to set forth the great mystery, "God manifest in the flesh."

The whole body of Christ was prepared for him and for his great work. To begin with, it was a sinless body, without taint of original sin, else God could not have dwelt therein. It was a body made highly vital and sensitive, probably far beyond what ours are; for sin has a blunting and hardening effect even upon flesh, and his flesh, though it was in the "likeness of sinful flesh," was not sinful flesh, but flesh which yielded prompt obedience to his spirit, even as his whole human nature was obedient unto death, even the death of the cross. His body was capable of great endurance, so as to know the griefs and agonies and unspeakable sorrows of a delicate, holy, and tender kind which it was necessary for him to bear. "A body hast thou prepared me." In the fullness of time he came into that body, which was admirably adapted to enshrine the Godhead. Wondrous mystery, that the infant of Bethlehem should be linked with the Infinite; and that the weary man by the shores of Galilee should be very God of very God, revealed in a body prepared for him! "A body hast thou prepared me": he had a prepared ear and a prepared body.

He who assumed that body was existent before that body was prepared. He says, "A body hast thou prepared me. Lo, I come." He from old eternity dwelt with God: the Word was in the beginning with God, and the Word was God. We could not any one of us have said that a body was prepared for us, and therefore we would come to it; for we had had no existence before our bodies were fashioned. From everlasting to everlasting our Lord is God, and he comes out of eternity into time—the Father bringing him into the world. He was before all worlds, and was before he came into the world to dwell in his prepared body.

Beloved, *the human nature of Christ was taken on him in order that he might be able to do for us that which God desired and required.* God desired to see an obedient man, a man who would keep his law to the full; and he sees him in Christ. God desired to see one who would vindicate the eternal justice, and show that sin is no trifle; and behold our Lord, the eternal Son of God, entering into that prepared body, was ready to do all this mighty work, by rendering to the law a full recompense for our dishonor of it! An absolutely perfect righteousness he renders unto God: as the second Adam, he presents it for all whom he represents. He bows his head a victim beneath Jehovah's sword, that the truth, and justice, and honor of God might suffer no detriment. His body was prepared to this end. Incarnation is a means to atonement. Only a man could vindicate the law, and therefore the Son of God became a man. This is a wonderful being, this God in our nature. "Emmanuel" is a glorious word. Surely for the incarnation and the atonement the world was made from the first. Was this the reason why the morning stars sang together when they saw the cornerstone of the world, because they had an inkling that here God would be manifest as nowhere else beside, and the Creator would be wedded to the creature? That God might be manifested in the Christ, it may even be that sin was permitted. Assuredly, there could have been no sacrifice on Calvary if there had not first of all been sin in Eden. The whole scheme, the whole of God's decrees and acts, worked up to an atoning Savior. Of the pyramid of creation and of providence Christ is the apex: he is the flower of all that God hath made. His divine nature in strange union with humanity constitutes a peerless personage, such as never was before, and can never be again. God in our nature one Being, and yet wearing two natures, is altogether unique. He saith, "A body hast thou prepared me. Lo, I come." Think of this: it is a truth fitter for meditation than for sermonizing. The Lord give us to know it well by faith!

III. But now, thirdly, I call your attention to THE DECLARATION OF THE CHRIST, made in the text: "Sacrifice and offering thou didst not desire. Then said I, Lo, I come." Observe *when* he says this. *It is in the time of failure.* All the sacrifices had failed. The candle flickered, and was dying out, and then the great light arose, even the eternal light, and like a trumpet the words rung out, "Lo, I come." All this has been of no avail; now I come. It is in the time of failure that Christ always does appear. The last of man is the first of God; and when we have come to the end of all our power and hope, then the eternal power and Godhead appears with its "Lo, I come."

When our Lord comes, *it is with the view of filling up the vacuum* which had now been sorrowfully seen. God does not desire these things; God does not require these things; but he does desire and he does require something better: and lo, the Christ has come to bring that something. That awful gap which was seen in human hope when Moses had passed away, and the Aaronic priesthood, and all the ordinances of it were gone, Christ was born to fill. It looked as if the light of ages had been quenched, and God's glorious revelation had been for ever withdrawn; and then, in the dark hour, Jesus cries, "Lo, I come!" He fills the blank abyss: he gives to man in reality what he had lost in the shadow.

When he appears, it is as the personal Lord. Lay the stress upon the pronoun, "Lo, *I* come." The infinite *Ego* appears. "Lo, I come." No mere man could talk thus, and be sane. No servant or prophet of God would ever say, "Lo, I come." Saintly men talk not so. God's prophets and apostles have a modest sense of their true position: they never magnify themselves, though they magnify their office. It is for God to say, "Lo, I come." He who says it takes the body prepared for him, and comes in his own proper personality as the I AM. "In him dwelleth all the fullness of the Godhead bodily." He comes forth from the ivory palaces to inhabit the tents of manhood. He takes upon himself the body prepared for him of the Lord God, and he stands forth in his matchless personality ready to do the will of God. "It pleased the Father that in him should all fullness dwell." Everything is stored up in his blessed person, and we are complete in him.

Observe the joyful avowal that he makes—"Lo, I come." This is no dirge: I think I hear a silver trumpet ring out—"Lo, I come." Here is a joyful alacrity and intense eagerness. The coming of the Savior was to him a thing of exceeding willingness. "For the joy that was set before him he endured the cross, despising the shame."

He comes with a word calling attention to it; for he is not ashamed to be made partaker of our flesh. "Lo," saith he, "I come. Behold, behold, I come." This is no clandestine union; he bids heaven behold him come into our nature. Earth is bidden to gaze upon it. O ye sinners, listen to this inviting "Lo!" Others have cried to you, "Lo, here! and Lo, there"; but Jesus looks on you, and cries, "Lo, I come." Look hither: turn all your thoughts this way, and behold your God in your nature ready to save you. Verily, the incarnate God is a subject meet for the loftiest thoughts of sages, and for the lowliest thoughts of children. Blessed are the children of grace who can sit at the feet of the incarnate God and look up, forgetting all the wisdom of the Greeks, and all the sign-seeking of the Jews in the satisfaction which they find in Jesus.

I think, too, *I hear in this declaration of the coming One a note of finality.* He takes away the sacrifice from Aaron's altar; but he says, "Lo, I come." There is an end of it. "Lo, I come." Is there anything after this? Can anything supersede this—"Lo, I come." "Lo, I come" has been the perpetual music of the ages. Read it, "Lo, I am come"; for it is in the present tense, and how sweet the sound! Christ is come, and joy with him. Read it as well in the future, if you will, "Lo, I come," for he comes "the second time without sin unto salvation"; here is our chief hope! "Lo, I come." He himself is the last word of God. "In the beginning was the Word"; and so he was God's first word. But he is the end as well as the beginning: God's last word to man; Christ is God's ultimatum. Look for no new revelation—"Lo, I am come," shines on for ever. Do not ask, "Art thou he that should come, or do we look for another?" He has come; look for no other. Behold, he came to give what God desires, what God requires; what would you more? Let him be all your salvation and all your desire. Let him be "the desire of all nations." He is the fulfillment of all the requirements of the human race, as well as the full amount of what God requires.

IV. Next, I beg you to note THE REFERENCE TO PRECEDING WRITINGS. He says, "Lo, I come: in the volume of the book it is written of me." If I preached from the passage in the Epistle to the Hebrews, I might fairly declare that in *the whole volume of Holy Scripture* much is written of our Lord and prescribed for him as Messiah. The page of inspiration is fragrant with the name of Jesus. He is the top line of the entire volume, and in the Greek word I see a half allusion to this. He is the head-line of contents to every chapter of Scripture. He is of all Scripture the sum. "In the beginning was the word." Everything speaks of him. The Pentateuch, and the books of the prophets, and the Psalms, and the gospels, and the epistles all speak of him. "In the volume of the book it is written of me."

Preaching as I am from the Psalms, I cannot take so long a range. I must look back and find what was written in David's day, and within *the Pentateuch certainly;* and where do I find it written concerning his coming? The Pentateuch drips with prophecies of Christ as a honeycomb overflowing with its honey. Chiefly is he to be found in the head and front of the book: so early as the opening chapters of the Book of Genesis, when Adam and Eve had sinned, and we were lost, behold he is spoken of in the volume of the book in these terms: "The seed of the woman shall bruise the serpent's head." So early was it written that the Redeemer would be born in our nature to vanquish our foe.

But I confess I do not feel shut out from another interpretation. I conceive that our Lord here refers to another book, *the book of the divine purposes,* the volume of the eternal covenant. There was a time before all time, when there was no day but the Ancient of Days, when all that existed was the Lord, who is all in all: then the sacred Three entered into covenant, in mutual agreement, for a sublime end. Man sinning, the Son of God shall be the surety. Christ shall bear the result of man's offense; he shall vindicate the law of God, and make Jehovah's name more glorious than ever it has been. The second person of the divine Unity was pledged to come, and take up the nature of men, and so become the firstborn among many brethren to lift up a fallen race, and to save a number that no man can number, elect of God the Father, and given to the Son to be his heritage, his portion, his bride. Then did the Well-beloved strike hands with the eternal God, and enter into covenant engagements on our behalf: "In the volume of the book it is written." That sealed book, upon whose secrets no angel's eye has looked, a book written by the finger of God long before he wrote the Book of the law upon tables of stone, that book of God may be spoken of in the Psalm, "And in thy book all my members were written, which in continuance were fashioned, when as yet there was none of them." Our Lord came to carry out all his suretyship engagements: his work is the exact fulfillment of his engagements recorded in the eternal covenant, "ordered in all things and sure." He acts out every mysterious line and syllable, even to the full. Then he said, "A body hast thou prepared me. Lo, I come: in the volume of the book it is written of me." It is ever a pleasing study to see our Lord, both in the written Word, and in the eternal covenant of grace.

V. I must close with the fifth point, THE DELIGHT OF HIM THAT COMETH. He said, "Lo, I come." As I have already told you, there is wonderful delight in that exclamation—"Lo, I come"; but lest we should mistake our Lord, he adds, "I delight to do thy will, O my God: yea, thy law is within my heart." There can be no denial of his joy in his service.

Note well, that *he came in compete subserviency to his Father, God.* "I delight to do"—what? "Thy will." His own will was absorbed in the divine will. His pleasure it was to say, "Not as I will, but as thou wilt." It was his meat and his drink to do the will of him that sent him, and to finish his work. Though he was Lord and God, he became a lowly servant for our sakes. Though high as the highest, he stooped low as the lowest. The King of kings was the servant of servants that he might save his people. He took upon him the form of a servant, and girded himself, and stood obediently at his Father's call.

He had a prospective delight as to his work. Before he came, he delighted in the thought of his incarnation. The Supreme Wisdom saith, "My delights were with the sons of men." Happy in his Father's courts, he yet looked forward to an access of happiness in becoming man. "Can that be?" saith one. Could the Son of God be happier than he was? As God, he was infinitely blessed; but he knew nothing by experience of the life of man, and into that sphere he desired to enter. To the Godhead there can be no enlargement, for it is infinite; but still there can be an addition; our Lord was to add the nature of man to that of God. He would live as man, suffer as man, and triumph as man, and yet remain God: and to this he looked forward with a strange delight, inexplicable except upon the knowledge of the great love he bore to us. He had given his heart so entirely to his dear bride, whom he saw in the glass of predestination, that for her he would endure all things.

> "Yea, saith the Lord, for her I'll go
> Through all the depths of care and woe,
> And on the cross will even dare
> The bitter pangs of death to bear."

It was wondrous love. Our Lord's love surpasses all language and even thought. I am talking prodigies and miracles at every word I utter. It was delightful to our Lord to come hither.

"What did he delight in?" saith one. Evidently he delighted in God's *law*. "Thy law is within my heart." He resolved that the beauties of the law of the Lord should be displayed by being embodied in his own life, and that its claims should be vindicated by his own death. To achieve this, he delighted to come and keep it and honor it by an obedience both active and passive. He delighted in God's will also, and that is somewhat more; for law is the expression of will, and this may be altered; but the will of the great King never changes. Our Lord delighted to carry out all the purposes and desires of the Most High God. He so delighted in the will of God that he came to do it, and to bear it, "by the which will we are sanctified through the offering of the body of Jesus Christ once for all."

He delighted also in *God*. He took an intense delight in glorifying the Father. He came to reveal the Father, and make him to be beloved of men. He did all things to please God. Moreover, he took a delight in *us;* and here, though the object of his love is less, the love itself is heightened by the conspicuous condescension. The Lord Jesus took a deep delight in his people, whose names were written on his heart, and graven on the palms of his hands. His heart was fixed on their redemption, and therefore he would present himself as a sacrifice on their behalf. The people whom the Father gave him from before the foundation of the world lay on his very soul; for them he had a baptism to be baptized with, and he was straitened till it was accomplished. He gave himself no rest till he had left both joy and rest to ransom his own.

May I go a step further and say that *he had an actual delight in his coming among men?* "I delight to do thy will, O my God"—not merely to think of doing it. When our Lord was here, he was the most blessed of men. Do you start? Do you remind me that he was "a man of sorrows"? I grant you that none was more afflicted; but I still stand to it, that within him dwelt a joy of the highest order. To him it was joy to be in sorrow, and honor to be put to shame. Do you think that lightens our estimate of his self-denial and disinterestedness? Nay, it adds weight to it. Some people fancy that there is no credit in doing a thing unless you are miserable in doing it. Nay, brethren, that is the very reverse. Obedience which is unwillingly offered and causes no joy in the soul, is not acceptable. We must serve God with our heart, or we do not serve him. Obedience rendered without delight in rendering it is only half obedience. You shall say what you will about the greatness of my Lord's agonies. You shall never go too far in your estimate of his unfathomable griefs; but going with you to the full in it all, I shall take liberty still to say that he had within himself a fountain of joy, which enabled him to endure the cross, and even to despise the shame. Blessed among men was he, even when he was made a curse for us! With delight he gave himself for us, and made a cheerful surrender of himself, that he might be the ransom for many. The text is express upon that fact.

And all this because *our Lord came with such intense heartiness.* He says, "Yea, thy law is within my heart." Our Lord is most thorough in all that he does. His work is never slovenly, nor in a half-hearted way. He does not even sit on the well and talk to a poor woman, but what his heart is there. He does not go into a fisherman's hut, but what his heart is there, and he heals the sick one. He does not sit down to supper with his followers, but what his heart is there, and he reveals his love. I wish we were always at home when the Lord calls for us! Sometimes we are all abroad, and our heart is away from the service of our Father; but he loved the Lord with all his heart, and mind, and strength. For us he gave his whole being, rejoicing to redeem us. He was always intense. Whether he preached or practiced, Jesus was all there and always there. Hence his delight; for what a man does with his heart he delights to do. These two sentences are melodious of joy to my ear. "I delight to do thy will, O my God: yea, thy law is within my heart."

Hear this one other word. It is all done now. Jesus has fulfilled the Father's will in the salvation in the midst of his ransomed ones. And shall I tell you, need I tell you, what must be the delight, *the heavenly joy of our lord, now that the work is finished?* He is now the focus, the center, the source of bliss. What must be his own delight! We often say of the angels that they rejoice over one sinner that repenteth. I doubt not that they do, but the Bible does not say so. The Bible says, "There is joy in the presence of the angels of God over one sinner that repenteth." What means the presence of the angels? Why, that the angels see the joy of Christ when sinners repent. Hear them say to one another, "Behold the Father's face! How he rejoices! Gaze on the countenance of the Son! What a heaven of delight shines in those eyes of his! Jesus wept for these sinners, but now he rejoices over them. How resplendent are the nail-prints to-day, for the redeemed of the Lord's death are believing and repenting! That blessed countenance which is always as a sun, shineth in the fullness of its strength, now that he sees of the travail of his soul." He who suffered feels a joy unsearchable,

> "The first-born sons of light
> Desire in vain its depths to see:
> They cannot read the mystery—
> The length, the breadth, the height."

Oh, the joy of triumphant love! The joy of the crucified, whose prepared body is the body of his glory as once it was the body of his humiliation! In that manhood he still rejoices, and delights to do the will of the Father.

My time has fled, and yet I am expected to say something about missions. What shall I say? My brothers, sisters, all of you, do you know anything about the truths I have spoken? Then go and tell the heathen that the Lord is come. Here is a message worth the telling. Mary Magdalene, and the other Maries, haste to tell the disciples that the Lord had risen; will you not go and tell them that he has come down to save? "Lo, I come," saith he. Will you not take up his words, and go to the people who have never heard of him, and say, "Lo, he has come." Tell the Ethiopians, the Chinese, the Hindus, and all the islands of the sea that God has come hither to save men, and has taken a prepared body, that he might give to God all he required, and all that he desired, that sinful men might be accepted in the Beloved, with whom God the Father is well pleased. Go, and take to the heathen this sacred Book. "In the volume of the book it is written of him." Do not begin to doubt the Book yourself. Why should you send missionaries to teach them about a book in which you do not yourself believe? Tell the nations that "In the volume of the book it is written of him." Believe this Book, and spread it. Help Bible societies, and all such efforts; and aid missionary societies, which carry the Book and proclaim the Savior. The men of the Book of God are the men of God, such as the world needs. Bid such men go and open the Book of God, and teach the nations its blessed news. Go, dear friends, and assure the heathen that there is happiness in obedience to God. So the Savior found it. He delighted in God's will, even to the death, and they will also know delight as in their measures they bow before the authority of the Word and the will of the one living and true God, the God of Abraham, of Isaac, and of Jacob. Jehovah, the I AM, must be worshipped, for beside him there is none else. Give glory unto God, whom our Lord Jesus has come to glorify. Amen.

PORTION OF SCRIPTURE READ BEFORE SERMON—Psalm 40.

HYMNS FROM "OUR OWN HYMN BOOK"

Hymn # 383— *High Priest and Surety*

JESUS, my great High Priest, Offer'd His blood, and died;
My guilty conscience seeks No sacrifice beside.
His powerful blood did once atone;
And now it pleads before the throne.

To this dear Surety's hand Will I commit my cause;
He answers and fulfills His Father's broken laws;
Behold my soul at freedom set!
My Surety paid the dreadful debt.

My Advocate appears For my defense on high;
The Father bows his ears, And lays His thunder by;
Not all that hell or sin can say,
Shall turn His heart, His love away.

Immense compassion reigns In my Immanuel's heart,
He condescends to act A Mediator's part:
He is my friend and brother, too,
Divinely kind, divinely true.
Isaac Watts, 1709

Hymn # 271—*Gethsemane*

MANY woes had He endured,
Many sore temptations met,
Patient, and to pains inured:
But the sorest trial yet
Was to be sustained in thee,
Gloomy, sad Gethsemane.

Came at length the dreadful night;
Vengeance with its iron rod
Stood, and with collected might
Bruised the harmless Lamb of God.
See, my soul, my Saviour see,
Prostrate in Gethsemane.

There my God bore all my guilt;
This through grace can be believed;
But the horrors which He felt
Are too vast to be conceived.
None can penetrate through thee,
Doleful, dark Gethsemane.

Sins against a holy God;
Sins against His righteous laws;
Sins against His love, His blood;
Sins against His name and cause;
Sins immense as is the sea—
 Hide me, O Gethsemane!

Here's my claim, and here alone;
None a Saviour more can need;
Deeds of righteousness I've none;
No, not one good work to plead:
Only a glimpse of hope for me,
 Only in Gethsemane.

Father, Son and Holy Ghost,
One almighty God of love,
Hymned by all the heavenly host
In Thy shining courts above,
We poor sinners, gracious Three,
 Bless Thee for Gethsemane.
Joseph Hart, 1759

Hymn # 229—*The Covenant God Extolled*

The God of Abraham praise, Who reigns enthroned above;
Ancient of everlasting days, and God of Love;
Jehovah, great I AM! by earth and Heav'n confessed;
I bow and bless the sacred Name forever blessed.

The God of Abraham praise, at Whose supreme command
From earth I rise—and seek the joys at His right hand;
I all on earth forsake, its wisdom, fame, and power;
And Him my only Portion make, my Shield and Tower.

The God of Abraham praise, Whose all sufficient grace
Shall guide me all my happy days, in all my ways.
He calls a worm His friend, He calls Himself my God!
And He shall save me to the end, thro' Jesus' blood.

He by Himself has sworn; I on His oath depend,
I shall, on eagle wings upborne, to Heav'n ascend.
I shall behold His face; I shall His power adore,
And sing the wonders of His grace forevermore.
Thomas Olivers, 1772

"Lo, I Come"
An Application Sermon

Delivered on Lord's-Day Morning, May 3rd, 1891, by
C. H. SPURGEON,
At the Metropolitan Tabernacle, Newington

"Then said I, Lo, I come."—Psalm 40:7.

TO MY GREAT SORROW, last Sunday night I was unable to preach. I had prepared a sermon upon this text, with much hope of its usefulness; for I intended it to be a supplement to the morning sermon, which was a doctrinal exposition. The evening sermon was intended to be practical, and to commend the whole subject to the attention of enquiring sinners. I came here feeling quite fit to preach, when an overpowering nervousness oppressed me, and I lost all self-control, and left the pulpit in anguish. I come hither this morning with the same subject. I have been turning it over, and wondering why it was so. Peradventure, this sermon was not to be preached on that occasion, because God would teach the preacher more of his own feebleness, and cast him more fully upon the divine strength. That has certainly been the effect upon my own heart. Perhaps, also, there are some here this morning who were not here last Lord's-day evening, whom God intends to bless by the sermon. The people were not here, peradventure, for whom the eternal decree of God had designed the message, and they may be here now. You that are fresh to this place, should consider the strange circumstance, which never happened to me before in the forty years of my ministry; and you may be led to enquire whether my bow was then unstrung that the arrow might find its ordained target in your heart. The two sermons will now go forth together from the press; and perhaps, going together, they may prove like two hands of love wherewith to embrace lost souls, and draw them to the Savior, who herein saith, "Lo, I come." God grant it may be so!

The times when our Lord says, "Lo, I come," have all a family likeness. There are certain crystals, which assume a regular shape, and if you break them, each fragment will show the same conformation; if you were to dash them to shivers, every particle of the crystal would be still of the same form. Now the goings forth of Christ which were of old, and his coming at Calvary, and that great advent when he shall come a second time to judge the earth in righteousness, all these have a likeness the one to the other. But there is a coming of what I may call a lesser sort, when Jesus cries "Lo, I come" to each individual sinner, and brings a revelation of pardon and salvation, and this has about it much which is similar to the great ones. My one desire this morning is to set forth the Lord Jesus as saying to you, as once he did to me, "Lo, I come." Still he cries to the weak, destitute, forlorn, hopeless sinner, "Lo, I come." I shall talk about that coming, and hope that you will experience it now, and thus be able to follow me in what I say. I speak to the unconverted mainly; but while I do so I shall hope to be refreshing the grateful memories of those already saved; but this will all depend upon the working of the Spirit of God. To him, then, lift up your hearts in prayer.

I. I will commence with this observation: THE LORD CHRIST HAS TIMES OF HIS FIRST COMINGS TO MEN; *"Then* said I, Lo, I come."

What are these times? Mayhap some here present have reached this season, and this very day is the time of blessing when the text shall be fulfilled: "Then said I, Lo, I come." Go with me to the first record in the volume of the Book, when it was said that he should come. You will find it in the early chapters of Genesis.

Jesus said, "Lo, I come" *when man's probation was a failure.* Man in the Garden of Eden had every advantage for obedience and life. He had a perfect nature, created without bias towards evil, and he was surrounded with every inducement to continue loyal to his Maker. He was placed under no burdensome law. The precept was simple and plain: "Of every tree of the garden thou mayest freely eat: but of the tree of the knowledge of good and evil, thou shalt not eat of it: for in the day that thou eatest thereof thou shalt surely die." Only one tree was reserved: all the rest were given up to be freely enjoyed. In a very short time—some think it was on the first day, but that we do not know—our mother Eve ate of the fruit, and father Adam followed her, and thus human probation ended in total failure. They were weighed in the balances, and found wanting: "Adam being in honor continued not." At that point we read in the volume of the Book that the Seed of the woman should bruise the serpent's head. *Then* our Redeemer said, "Lo, I come." Hearken to me, my friend: you also have had your probation, as you have thought it to be. You quitted your father's roof with every hope, your mother judged you to be of a most amiable character, and your friends expected to see in you one whose life would honor the family. You thought so yourself. Your probation has reversed that hope: you have turned out far other then you should have been; and looking back upon the whole of your life to this moment, you ought to be ashamed. It has been a terrible breaking down for you, and for all who know you; and you are sitting in this place feeling, "Yes, it is so; the tests have proved me to be as a broken reed. I am under condemnation by reason of my transgressions against God." How rejoiced I am to tell you that, at such a time when you are conscious that you are a dead failure, Jesus says, "Lo, I come!" If you had not been a failure you would not have wanted him, and he never comes as a superfluity; but now in your complete break-down you must have him or perish, and in infinite pity he cries, "Lo, I come." Is not this good news for you? Believe it and live.

That also was *a time when man's clever dealings with the devil had turned out a great failure.* The serpent came and said, "God doth know that in the day ye eat thereof, then your eyes shall be opened, and ye shall be as gods, knowing good and evil." How craftily he put it! How cunningly he insinuated that God was jealous of what man might become, and was keeping him back from a nobler destiny! He even dared to say, "Ye shall not surely die," thus giving the Lord the lie direct. He seemed to say— His threat is a mere bugbear, a thing to scare you from a great advance in knowledge and position. "Ye shall not surely die." Eve, in her supposed wisdom, was not able to cope with the serpent's subtlety. "And when the woman saw that the tree was good for food, and that it was pleasant to the eyes, and a tree to be desired to make one wise, she took of the fruit thereof, and did eat, and gave also unto her husband with her; and he did eat." The devil had played his cards so well that man was left bankrupt of virtue, bankrupt of happiness, bankrupt of hope. *Then,* in the volume of the Book, it was written, "I said, Lo, I come." Yes, in the hour when hellish falsehood had robbed man of everything. No man hath yet dealt with the devil without being a loser. The arch-deceiver promises very fairly; but he lies from beginning to end. I know he promised you pleasure unbounded, and liberty unrestrained. Now, the pleasure is burnt out, and the ashes of that which once blazed and crackled, are terrible to look upon. As for liberty, where is it? You have become the bond-slave of sin. You were to enjoy life, and lo, you are plunged in death! It may be, there are in this house persons who bear in their bodies the marks, not of the Lord Jesus, but of the devil's temptations. He has made you so to sin that your bones are filled with the sins of your youth; and you know it. He needs a long spoon who eats out of the same dish as the devil, and your spoon has not been long enough. Sin has overreached and betrayed you; and you stand trembling before God as the result of having listened to the falsehoods of hell, and having rejected the commands of heaven. Supposing such a person to be present—and I feel sure he is—I pray that he may hear my text as from the Lord Jesus himself. "Then said I, Lo, I come." The devil has trodden you down, but Jesus comes to raise you up. Your paradise is lost, and by him it is to be restored. Jesus has come to give repentance and remission of sins. That crafty head which deceived you, the Lord Jesus has broken; he came for this purpose. If you had not been betrayed, you would not have needed a deliverer; but your misery has made room for his mercy. Not while Adam is perfect in paradise is there any news of the Seed of the woman bruising the serpent's head; but after the serpent has done his deceitful work, and has ruined the race, then we hear that ancient gospel of God, and see the sole hope of fallen man. Here is good cheer for you who look with shame upon your foolish yielding to Satan's deceits. You are caught as silly birds in a snare; you have been as foolish as the fish of the sea which are taken in a net; but when you are captives, Christ comes to be your Liberator, and God commends his love towards you in that while you are yet sinners Christ died for the ungodly.

Further than this, when we find the first promise of our Lord's coming, "in the volume of the Book," we find that *man's covering was a failure.* The guilty pair had gathered the leaves of the fig-tree, and had made themselves aprons, for they knew that they were naked. This was the first fruit of that boasted tree of knowledge, and it is the principal one to this day. Their scant coverlet contented them for a little while; but when the voice of the Lord God was heard in the garden they confessed that their aprons were good for nothing; for Adam owned that he was afraid because he was naked, and that therefore he had hidden himself in the thick groves of the garden. It is easy to make a covering which pleases us for a season; but self-righteousness, presumption, pretended fidelity, and fancied natural excellence—all those things are like green fig-leaves, which shrivel up before long, lose their freshness, and are rather an exposure than a covering. It may be that my hearer has found his imaginary virtues failing him. It was when our first parents knew that they were naked that the Savior said, "Lo, I come." My downcast hearer, if you are no longer in your own esteem as good as you used to be; if you can no longer hide the fact that you have broken God's law, and deserve his wrath; if you no longer believe the devil's lie that you shall suffer no penalty, but may even be the better for sin, then the Lord the Savior says to you, "Lo, I come." To you, O naked sinner, shivering in your own shame, blushing scarlet with conviction—to you he comes. When you have nothing left of your own, he comes to be your robe of righteousness, wherein you may stand accepted with God.

That first news of the coming Champion came at a time *when all man's pleas were failures.* Adam had thrown the blame on Eve—"The woman whom thou gavest to be with me, she gave me of the tree, and I did eat." Eve had also thrown the blame on the serpent; but the Lord God had silenced all such excuses, and driven them from their refuges. He had made them feel their guilt, and had pronounced upon them the inevitable sentence; and then it was that he spake of the "Seed of the woman." Here was man's first, and last, and best hope. So too, my friend, when you dare no longer plead your innocence, nor mention extenuations and excuses, then Jesus comes in. If conscience oppresses you so sorely that you cannot escape from it; if it be so that all you can say is "Guilty, Willfully Guilty," then Jesus comes. If you neither blame your surroundings, nor your companions, nor the providence of God, nor your physical weakness, nor anything else, but just take all the blame to yourself because you cannot help doing so, then Jesus comes in. Verily you have sinned against God, against your parents, against your fellowmen, against light, against knowledge, against conscience, and against the Holy Ghost; no wonder, therefore, that you stand speechless, unable to offer any plea by way of self-justification. It is in that moment of shame and confusion that the Savior says, "Lo, I come." For such as you are he is an Advocate. When a sinner cannot plead for himself, Christ pleads for him; when his excuses have come to an end, then will the Lord put away his sin, through his own great sacrifice. Is not this a precious gospel word?

When our Lord did actually arrive, fulfilling the text by being born of a woman, it was *when man's religion had proved a failure.* Sacrifices and offerings had ceased to be of any value: God had put them away as a weariness to him. The scribes and the Pharisees, with all their phylacteries and wide-bordered garments, were a mere sham. There seemed to be no true religion left upon the earth. Then said Christ, "Lo, I come." There was never a darker thirty years than when Herod slew the innocents, and the chief priests and scribes pursued the Son of God, and at last nailed him to the tree. It was *then* that Jesus came to us to redeem us by his death. Do I speak to any man here whose religion has broken down? You have observed a host of rites and ceremonies: you were christened in your infancy, you were duly confirmed, you have taken what you call "the blessed sacrament"; or it may be you have sat always in the most plain of meeting-houses, and listened to the most orthodox of preachers, and you have been amongst the most religious of religious people; but now, at length, the Spirit of God has shown you that all these performances and attendances are worthless cobwebs which avail you nothing. You see now that—

> "Not all the outward forms on earth,
> Nor rites that God has given,
> Nor will of man, nor blood, nor birth,
> Can raise a soul to heaven."

You are just now driven to despair, because the palace of your imaginary excellence has vanished like the baseless fabric of a vision. If I had told you that your religiousness was of no value, you would have been very angry with me, and perhaps you would have said, "That is a bigoted remark, and you ought to be ashamed of making it." But now the Spirit of God has told it you, and you feel its force: he is great at convincing of sin. When the Spirit of truth comes to deal with the religiousness of the flesh, he withers it in a moment. All religion which is not spiritual is worthless. All religion which is not the supernatural product of the Holy Ghost is a fiction. One breath from the Spirit of God withers all the beauty of our pride, and destroys the comeliness of our conceit; and *then*, when our own religion is dashed to shivers, the Lord Jesus comes in, saying, "Lo, I come." He delights to come in his glorious personality, when the Pharisee can no longer say, "God, I thank thee, that I am not as other men"; and when the once bold fisherman is crying, "Lord, save, or I perish." If you feel that you need something infinitely better than Churchianity, or Dissenterism, or Methodism—in fact, that you need Christ himself to be formed in you—*then* to you, even to you, Jesus says, "Lo, I come." When man is at his worst, Christ is seen at his best. The Lord walks to us on the sea in the middle watch of the night. He draws nigh to those souls which draw nigh to death. When you part with self you meet with Christ. When no shred of hope remains, then Jesus says, "Lo, I come."

Once more. The Lord Jesus is to come a second time; and when will he come? He will come *when man's hope is a failure*. He will come when iniquity abounds, and the love of many hath waxed cold. He will come when dreams of a golden age shall be turned into the dread reality of abounding evil. Do not dream that the world will go on improving and improving, and that the improvement will naturally culminate in the millennium. No such thing. It may grow better for a while, better under certain aspects; but, afterwards the power of the better element will ebb out like the sea, even though each wave should look like an advance. That day shall not come except there be a falling away first. Even the wise virgins will sleep, and the men of the world will be, as in the days of Noah, eating and drinking, marrying and being given in marriage. On a sudden, the Lord will come as a thief in the night. The deluge of fire will find men as unprepared as did the deluge of water. He will come taking vengeance on his adversaries. When things wax worse and worse we see the tokens of his speedy coming. He will shortly appear, for the sky is darkening. When every hope will seem blotted out, and nothing but grim ages of anarchy and ungodliness are to be expected, then our Deliverer will come. When the tale of bricks was doubled in Egypt, Moses came; and when the world attains to its utmost unbelief and iniquity, Jesus will come. So at this moment my hearer may be saying, "I cannot be worse than I am; if I am not actually in hell already, yet I feel a fire within which tortures my soul. The sword of vengeance hangs over my head suspended by a single hair. I tremble to live, and I fear to die. Lost! Lost! Lost! I am past hope!" This is the time for my text: *"Then* said I, Lo, I come." He who is able to save to the uttermost appears to the soul when every other hope disappears. In your deep distress I see a token for good. You are now reduced to spiritual death, and now I trust the eternal life will visit you.

Now all this I put before you in simple language, believing what I say, and trusting that if I describe your case, you will know that I mean it for you. I have heard of a preacher who was so fearful lest he should be thought personal, that he said to his congregation, "Lest any of you should think that what I have said was meant for you, I would observe that the sermon I am preaching was prepared for a congregation in Massachusetts." I can plead nothing of the sort. I refer to you, my hearer, in the most pointed manner. I will attend to Massachusetts, if ever the Lord sends me there; but just now *I mean you.* Oh, that you may have grace to take home these thoughts to yourselves; for if you do so, they will by the Spirit's power bring the light of hope into your souls!

II. Secondly, I would remark that CHRIST COMES TO SINNERS IN THE GLORY OF HIS PERSON: "Then said I, Lo, I come." Note that glorious *I!* Have you not seen people engaged in urgent work who did not understand their business? Apprentices, and other unskillful people, are muddling time away. They are making bad worse, and running great risk. Perhaps a great calamity will occur if the work is not done well and quickly. A first-rate worker is sent for. See, the man has come who understands the business. He cries, "Let me come! Stand out of my way! You are on the wrong tack: let me do it myself!" You have not blamed him for egotism, for the thing needed to be done, and *he* could do it, and the others could not. Everybody recognized the master workman, and gave place to him. The announcement of his coming was the end of the muddle, and the signal of hope. Even so Jesus comes to you sinners, and his presence is your salvation. He says, "Lo, I come." What does he mean?

He means, *the setting of all else on one side.* There is the priest—he has not helped you much; he may go, for Jesus says, "Lo, I come." There are your own efforts and doings; there are your feelings and thinkings; there are your ceremonies and austerities; there are your prayers and tears; there are your hearings and readings—all these must be laid aside as grounds of confidence, and Jesus alone must be your trust. He can do for you what none of these can. You are trying to work yourself up to repentance and faith, and you cannot succeed. Let him come, and he will bring every good thing with him. It is glorious to see our Lord throwing down all our bowing walls and tottering fences, and to hear him cry, "Behold, I lay in Zion for a foundation." Everything else vanishes before his perfect salvation.

Before him there is *a setting of self aside.* You have been your own confidence. What you could feel, or do, or think, or resolve, had become the ground of your confidence; but now Jesus puts self down, and he is himself exalted. By working yourself to death, you cannot effect your own salvation. Lo, Jesus comes to save you. You cannot weave yourself a garment. Lo, he comes to clothe you from heed to foot with his own seamless robe of righteousness. He annihilates self that he may fill all things.

Here is a glorious *setting of himself at our side and in our place.* Mr. Moody tells a story, which I would fain hope may be true; for one would like to hear something good about a Czar of Russia, and especially about our once enemy, the Emperor Nicholas. The story concerns a soldier in the barracks who was much distressed by his heavy debts. He was in despair, for he owed a great deal of money, and could not tell where to get it. He took a piece of paper, and made a list of his debts, and underneath the list he wrote, "Who will pay these debts?" He then lay down on the barrack bed, and fell asleep, with the paper before him. The Emperor of Russia passed by, and, taking up the paper, read it, and being in a gracious mood signed at the bottom, "NICHOLAS." Was not that a splendid answer to the question? When the soldier woke up and read it, he could scarcely believe his own eyes. "Who will pay these debts?" was the despairing question. "Nicholas" was the all-sufficient answer. So are we answered, Who will bear our sins? The grand reply is "JESUS." He puts his own name to our liabilities, and in effect, that he may meet them, he says, "Lo, I come." Your debt of sin is discharged when you believe in Christ Jesus. "Without shedding of blood is no remission;" but the blood of Jesus Christ, God's dear Son, cleanseth us from all sin. You are not now to bear your own sins. Behold the scape-goat, who carries them away into the wilderness! Yea, Jesus says, "Lo, I come!" He takes our sins upon himself, he bears their penalty, and we go free. Blessed word—"Lo, I come": I come to take your weight of sin, your burden of punishment. I come to be made a curse for you, that you may be made the righteousness of God in me. Sinner, stand out of the way, and let Jesus appear for you, and fill your place! He sets you on one side, and then he sets himself where you have been. Jesus is now the one pillar on which to lean, the one foundation on which to build, the one and only rest of our weary souls.

He sets himself where we can see him; for he cries, *"Lo,* I come"; that is to say, "See me come." He comes openly, that we may see him clearly. How I wish the Lord would reveal himself at this moment to each one of those who are weary of earth, of self, of sin, and possibly even weary of life itself! Oh, if you could but see Jesus standing in your room and stead, you would have faith to stand in his place, and so become "accepted in the Beloved"! O Lord, hear my prayer, and cause poor hearts to see thee descending from the skies, to uplift sinners from the dark abyss! Holy Spirit, touch that young man's eyes with heavenly salve, that he may see where salvation lies. Deal with that poor woman's dim eyes also, that she may perceive the Lord Christ, and find peace in him. Jesus cries, "Lo, I come! Look unto me, and be ye saved, all the ends of the earth."

> "There is life for a look at the Crucified One;
> There is life at this moment for thee.
> Then look, sinner—look unto him, and be saved—
> Unto him who was nail'd to the tree."

Should you even lie in all the despair and desolation which I described, I would persuade you to believe in Jesus. Trust him, and you shall find him all that you want.

Our Lord sets himself to be permanently our all in all. When he came on earth, he did not leave his work till he had finished it. Even when he rose to glory, he continued his service for his chosen, living to intercede for them. Jesus was a Savior nineteen hundred years ago, and he is a Savior still; and he will be a Savior until all the chosen race shall have been gathered home. He tells us, "I said, Lo, I come"; but he does not say, "I said, I will go away, and quit the work." Our Lord's ear is bored, and he goes out no more from the service of salvation. It is not written of any penitent souls, "Ye shall seek me, but shall not find me"; but it is written, "If thou seek him, he will be found of thee." O my hearer, you are now in the place where the gospel is preached to you—yes, to you, for we are sent to preach the gospel to every creature; and though you should be the worst, and most benighted, and most guilty of all the creatures out of hell, yet you are a creature, and we preach Christ to you. O poor heart, may the Lord Jesus say to you "Lo, I come!" for he comes to stay,—to stay until he has worked salvation *in* you as he has worked out salvation *for* you. He will not leave a believer till he has presented him spotless before the throne of God with exceeding joy. I wish I could make all this most clear and plain. You are altogether ruined by your own fault, and you cannot undo the evil. You have done all you can, and it has come to nothing. You are steeped in sin up to your throat; yea the filth has gone over your head: you are as one drowned in black waters. Despairing one, cast not your eyes around to seek for a friend, for you will look in vain to men. No arm can rescue you, save one; and that is the arm of Jesus, who now cries "Lo, I come." Set everything else on one side, and trust yourself with the Savior, Christ the Lord.

III. Oh, that many may be comforted while I dwell on a third head! **CHRIST IN HIS COMING IS HIS OWN INTRODUCTION.**

Here our Lord is his own herald, "Lo, I come." He does not wait for an eloquent preacher to act as master of the ceremonies to him: he introduces himself. Therefore even I, the simplest talker on earth, may prove quite sufficient for my Lord's purpose if he will graciously condescend to bless these plain words of mine. It is not I that say that Jesus comes, but in the text our Lord himself declares, "Then said I, Lo, I come." You need not do anything to draw Christ's attention to you; it is Christ who draws your attention to himself. Do you see this? You are the blind bat; and he is all eye towards you, and bids you look on him. I hear you cry, "Lord, remember me," and I hear him answer, "Soul, remember me." He bids you look on him when you beseech him to look on you.

He comes when quite unsought, or sought for in a wrong way. To many men and women Christ has come though they had not even desired him. Yea, he has come even to those who hated him. Saul of Tarsus was on his way to worry the saints at Damascus, but Jesus said, "Lo, I come"; and when he looked out of heaven he turned Saul, the persecutor, into Paul, the apostle. The promise is fulfilled, "I was found of them that sought me not; I was made manifest unto them that asked not after me." Herein is the glorious sovereignty of his love fully exercised, and grace reigns supreme. "Lo, I come," is the announcement of majestic grace which waiteth not for man, neither tarrieth for the sons of men.

Our Lord Jesus is the way to himself. Did you ever notice that? He comes himself to us, and so he is the way by which we meet him. He is our rest, and the way to our rest; he says, "I am the way." You want to know how to get to Christ? You have not to get to Christ, for he has come to you. It is well for you to come to Christ; but that is only possible because Christ has come to you. Jesus is near you: near you *now*. Backslider, he comes to you! Wandering soul, roving to the very brink of perdition, the good Shepherd cries, "Lo, I come." He is the way to himself.

Remember, also, that *he is the blessing which he brings.* Jesus not only gives life and resurrection, but he says, "I am the resurrection and the life." Christ is salvation, and everything needful to salvation is in him. If he comes, all good comes *with* him, or rather *in* him. An enquirer once said to a minister, "The next step for me is to get a deeper conviction of sin." The minister said, "No such thing, my friend: the next step is to trust in Jesus, for he says, Come unto me." To come to Jesus, or rather to receive Jesus who has come to us, is the one essential step into eternal salvation. Though our Lord does say, "Come unto me," he has preceded it with this other word, "Lo, I come." Poor cripple, if you cannot come to Jesus, ask him to come to you; and he will. Here you lie, and you have been for years in this case; you have no man to put you into the pool, and it would do you no good if he did; but Jesus can make you whole, and he is here. You cannot stir hand or foot because of spiritual paralysis; but your case is not hopeless. Listen to my Lord in the text, "Then said I, Lo, I come." He has no paralysis. He can come, leaping over the mountains of division. I know my Lord came to me, or I should never have come to him: why should he not come to you? I came to him because he came to me.

> "He drew me, and I followed on,
> Charmed to confess the voice divine."

Why should he not draw us also? Is he not doing so? Yield to the pressure of his love.

"Then said I, Lo, I come." You see *our Lord is his own spokesman*. He says to me, "Go and tell those people about my coming"; and I gladly do so; but you will forget my words, and refuse to accept the Coming One. Your consciences will be unawakened, your hearts unmoved: I fear it will be so. But if this text be fulfilled concerning our Lord this day—"Then said I, Lo, I come"—you will hear HIM. If he speaks he is himself the Almighty Word, and his voice will reach your hearts, and accomplish his purpose. Dear Christian people, join with me in this prayer: Lord, speak to thy chosen ones that lie here in their death-like despair, far off from thee, and say to each one of them, "Lo, I come." O downcast soul, this is your morning: this is the set time to favor you: this day is salvation come to your house and to your heart. Make haste and come down from the tree of your frivolity or your self-righteousness. Receive the Lord Jesus, for to-day he must abide in your house and in your heart: the hour for the imperial *"must"* of the eternal purpose has arrived. God grant it may be so! May this be an hour of which Jesus shall declare,—"Then said I, Lo, I come!"

IV. Our next point is this—CHRIST, TO CHEER US, REVEALS HIS REASONS FOR COMING. Only a few words on this. Note the rest of the verse: "Lo, I come: in the volume of the book it is written of me." When we were yet without strength, in due time Christ died for the ungodly, because it was the due time *according to covenant purposes*. Christ comes to a guilty sinner, just as he once came to a manger and a stable, because so it was appointed. There is nothing for him to get, but everything for him to give; but he comes because so it is written in the volume of the divine decrees—

"Thus the eternal counsel ran,—
Almighty grace, arrest that man."

Therefore in love the Savior appears to the sinner, and by grace arrests him in his mad career.

It is his Father's will. Christ's coming to save a soul is with his Father's full consent and aid. The Father wills that you who believe in him, lost though you be, should now be saved, and Jesus comes to do the will of the Father.

He comes because his heart is set on you. He loves you, and so he hastens to your rescue. Your salvation is his delight. Though your soul is sunk in a sea of need, and you are in despair because of that need, Jesus loves you, and comes to meet your case. The best of all is that Jesus loves you. One asked an old man of ninety, "Do you love Jesus?" and the old man answered with a smile, "I do, indeed; but I can tell you something better than that." His friend said, "Something better than loving Jesus! What is that?" The old disciple replied, *"He loves me."* O soul, I wish you could see this fact, which is indeed better than your love to Jesus, namely, his love to you! Because he loved his redeemed from before the foundation of the world, therefore in due time he says, "Lo, I come."

The fact is, *you have need, and he has love, and so he comes.* There is no hope for you unless he does come, and that is why he comes. If you had a penny of your own, he would not give you his purse; if you had a rag of your own, he would not give you his robe; if you had a breath of your own, he would not give you his life. But now you are naked, and poor, and miserable, and lost, and dead, Jesus reveals himself, and you read concerning him, "Then said I, Lo, I come." He gives you his reasons—reasons not in yourself, but all in *his* grace. There is no good in you; there is no reason in you why the Lord should save you; but because of his free, spontaneous, rich, sovereign, almighty grace, he leaps out of heaven, he descends to earth, he plunges into the grave to pluck his beloved from destruction.

V. Here is my last word: CHRIST'S COMING IS THE BEST PLEA FOR OUR RECEIVING HIM, and receiving him now. O sirs, remember you have not to raise the question whether he will come or not. He is come. You have not to say, "How can I come to him?" He comes to you. You do want a Mediator between your soul and God; but you do *not* want any mediator between yourself and Jesus; for he says, "Lo, I come." To you in all your filthiness, in all your condemnation, in all your hopelessness, he comes. Wait not for anybody to introduce you to him, or him to you; he has introduced himself, and here is his card—"Then said I, Lo, I come." No pleas are needed to persuade him to come to you, for he says, "Lo, I come." Though you cannot think of a single argument why he should appear to you in mercy, he does so appear. It is written, "I will have mercy upon her that had not obtained mercy; and I will say to them which were not my people, Thou art my people; and they shall say, Thou art my God." O words of wondrous grace! Our gracious Lord does not wait for our entreaties; but of his own accord he says, "Lo, I come." Without asking you, and without your asking him, he puts in an appearance in the sovereignty of his grace.

No search is needed to find the Lord, for he comes in manifested grace, and calls upon us to see him. "I have long been searching for Christ" murmurs one. What! seeking for the sun at noonday? Jesus is not lost. It is you that are lost, and he is searching for you. He says, "Lo, I come": it is *you* that will not come. Still one declares that he has been seeking the Lord Jesus for many a day. This is sadly strange, for Jesus is near. "Say not in thine heart, Who shall ascend into heaven? or, Who shall descend into the deep? The word is nigh thee, even in thy mouth, and in thy heart, that if thou wilt confess with thy mouth the Lord Jesus, and shalt believe in thy heart that God hath raised him from the dead, thou shalt be saved." If thou believest in the Lord Jesus Christ, thou shalt be saved. Searching after Christ? Nay, verily he saith, "Lo, I come."

Moreover, no waiting is needed, and no preparation is to be made by you. Why do you wait? HE does not wait, but cries, "Lo, I come!" "I will get ready for Christ", say you; but it is too late to talk so, when he cries, "Lo, I am come." Receive him! If you are in yourself sadly unready, yet he himself will make everything ready for himself. Only open wide the door, and let him in. Do you say, "But I am ashamed"? Be ashamed. He bids you be ashamed, and be confounded, while he declares, "I do not this for your sakes." Yet be not so ashamed as to commit another shameful deed by shutting the door in your Redeemer's face. Shut not out your own mercy. A pastor in Edinburgh, in going round his district, knocked at the door of a poor woman, for whom he had brought some needed help; but he received no answer. When next he met her, he said to her, "I called on Tuesday at your house." She asked, "At what time?" "About eleven o'clock; I knocked, and you did not answer. I was disappointed, for I called to give you help." "Ah, sir!" said she, "I am very sorry. I thought it was the man coming for the rent, and I could not pay it, and therefore I did not dare to go to the door."

Many a troubled soul thinks that Jesus is one who comes to ask of us what we cannot give; but indeed he comes to give us all things. His errand is not to condemn, but to forgive. Miss not the charity of God through unbelief. Run to the door, and say to your loving Redeemer, "Lord, I am not worthy that thou shouldest come under my roof; but as thou hast come to me, I welcome thee with all my heart."

No assistance is wanted by Christ on your part. He does not come with half a salvation, and look to you to complete it. He does not come to bring you a robe half woven, which you are to finish. How could you finish it? Could the best saint in the world add anything to Christ's righteousness? No good man would even dream of adding his home-spun to that raiment which is of wrought gold. What! are *you* to make up the deficient ransom price? Is it deficient? Would you bring your clods of mud into the royal treasury, and lay them down side by side with sapphires? Would you help Christ? Go, yoke a mouse with an elephant! Go harness a fly side by side with an archangel. But dream not of yoking yourself with Christ.

He says, "Lo, I come", and I trust you will reply, "My Lord, if thou art come, all is come, and I am complete in thee."

> "Thou, O Christ art all I want,
> More than all in thee I find."

Receive him: receive him at once. Dear children of God, and sinners that have begun to feel after him, say with one accord, "Even so, come quickly, Lord Jesus." If he says, "Lo, I come," and the Spirit and the bride say, Come; and he that heareth says, Come, and he that is athirst comes, and whosoever will is bidden to come and take the water of life freely; then let us join the chorus of comes, and come to Christ ourselves. "Behold, the Bridegroom cometh; go you out to meet him!" Ye who most of all need him, be among the first and gladdest, as you hear him say, "Lo, I come."

All that I have said will be good for nothing as to saving results unless the Holy Ghost shall apply it with power to your hearts. Join with me in prayer that many may see Jesus just now, and may at once behold and accept the present salvation which is in him.

{*Sadly, we do not have either the Scripture Portion or the Hymns that were sung for this service, as they are not included in the volumes of the Metropolitan Tabernacle Pulpit.*}

"My Times Are In Thy Hand"

Delivered on Lord's-Day Morning, May 17th, 1891, by
C. H. SPURGEON,
At the Metropolitan Tabernacle, Newington

"My times are in thy hand."—Psalm 31:15.

DAVID WAS SAD: his life was spent with grief, and his years with sighing. His sorrow had wasted his strength, and even his bones were consumed within him. Cruel enemies pursued him with malicious craft, even seeking his life. At such a time he used the best resource of grief; for he says in verse 14, "But I trusted in thee, O Lord." He had no other refuge but that which he found in faith in the Lord his God. If enemies slandered him, he did not render railing for railing; if they devised to take away his life, he did not meet violence with violence; but he calmly trusted in the Lord. They ran hither and thither, using all kinds of nets and traps to make the man of God their victim; but he met all their inventions with the one simple defense of trust in God. Many are the fiery darts of the wicked one; but our shield is one. The shield of faith not only quenches fiery darts, but it breaks arrows of steel. Though the javelins of the foe were dipped in the venom of hell, yet our one shield of faith would hold us harmless, casting them off from us. Thus David had the grand resource of faith in the hour of danger. Note well that he uttered a glorious claim, the greatest claim that man has ever made: "I said, Thou art my God." He that can say, "This kingdom is mine," makes a royal claim; he that can say, "This mountain of silver is mine," makes a wealthy claim; but he that can say to the Lord, "Thou art my God," hath said more than all monarchs and millionaires can reach. If this God is your God by his gift of himself to you, what can you have more? If Jehovah has been made your own by an act of appropriating faith, what more can be conceived of? You have not the world, but you have the Maker of the world; and that is far more. There is no measuring the greatness of his treasure who hath God to be his all in all.

Having thus taken to the best resource by trusting in Jehovah, and having made the grandest claim possible by saying, "Thou art my God", the Psalmist now stays himself upon a grand old doctrine, one of the most wonderful that was ever revealed to men. He sings, "My times are in thy hand." This to him was a most cheering fact: he had no fear as to his circumstances, since all things were in the divine hand. He was not shut up unto the hand of the enemy; but his feet stood in a large room, for he was in a space large enough for the ocean, seeing the Lord had placed him in the hollow of his hand. To be entirely at the disposal of God is life and liberty for us.

The great truth is this—all that concerns the believer is in the hands of the Almighty God. "My times", these change and shift; but they change only in accordance with unchanging love, and they shift only according to the purpose of One with whom is no variableness nor shadow of a turning. "My times", that is to say, my ups and my downs, my health and my sickness, my poverty and my wealth—all those are in the hand of the Lord, who arranges and appoints according to his holy will the length of my days, and the darkness of my nights. Storms and calms vary the seasons at the divine appointment. Whether times are reviving or depressing remains with him who is Lord both of time and of eternity; and we are glad it is so.

We assent to the statement, "My times are in thy hand," as to their result. Whatever is to come out of our life, is in our heavenly Father's hand. He guards the vine of life, and he also protects the clusters which shall be produced thereby. If life be as a field, the field is under the hand of the great Husbandman, and the harvest of that field is with him also. The ultimate results of his work of grace upon us, and of his education of us in this life, are in the highest hand. We are not in our own hands, nor in the hands of earthly teachers; but we are under the skillful operation of hands which make nothing in vain. The close of life is not decided by the sharp knife of the fates; but by the hand of love. We shall not die before our time, neither shall we be forgotten and left upon the stage too long.

Not only are we ourselves in the hand of the Lord, but all that surrounds us. Our times make up a kind of atmosphere of existence; and all this is under divine arrangement. We dwell within the palm of

God's hand. We are absolutely at his disposal, and all our circumstances are arranged by him in all their details. We are comforted to have it so.

How came the Psalmist's times to be thus in God's hand? I should answer, first, that they were there in the order of nature, according to the eternal purpose and decree of God. All things are ordained of God, and are settled by him, according to his wise and holy predestination. Whatsoever happeneth here happeneth not by chance, but according to the counsel of the Most High. The acts and deeds of men below, though left wholly to their own wills, are the counterpart of that which is written in the purpose of heaven. The open acts of Providence below tally exactly with that which is written in the secret book, which no eye of man or angel as yet has scanned. This eternal purpose superintended our birth. "In thy book all my members were written, which in continuance were fashioned, when as yet there was none of them." In thy book, every footstep of every creature is recorded before the creature is made. God has mapped out the pathway of every man who traverses the plains of life. Some may doubt this; but all agree that God foresees all things; and how can they be certainly foreseen unless they are certain *to be?* It is no mean comfort to a man of God that he feels that, by divine arrangement and sacred predestination, his times are in the hand of God.

But David's times were in God's hand in another sense; namely, that he had by faith committed them all to God. Observe carefully the fifth verse: "Into thine hand I commit my spirit: thou hast redeemed me, O Lord God of truth." In life we use the words which our Lord so patiently used in death: we hand over our spirits to the hand of God. If our lives were not appointed of heaven, we should wish they were. If there were no overruling Providence, we would crave for one. We would merge our own wills in the will of the great God, and cry, "Not as we will, but as thou wilt." It would be a hideous thought to us if any one point of our life-story were left to chance, or to the frivolities of our own fancy; but with joyful hope we fall back upon the eternal foresight and the infallible wisdom of God, and cry, "Thou shalt choose our inheritance for us." We would beg him to take our times into his hand, even if they were not there.

Moreover, beloved brethren, our times are in the Lord's hands, because we are one with Christ Jesus. "We are members of his body, of his flesh, and of his bones." Everything that concerns Christ touches the great Father's heart. He thinks more of Jesus than of all the world. Hence it follows that when we become one with Jesus, we become conspicuous objects of the Father's care. He takes us in hand for the sake of his dear Son. He that loves the Head loves all the members of the mystical body. We cannot conceive of the dear Redeemer as ever being out of the Father's mind; neither can any of us who are in Christ be away from the Father's active, loving care: our times are ever in his hand. All his eternal purposes work towards the glorifying of the Son, and quite as surely they work together for the good of those who are in his Son. The purposes which concern our Lord and ourselves are so inter-twisted as never to be separated.

To have our times in God's hand must mean not only that they are at God's disposal, but that they are arranged by the highest wisdom. God's hand never errs; and if our times are in his hand, those times are ordered rightly. We need not puzzle our brains to understand the dispensations of Providence: a much easier and wiser course is open to us; namely, to believe the hand of the Lord works all things for the best. Sit thou still, O child, at thy great Father's feet, and let him do as seemeth him good! When thou canst not comprehend him, know that a babe cannot understand the wisdom of its sire. Thy Father comprehends all things, though thou dost not: let his wisdom be enough for thee. Everything in the hand of God is where it may be left without anxiety; and it is where it will be carried through to a prosperous issue. Things prosper which are in his hand. "My times are in thy hand," is an assurance that none can disturb, or pervert, or poison them. In that hand we rest as securely as rests a babe upon its mother's breast. Where could our interests be so well secured as in the eternal hand? What a blessing it is to see by the eye of faith all things that concern you grasped in the hand of God! What peace as to every matter which could cause anxiety flows into the soul when we see all our hopes built upon so stable a foundation, and preserved by such supreme power! "My times are in thy hand!"

Before I go into this subject, to show the sweetness of this confidence, I pray every Christian here to read the text, and take it in the singular, and not as we sang it just now—

> "Our times are in thy hand,
> Whatever they may be,
> Pleasing or painful, dark or bright,
> As best may seem to thee."

We find it in the psalm, *"My* times are in thy hand." This does not exclude the whole body of the saints enjoying this safety together; but, after all, truth is sweetest when each man tastes the flavour of it for himself. Come, let each man take to himself this doctrine of the supreme appointment of God, and believe that it stands true as to his own case, *"My* times are in thy hand." The wings of the cherubim cover *me*. The Lord Jesus loved me, and gave himself for me, and my times are in those hands which were nailed to the cross for my redemption. What will be the effect of such a faith, if it be clear, personal, and enduring? This shall be our subject at this season. May the Holy Spirit help us!

I. A clear conviction that our times are in the hand of God WILL CREATE WITHIN US A SENSE OF THE NEARNESS OF GOD. If the hand of God is laid upon all our surroundings, God himself is near us. Our Puritanic fathers walked with God the more readily because they believed in God as arranging everything in their daily business and domestic life; and they saw him in the history of the nation, and in all the events which transpired. The tendency of this age is to get further and further from God. Men will scarcely tolerate a Creator now, but everything must be evolved. To get God one stage further back is the ambition of modern philosophy; whereas, if we were wise, we should labor to clear out all obstacles, and leave a clear channel for drawing near to God, and for God to draw near to us. When we see that in his hand are all our ways, we feel that God is real and near.

"My times are in thy hand." Then there is nothing left to chance. Events happen not to man by a fortune which has no order or purpose in it. "The lot is cast into the lap; but the whole disposing thereof is of the Lord." Chance is a heathenish idea which the teaching of the Word has cast down, even as the ark threw down Dagon, and brake him in pieces. Blessed is that man who has done with chance, who never speaks of luck; but believes that, from the least even to the greatest, all things are ordained of the Lord. We dare not leave out the least event. The creeping of an aphis upon a rosebud, is as surely arranged by the decree of Providence, as the march of a pestilence through a nation. Believe ye this; for if the least be omitted from the supreme government, so may the next be, and the next, till nothing is left in the divine hand. There is no place for chance, since God filleth all things.

"My times are in thy hand" is an assurance which also puts an end to the grim idea of an iron fate compelling all things. Have you the notion that fate grinds on like an enormous wheel, ruthlessly crushing everything that lies in its way, not pausing for pity, nor turning aside for mercy? Remember that, if you liken Providence to a wheel, it must be a wheel which is full of eyes. Its every revolution is in wisdom and goodness. God's eye leaves nothing in providence blind; but fills all things with sight. God works all things according to his purpose; but then *He* himself works them. There is all the difference between the lone machinery of fixed fate, and the presence of a gracious, loving Spirit ruling all things. Things do happen as he plans them; but he himself is there to make them happen, and to moderate, and guide, and secure results. Our great joy is not, "My times are in the wheel of destiny"; but, "My times are in thy hand." With a living, loving God to superintend all things, we feel ourselves at home, resting near our Father's heart.

"My times are in thy hand." Does not this reveal the condescension of the Lord? He has all heaven to worship him, and all worlds to govern; and yet "my times"—the times of such an inconsiderable and unworthy person as I am—are in his hand. Now, what is man that it should be so? Wonder of wonders, that God should not only think of me, but should make my concerns his concerns, and take my matters into his hand! He has the stars in his hand, and yet he puts *us* there. He deigns to take in hand the passing interests of obscure men and lowly women.

Beloved, God is near his people with all his attributes; his wisdom, his power, his faithfulness, his immutability; and these are under oath to work for the good of those who put their trust in him. "All things work together for good to them that love God, to them who are the called according to his purpose." Yes, God considers our times, and thinks them over; with his heart and soul planning to do us good. That august mind, out of which all things spring, bows itself to us; and those eternal wings, which cover the universe, also brood over us and our household, and our daily wants and woes. Our God sits not still as a listless spectator of our griefs, suffering us to be drifted like waifs upon the waters of circumstance; but is busily occupying himself at all times for the defense and perfecting of his children. He leads us that he may bring us home to the place where his flock shall rest for ever.

What a bliss this is! Our times, in all their needs and aspects, are in God's hand, and therefore God is always caring for us. How near it brings God to us, and us to God! Child of God, go not thou tomorrow into the field, lamenting that God is not there! He will bless thy going out. Come not home to thy chamber, crying, "Oh, that I knew where I might find him!" He will bless thy coming in. Go not to thy bed, dreaming that thou art left an orphan; neither wake up in the morning with a sense of loneliness upon thee: thou art not alone, for the Father is with thee.

Wilt thou not feel how good it is that God should come so close to thee, and handle thy bread and thy water, and bless thy bed and thy board? Art thou not happy to be allowed to come so close to God, as to say, "My times are in thy hand"? There is a great deal in this first point as to the nearness of the Lord; and if you will turn it over, you will see more and more that a conviction that our times are in God's hand tends to create a happy and holy sense of the nearness of God to us.

II. THIS TRUTH IS A COMPLETE ANSWER TO MANY A TEMPTATION. You know how craftily Satan will urge a temptation. He says, "Now you have a large family, and your chief duty is to provide for them. Your position brings with it many wants. Here is a plan of making money; others follow it. It may not be quite straight, but you must not be particular in such a world as this, for nobody else is." How will you meet this? If you can say to Satan, "It is not my business to provide for myself or for my family: my times are in God's hand; and his name is Jehovah-Jireh, the Lord will provide; and I will not do a questionable thing, though it would fill my house with silver and gold from the cellar to the chimney-pot. I shall not meddle with my Lord's business. It is his to provide for me: it is mine to walk uprightly, and obey his Word." This is a noble answer to the arch-enemy. But supposing he says, "Well, but you are already in difficulties, and you cannot extricate yourself if you are too precise. A poor man cannot afford to keep a conscience: it is an expensive luxury in these days. Give your conscience a holiday, and you can soon get out of your trouble." Let your reply be, "O prince of darkness, it is no business of mine to extricate myself! My times are in God's hand. I have taken my case to him, and he will work for me in this matter better than I can do for myself! He does not wish me to do a wrong thing, that I may do for myself what he has promised to do for me." We are not called upon to eke out God's wisdom with a bit of our own wickedness. God forbid! Do the right, even if the heavens should fall. The Lord who has taken your business into his hand will bear you through.

"Well", says one, "we may use a little discreet policy in religious matters, and keep the peace by wise compromise. We may accomplish our end all the sooner by going a little roundabout. If you can just let truth wait for a little until the fine weather comes, and the silver slippers are in season, then she will be saved a good deal of annoyance!" Brethren, it is not for us to pick and plan times in this fashion. God's cause is in God's hand, and God would not have us help his cause by a compromising hand being laid on his ark. Remember what the hand of Uzzah brought on him, though he meant it well. Let us continue steadfast in the integrity of our walk, and we shall find our times are in

God's hand, and that they are well ordered, and need no hasty and unholy interposition on our part.

Brethren, is it not a delightful thing for us to know that though we are on a stormy voyage, the Lord himself is at the helm? The course we do not know; nor even our present latitude and longitude; but the Pilot knows all about us, and about the sea also. It will be our wisdom not to interfere with our Captain's orders. They put up a notice on the steamboats, "Do not speak to the man at the wheel." We are very apt, in our unbelief, to dispute with him to whom the steering of our vessel is entrusted. We shall not confuse him, thank God; but we often confound and confuse ourselves by our idle complaining against the living Lord. No, when you are tempted to presume, or to act in a despairing haste, or to hide your principles, or to do something which is not defensible, in order that you may arrange your times more comfortably, answer with a decided "No," and say, "My times are in God's hand," and there I will leave them.

When the devil comes with his subtle questions and insinuations, refer him to your Lord, in whose hand your times are placed. When you have a lawsuit, the opposite side will like to come and talk with you, to see if they can get something out of you. It will be your wisdom to reply, "If you have anything to say, say it to my solicitor." If the devil comes to you, and you get into an argument with him, he will beat you; for he is a very ancient lawyer, and he has been at the business for so many ages that you cannot match him. Send him to your Advocate. Refer him to the Wonderful, the Counselor. Ever shelter beneath this fact, "My times are in his hand. I have left the whole business to another, and I cannot dishonor him by intermeddling." Satan knows the Christ too well to go to him; he knows the taste of his broad-sword, of "It is written." He will not contest with Jesus, if we leave him to plead the causes of our soul.

III. In the third place, THIS CONVICTION IS A SUFFICIENT SUPPORT AGAINST THE FEAR OF MEN. We may say to ourselves, when our enemies bear very hard upon us, "I am not in their hands. My times are in thy hand." Here are gentlemen judging and condemning us with great rapidity. They say, "He has made a great mistake: he is an old bigot; he has snuffed himself out." This is easier said than done. The candle shines still. They say of you, "He is foolish and headstrong, and on religious matters he is as obstinate as a mule; and he will come to grief." You have not come to grief yet in the way they predict, and they had better not prophesy till they know. The godly are not in the hands of those who mock them. The wicked may gnash their teeth at believers, but they cannot destroy them. Here is their comfort, they have committed their spirit to the hand of God, and he will sacredly preserve the precious deposit. Fear not the judgments of men. Appeal to a higher court. Take the case to the King's Bench. Go to God himself with the matter, and he will bring forth your judgment as the light, and your righteousness as the noonday.

Do the malicious resolve to crush you? They will use to the utmost their little power; but there is a higher power which will hold them in. Rejoicingly say, "My times are in thy hand." Do they treat you with contempt? Do they sneer at you? What does that matter? Your honor comes not from men. Their contempt is the highest compliment the wicked can pay you.

Alas, many professors place their times in the hands of the world! If they prosper and grow rich, they see an opportunity of social advantage, and they quit their humbler friends to join a more respectable sect. How many are lost to fidelity because their prosperous times are not in God's hand, but in their own! Some, on the other hand, when they are in adversity, get away from the Lord. The excuse is, "I cannot go to the house of God any more; for my clothes are not so respectable as they used to be." Is your poverty to take you out of your Lord's hands? Never let it be so; but say, "My times are in thy hand." Cleave to the Lord in losses as well as in gains, and so let all your times be with him.

How often we meet with people who are staggered by slander! It is impossible to stop malicious tongues. They wound, and even slay, the characters of the godly. The tried one cries, "I cannot bear it: I shall give all up." Why? Why yield to mere talk? Even these cruel tongues are in God's hand. Can you not brave their attacks? They cannot utter a single whisper more than God permits. Go on thy way, O righteous man, and let false tongues pour forth their poison as they will. "Every tongue that shall rise against thee in judgment thou shalt condemn." If my times are in God's hand, no man can do me harm unless God permit. Though my soul is among lions, yet no lion can bite me while Jehovah's angel is my guard.

This feeling, that our interests are safe in the highest keeping, breeds an independent spirit. It prevents cringing before the great, and flattering the strong. At the same time, it removes all tendency to envy; so that you do not wish for the prosperity of the wicked, nor fret yourself because of evil-doers. When one knows that his times are in God's hand, he would not change places with a king; nay, nor with an angel.

IV. A full belief in the statement of our text is A CURE FOR PRESENT WORRY. O Lord, if my times are in thy hand, I have cast my care on thee, and I trust and am not afraid! Why is it, my sister—for this habit of worrying abounds among the gracious sisterhood—why do you vex yourself about a matter which is in the hand of God? If he has undertaken for you, what cause have you for anxiety? And you, my brother—for there are plenty of men who are nervous and fretful—why do you want to interfere with the Lord's business? If the case is in his hand, what need can there be for you to be prying and crying? You were worrying this morning, and fretting last night, and you are distressed now, and will be worse to-morrow morning. May I ask you a question? Did you ever get any good by fretting? When there was not rain enough for your farm, did you ever fret a shower down? When there was too much wet, or you thought so, did you ever worry the clouds away? Tell me, did you ever make a sixpence by worrying? It is a very unprofitable business. Do you answer, "What, then, are we to do in troublous times"? Why, go to him into whose hand you have committed yourself and your times. Consult with infinite wisdom by prayer; console yourself with infinite love by fellowship with God. Tell the Lord what you feel, and what you fear. Ten minutes' praying is better than a year's murmuring. He that waits upon God, and casts his burden upon him, may lead a royal life: indeed, he will be far happier than a king.

To leave our times with God is to live as free from care as the birds upon the bough. If we fret, we shall not glorify God; and we shall not constrain others to see what true religion can do for us in the hour of tribulation. Fret and worry put it out of our power to act wisely; but if we can leave everything with God because everything is really in his hand, we shall be peaceful, and our action will be deliberate; and for that very reason it will be more likely to be wise. He that rolls his burden upon the Lord will be strong to do or to suffer; and his days shall be as the days of heaven upon the earth. I admire the serenity of Abraham. He never seems to be in a fluster; but he moves grandly, like a prince among men. He is much more than the equal of the greatest man he meets: we can hardly see Lot with a microscope when we have once seen Abraham. Why was that? Because he believed in God, and staggered not.

Half the joy of life lies in expectation. Our children get greater pleasure out of expecting the holiday than they do out of the day itself. It is much the same with ourselves. If we believe that all our times are in God's hand, we shall be expecting great things from our heavenly

Father. When we get into a difficulty we shall say, "I am now going to see the wonders of God, and to learn again how surely he delivers them that trust in him." I thank God I have learned at times to glory in necessities, as opening a window into heaven for me, out of which the Lord would abundantly pour forth his supplies. It has been to me so unspeakable a delight to see how the Lord has supplied my needs for the Orphanage, the College, and other works, that I have half wished to be in straits, that I might see how the Lord would appear for me. I remember, some time ago, when year after year all the money came in for the various enterprises, I began to look back with regret upon those grand days when the Lord permitted the brook Cherith to dry up, and called off the ravens with their bread and meat, and then found some other way of supplying the orphans' needs. In those days, the Lord used to come to me, as it were, walking on the tops of the mountains, stepping from peak to peak, and by marvelous deeds supplying all my needs, according to his riches in glory by Christ Jesus. Do you know, I almost wished that the Lord would stop the streams, and then let me see how he can fetch water out of the rock. He did so, not very long ago. Funds ran very low, and then I cried to him, and he heard me out of his holy hill. How glad was I to hear the footfall of the ever-present Lord, answering to his child's prayer, and letting him know that his times were still in his Father's hand! Surely it is better to trust in the Lord than to put confidence in man. It is a joy worth worlds to be driven where none but the Lord can help you, and then to see his mighty hand pulling you out of the net. The joy lies mainly in the fact that you are sure it is the Lord, and sure that he is near you. This blessed realization of the Lord's interposition causes us to glory in tribulation. Is not that a cure for worry, a blessed cure for anxiety?

V. Fifthly, a firm conviction of this truth is A QUIETUS AS TO FUTURE DREAD. "My times are in thy hand." Do you wish to know what is going to happen to you in a short time? Would you look between the folded leaves of the future? You can buy a penny newspaper which will tell you the fate of nations this very year. You may be well-nigh sure that nothing will happen which is thus predicted, and thus it may be of some little use to you. Be you content with the prophecies of Scripture, but follow not every interpreter of them. Many people would pay largely to have the future made known to them. If they were wise, they would rather desire to have it concealed. Do not want to know; such knowledge would answer no useful purpose. The future is intended to be a sealed book. The present is all we need to have before us. Do thy day's work in its day, and leave to-morrow with thy God. If there were ways of reading the future, it would be wise to decline to use them. The knowledge would create responsibility, arouse fear, and diminish present enjoyment; why seek after it? Famish idle curiosity, and give your strength to believing obedience. Of this you may be quite sure, that there is nothing in the book of the future which should cause distrust to a believer. Your times are in God's hand; and this secures them.

The very word "times" supposes change for you; but as there are no changes with God, all is well. Things will happen which you cannot foresee; but your Lord has foreseen all, and provided for all. Nothing can occur without his divine allowance, and he will not permit that which would be for your real or permanent injury. "I should like to know", says one, "whether I shall die soon." Have no desire in that direction: your time will come when it should. The best way to live above all fear of death is to die every morning before you leave your bedroom. The apostle Paul said, "I die daily." When you have got into the holy habit of daily dying, it will come easy to you to die for the last time. It is greatly wise to be familiar with our last hours. As you take off your garments at night, rehearse the solemn scene when you shall lay aside your robe of flesh. When you put on your garments in the morning, anticipate the being clothed upon with your house which is from heaven in the day of resurrection. To be fearful of death is often the height of folly. A great prophet once ran away many miles to escape from death by an imperious queen. He was one of the bravest of the brave, and yet he hurried into solitude to escape a woman's threat. When he had finished his weary walk, he sat down, and actually prayed, "Let me die." It was a singular thing to do, to run for his life, and then to cry, "Let me die." That man never did die; for we speak of Elijah, who rode to heaven in a chariot of fire. God does not answer all his people's prayers, for he has better things for them than they ask. Do not tremble about what may never happen. Even we may never die; for it is written, "We shall not all sleep, but we shall all be changed, in a moment, in the twinkling of an eye, at the last trump." Some of us may be alive and remain at the coming of the Lord. Who knows? Behold, he comes quickly. At any rate, do not let us worry about death, for it is in his hands.

VI. Again, a full conviction that our times are in his hand will be A REASON FOR CONSECRATED SERVICE. If God has undertaken my business for me, then I may most fitly undertake such business for him as he may appoint. Queen Elizabeth wished one of the leading merchants of London to go to Holland to watch her interests there. The honest man told her Majesty that he would obey her commands; but he begged her to remember that it would involve the ruin of his own trade for him to be absent. To this the Queen replied, "If you will see to my business, I will see to your business." With such a royal promise he might willingly let his own business go; for a queen should have it in her power to do more for a subject than he can do for himself. The Lord, in effect, says to the believer, "I will take your affairs in hand, and see them through for you." Will you not at once feel that now it is your joy, your delight, to live to glorify your gracious Lord? To be set free to serve the Lord is the highest freedom. How beautiful it is to read in the book of Isaiah, "And strangers shall stand and feed your flocks, and the sons of the alien shall be your plowmen and your vinedressers"! Outsiders shall do the drudgery for you, and set you free for higher service. Read on and see: "But ye shall be named the Priests of the Lord: men shall call you the Ministers of our God." Faith sets us free from the wear and tear of carking care, that we may give ourselves up wholly to the service of the Lord our God. Faith causes us to live exempt from fret, to serve the blessed God alone. Set free from the burden of earthly things by God's kind care of us, we present our bodies as living sacrifices unto the Lord our God. He hath not made us slaves and drudges, but priests and kings unto God.

I am sure, dear friends, if we get this truth fully saturating our souls, that our times are in God's hand, it will make life a grander thing than it has ever seemed to be. Do you believe that God's hand is working with you and for you? Then art thou lifted above the dumb-driven cattle that surround thee; for the God of heaven thinketh upon thee, and puts his hand to thine affairs. This connection with the divine puts heart into a man, and rises him to high endeavor, and great belief. We feel we are immortal till our work is done; we feel that God is with us, and that we are bound to be victorious through the blood of Jesus. We shall not be defeated in the campaign of life, for the Lord of hosts is with us, and we shall tread down our enemies. God will strengthen us, for our times are in his hand; therefore we will serve him with all our heart, and with all our soul, being fully convinced that "our labor is not in vain in the Lord."

VII. Lastly, if our times are in God's hand, here is A GRAND ARGUMENT FOR FUTURE BLESSEDNESS. He that takes care of our times, will take care of our eternity. He that has brought us so far, and wrought so graciously for us, will see us safely over the rest of the road. I marvel at some of you older folks, when you begin to doubt. You will say, "Look at yourself." Well, so I do; and I am heartily ashamed that ever a grain of mistrust should get into the eye of my faith. I would weep it out, and keep it out for the future. Still, some of you are older than I am, for you are seventy or eighty years of age. How much longer do you expect to travel in this wilderness? Have you another ten years, think you? God has been gracious to you for seventy years, and will you fret about the last ten, which, indeed, may never come? That will never do. God has delivered some of you out of such great trials, that your present ones are mere flea-bites. Sir Francis Drake, after he had sailed round the world, came up the Thames, and when he had passed Gravesend there came a storm which threatened the ship. The brave commander said, "What! Go round the world safely, and then get drowned in a ditch? Never!" So we ought to say. God has upheld us in great tribulations, and we are not going to be cast down about trials which are common to men. A man of energy, if he takes a work in hand, will push it through and the Lord our God never undertakes what he will not complete. "My times are in thy hand," and therefore the end will be glorious. My Lord, if my times were in my own hand, they would prove a failure; but since they are in thy hand, thou wilt not fail, nor shall I. The hand of God ensures success all along the line. In that day when we shall see the tapestry which records our lives, we shall see all the scenes therein with wondering eye; we shall see what wisdom, what love, what tenderness, what care was lavished upon them. When once a matter is in God's hand it is never neglected or forgotten, but it is carried out to the end. Wherefore, comfort one another with these words.

I have not been able to preach on this text as I hoped to do, for I am full of pain, and have a heavy headache; but, thank God, I have no heartache, with such a glorious truth before me. Sweet to my soul are these words—"My times are in thy hand." Take the golden sentence home with you. Keep this truth in your mind. Let it lie on your tongue like a wafer made with honey. Let it dissolve until your whole nature is sweetened by it. Yes, dear old lady, you that have come out of the workhouse this morning to hear this sermon, say to yourself, "My times are in thy hand." Yes, you, dear friend, who cannot find a situation, and have been walking the shoes off your feet in the vain endeavor to seek one: you also may say, "My times are in thy hand." Yes, my dear sister, pining away with consumption, this may be your song: "My times are in thy hand." Yes, young man, you that have just started in business, and have met with a crushing loss, it will be for your benefit after all; therefore say, "My times are in thy hand." This little sentence, to my mind, swells into a hymn: it buds and blossoms into a psalm. Few are the words, but mighty is the sense, and full of rest.

Now, remember, it is not everybody that can find honey in this hive. O sinners, you are in the hands of an angry God; and this is terrible! The God against whom you continually sin, and whom you provoke by refusing his grace, has absolute power over you. Beware, ye that forget God, lest he tear you in pieces. You have provoked, offended, and grieved him; but yet there is hope, for his mercy endureth for ever. Though you have vexed his Holy Spirit, yet return unto him, and he will have mercy upon you, and abundantly pardon you. It is certain that you are in his hands, and that you cannot escape from him. If you should climb to heaven, or dive to hell, you would not be out of his reach. No strength of yours can resist him, no speed can outrun him. Yield yourselves unto God; and then this great power of God, which now surrounds you, shall become your comfort. At present it ought to be your terror. The eyes of God are fixed upon you; the hand of God is against you; and if you are unsaved, one touch of that hand will mean death and everlasting destruction. That hand which the believer devoutly kisses, is the hand which you may well dread. Oh, that you would flee to Christ Jesus, and find shelter from wrath beneath the crimson canopy of his precious blood! Amen.

PORTION OF SCRIPTURE READ BEFORE SERMON—Psalm 31.

HYMNS FROM "OUR OWN HYMN BOOK"

Hymn # 910— *Sweet Day, so calm, so bright*

Sweet is the task, O Lord,
Thy glorious acts to sing,
To praise Thy name, and hear Thy word,
And grateful offerings bring.

Sweet at the dawning hour,
Thy boundless love to tell,
And when the night-wind shuts the flower,
Still on the theme to dwell.

Sweet, on this day of rest,
To join in heart and voice
With those who love and serve Thee best,
And in Thy name rejoice.

To songs of praise and joy
Be every Sabbath given,
That such may be our best employ
Eternally in heaven.

Henry Francis Lyte, 1841

Hymn # 701 — *My Times are in Thy Hand*

OUR times are in Thy hand,
Father, we wish them there;
Our life, our soul, our all, we leave
Entirely to Thy care.

Our times are in Thy hand,
Whatever they may be,
Pleasing or painful, dark or bright,
As best may seem to Thee.

Our times are in Thy hand;
Why should we doubt or fear?
A Father's hand will never cause
His child a needless tear.

Our times are in Thy hand;
Jesus the Crucified!
The hand our many sins had pierced,
Is now our guard and guide.

Our times are in Thy hand,
We'd always trust in Thee,
Till we have left this weary land,
And all Thy glory see.

William Freeman Lloyd, 1835

Hymn # 703 — *He shall choose our inheritance for us.*

Thy way, not mine, O Lord,
However dark it be;
Lead me by Thine own hand,
Choose out the path for me.

Smooth let it be or rough,
It will be still the best;
Winding or straight, it matters not,
It leads me to Thy rest.

I dare not choose my lot;
I would not, if I might;
But choose Thou for me, O my God,
So I shall walk aright.

Take Thou my cup, and it
With joy or sorrow fill;
As ever best to Thee may seem;
Choose Thou my good and ill.

Choose Thou for me my friends,
My sickness or my health;
Choose Thou my joys and cares for me
My poverty or wealth.

Not mine, not mine the choice
In things or great or small;
Be Thou my Guide, my Guard, my Strength,
My Wisdom, and my All.

Horatius Bonar, 1856

"The Statute of David for the Sharing of the Spoil"

Delivered on Lord's-Day Morning, June 7th, 1891, by
C. H. SPURGEON,
At the Metropolitan Tabernacle, Newington

{This is the last sermon Charles Spurgeon ever preached at the Metropolitan Tabernacle in London. He struggled with illness for most of 1891. He finally went to Mentone on the French Riviera to try to rest and recover, but he succumbed on January 31, 1892 and never made it back to his pulpit.}

"And David came to the two hundred men, which were so faint that they could not follow David, whom they had made also to abide at the brook Besor: and they went forth to meet David, and to meet the people that were with him: and when David came near to the people, he saluted them. Then answered all the wicked men and men of Belial, of those that went with David, and said, Because they went not with us, we will not give them ought of the spoil that we have recovered, save to every man his wife and his children, that they may lead them away, and depart. Then said David, Ye shall not do so, my brethren, with that which the Lord hath given us, who hath preserved us, and delivered the company that came against us into our hand. For who will hearken unto you in this matter? but as his part is that goeth down to the battle, so shall his part be that tarrieth by the stuff: they shall part alike. And it was so from that day forward, that he made it a statute and an ordinance for Israel unto this day. And when David came to Ziklag, he sent of the spoil unto the elders of Judah, even to his friends, saying, Behold a present for you of the spoil of the enemies of the Lord"
—1 Samuel 30:21-26.

THOSE WHO ASSOCIATE themselves with a leader must share his fortunes. Six hundred men had quitted their abodes in Judaea; unable to endure the tyranny of Saul they had linked themselves with David, and made him to be a captain over them. They were, some of them, the best of men, and some of them were the worst: in this, resembling our congregations. Some of them were choice spirits, whom David would have sought, but others were undesirable persons, from whom he might gladly have been free. However, be they who they may, they must rise or fall with their leader and commander. If he had the city Ziklag given to him, they had a house and a home in it; and if Ziklag was burned with fire, their houses did not escape. When David stood amid the smoking ruins, a penniless and a wifeless man they stood in the same condition. This rule holds good with all of us, who have joined ourselves to Christ and his cause; we must be partakers with him. I hope we are prepared to stand to this rule to-day. If there be ridicule and reproach for the gospel of Christ, let us be willing to be ridiculed and reproached for his sake. Let us gladly share with him in his humiliation, and never dream of shrinking. This involves a great privilege, since they that are with him in his humiliation shall be with him in his glory. If we share his rebuke in the midst of an evil generation we shall also sit upon his throne, and share his glory in the day of his appearing. Brethren, I hope the most of us can say we are in for it, to sink or swim with Jesus. In life or death, where he is, there will we, his servants, be. We joyfully accept both the cross and the crown which go with our Lord Jesus Christ: we are eager to bear our full share of the blame that we may partake in his joy.

It frequently happens that when a great disaster occurs to a band of men, a mutiny follows thereupon. However little it may be the leader's fault, the defeated cast the blame of the defeat upon him. If the fight is won, "it was a soldiers' battle"; every man at arms claims his share of praise. But if the battle is lost, cashier the commander! It was entirely his fault; if he had been a better general he might have won the day. This is how people talk: fairness is out of the question. So in the great disaster of Ziklag, when the town was burned with fire, and wives and children were carried away captive; then we read that they spoke of stoning David. Why David? Why David more than anybody else, it is hard to see, for he was not there, nor any one of them. They felt so vexed, that it would be a relief to stone somebody, and why not David? Brethren, it sometimes happens, even to the servants of Christ, that when they fall into persecution and loss for Christ's sake, the tempter whispers to them to throw up their profession. "Since you have been a Christian, you have had nothing but trouble. It seems as if the dogs of hell were snapping at your heels more than ever since you took upon you the name of Christ. Therefore, throw it up, and leave the ways of godliness." Vile suggestion! Mutiny against the Lord Jesus? Dare you do so? Some of us cannot do so, for when he asks us, "Will ye also go away?" we can only answer, "Lord, to whom should we go? Thou hast the words of eternal life." No other leader is worth following. We must follow the Son of David. Mutiny against him is out of the question.

> "Through floods or flames, if Jesus lead,
> We'll follow where he goes."

When a dog follows a man, we may discover whether the man is his master by seeing what happens when they come to a turn in the road. If the creature keeps close to its master at all turnings, it belongs to him. Every now and then you and I come to turns in the road, and many of us are ready, through grace, to prove our loyalty by following Jesus even when the way is hardest. Though the tears stand in his eyes and in ours; though we weep together till we have no more power to weep, we will cling to him when the many turn aside, and witness that he hath the living Word, and none upon earth beside. God grant us grace to be faithful unto death!

If we thus follow our leader and bear his reproach, the end and issue will be glorious victory. It was a piteous sight to see David leaving two hundred men behind him, and marching with his much diminished forces after an enemy who had gone, he scarce knew where, who might be ten times stronger than his little band, and might slay those who pursued them. It was a melancholy spectacle for those left behind to see their leader a broken man, worn and weary like themselves, hastening after the cruel Amalekite. How very different was the scene when he came back to the brook Besor more than a conqueror! Do you not hear the song of them that make merry? A host of men in the front are driving vast herds of cattle and flocks of sheep, and singing as they march, "This is David's spoil!" Then you see armed men, with David in the midst of them, all laden with spoil, and you hear them singing yet another song; those that bring up the rear are shouting exultingly, "David recovered all! David recovered all!" They, the worn-out ones that stayed at the brook Besor, hear the mingled song, and join first in the one shout, and then in the other; singing, "This is David's spoil! David recovered all!"

Yes, we have no doubt about the result of our warfare. He that is faithful to Christ shall be glorified with him. That he will divide the spoil with the strong is never a matter of question. "The pleasure of the Lord shall prosper in his hand."

> "The old truth by which we stand
> shall never be blotted out.
> Engraved as in eternal brass
> The mighty promise shines;
> Nor shall the powers of darkness rase
> Those everlasting lines."

We are certain as we live that the exiled truth shall celebrate its joyful return. The faith once for all delivered to the saints may be downtrodden for a season; but rejoice not over us, O our adversaries: though we fall we shall rise again! Wherefore we patiently hope, and quietly wait, and calmly believe. We drink of the brook Besor by the way and lift up our heads.

This morning I want to utter God-given words of comfort to those who are faint and weary in the Lord's army. May the divine Comforter make them so!

I. I shall begin by saying, first, that FAINT ONES OCCUR EVEN IN THE ARMY OF OUR KING. Among the very elect of David's army heroes who were men of war from their youth up—there were hands that hung down, and feeble knees that needed to be confirmed. There are such in Christ's army at most seasons. We have among us soldiers whose faith is real, and whose love is burning; and yet, for all that, just now their strength is weakened in the way, and they are so depressed in spirit that they are obliged to stop behind with the baggage.

Possibly some of these weary ones had grown faint because *they had been a good deal perplexed.* David had so wrongfully entangled himself with the Philistine king, that he felt bound to go with Achish to fight against Israel. I dare say these men said to themselves, "How will this end? Will David really lead us to battle against Saul? When he could have killed him in the cave he would not, but declared that he would not lift up his hand against the Lord's anointed; will he now take us to fight against the anointed of God? This David, who was so great an enemy of Philistia, and slew their champion, will he wax on their behalf?" They were perplexed with their leader's movements. I do not know whether you agree with me, but I find that half-an-hour's perplexity takes more out of a man than a month's labour. When you cannot see your bearings, and know not what to do, it is most trying. When to be true to God it seems that you must break faith with man, and when to fulfill your unhappy covenant with evil would make you false to your Christian professions, things are perplexing. If you do not walk carefully, you can easily get into a snarl. If Christians walk in a straight line it is comparatively easy going, for it is easy to find your way along a straight road; but when good men take to the new out, that bypath across the meadow, then they often get into ditches that are not in the map, and fall into thickets and sloughs that they never reckoned upon. Then is the time for heart-sickness to come on. These warriors may very well have been perplexed; and perhaps they feared that God was against them, and that now their cause would be put to shame; and when they came to Ziklag, and found it burned with fire, the perplexity of their minds added intense bitterness to their sorrow, and they felt bowed into the dust. They did not pretend to be faint, but they were really so; for the mind can soon act upon the body, and the body fails sadly when the spirits are worried with questions and fears. This is one reason why certain of our Lord's loyal-hearted ones are on the sick list, and must keep in the trenches for a while.

Perhaps, also, *the pace was killing to these men.* They made forced marches for three clays from the city of Achish to Ziklag. These men could do a good day's march with anybody; but they could not foot it at the double quick march all day long. There are a great many Christians of that sort—good, staying men who can keep on under ordinary pressure, doing daily duty well, and resisting ordinary temptations bravely; but at a push they fare badly: who among us does not? To us there may come multiplied labours, and we faint because our strength is small.

Worst of all, *their grief came in just then.* Their wives were gone. Although, as it turned out, they were neither killed nor otherwise harmed; yet they could not tell this, and they feared the worse. For a man to know that his wife is in the hands of robbers, and that he may never see her again, is no small trouble. Their sons and daughters also were gone: no prattlers climbed their father's knee; no gentle daughters came forth to bid them "Welcome home." Their homes were still burning, their goods were consumed, and they lifted up their voice and wept: is it at all wonderful that some of them were faint after performing that doleful *miserere?* Where would you be if you went home this morning, and found your home burned, and your family gone, you knew not where? I know many Christians who get very faint under extraordinary troubles. They should not, but they do. We have reason to thank God that no temptation has happened to us but such as is common to men; and yet it may not seem so; but we may feel as if we were specially tried, like Job. Messenger after messenger has brought us evil tidings, and our hearts are not fixed on the Lord as they ought to be. To those who are faint through grief I speak just now. You may be this, and yet you may be a true follower of the Lamb; and as God has promised to bring you out of your troubles, he will surely keep his word. Remember, he has never promised that you shall have no sorrows, but that he will deliver you out of them all. Ask yon saints in heaven! Ask those to step out of the shining ranks who came thither without trial. Will one of the leaders of the shining host give the word of command that he shall step forward who has washed his robes and made them white in the blood of the Lamb, but who never knew what affliction meant while here below? No one stirs in all that white-robed host. Does not one come forward? Must we wait here for ever without response? See! instead of anyone stirring from their ranks, I hear a voice that says, "These are they which came out of great tribulation." All of them have known, not only tribulation, but *great* tribulation. One promise of the New Testament is surely fulfilled before our eyes—"In the world ye shall have tribulation." When trouble came so pressingly on David's men they felt their weakness and needed to halt at the margin of the brook.

Perhaps, also, *the force of the torrent was too much for them.* As I have told you, in all probability the brook Besor was only a hollow place, which in ordinary times was almost dry; but in a season of great rain it filled suddenly with a rushing muddy stream, against which only strong men could stand. These men might have kept on upon dry land, but the current was too fierce for them, and they feared that it would carry them off their feet and drown them. Therefore, David gave them leave to stop there and guard the stuff. Many there are of our Lord's servants who stop short of certain onerous service: they are not called to do what their stronger comrades undertake with joy. They can do something, but they fail to do more; they can also bear certain trials, but they are unable to bear more; they faint because they have not yet come to fullness of growth in grace. Their hearts are right in the sight of God, but they are not in condition to surmount some peculiar difficulty. You must not overdrive them, for *they* are the feeble of the flock. Many are too faint for needful controversy. I have found a great many of that sort about lately: the truth is very important, but they love peace. It is quite necessary that certain of us should stand up for the faith once delivered to the saints; but they are not up to the mark for it. They cannot bear to differ from their fellows; and they hold their tongues rather than contend for the truth. There are true hearts that, nevertheless, cannot defend the gospel. They wish well to the champions; but they seek the rear rank for themselves. And some cannot advance any further with regard to knowledge; they know the fundamentals, and feel as if they could master nothing more. It is a great blessing that they know the gospel, and feel that it will save them; but the glorious mysteries of the everlasting covenant, of the sovereignty of God, of his eternal love and distinguishing grace, they cannot compass—these are a brook Besor which as yet they cannot swim. It would do them a world of good if they could venture in; but, still, they are not to be tempted into these blessed deeps. To hear of these things rather wearies them than instructs them: they have not strength enough of mind for the deep things of God. I would have every Christian wish to know all that he can know of revealed truth. Somebody whispers that the secret things belong not to us. You may be sure you will never know them if they are secret; but all that is revealed you ought to know, for these things belong to you and to your children. Take care you know what the Holy Ghost teaches. Do not give way to a fainthearted ignorance lest you be great losers thereby. That which is fit food for babes should not be enough for young men and fathers: we should eat strong meat, and leave milk to the little ones.

Yet these fainting ones were, after all, in David's army. Their names were in their Captain's Register as much as the names of the strong. And they did not desert the colours. They had the same captain as the stoutest-hearted men in the whole regiment; they could call David "Master" and "Lord" as truly as the most lion-like man amongst them. They were in for the same dangers; for if the men in front had been beaten and had retreated, the enemy would have fallen on those who guarded the stuff. If the Amalekites had slain the four hundred, they would have made short work of the two hundred. They had work to do as needful as that of the others. Though they had not to fight, they had to take care of the stuff; and this eased the minds of the fighting men. I will be bound to say it was a great trial to them not to be allowed to march into the fight. For a brave man to see the troops go past him, and hear the last footfall of his comrades, must have been sickening. Who could pleasantly say, "I am left out of it. There is a glorious day coming, and I shall be away. I shall, until I die, think myself accursed I was not there, and hold my manhood cheap that I fought not with them on that glorious day?" It is hard to brave men to be confined to hospital, and have no drive at the foe. The weary one wishes he could be to the front, where his Captain's eye would be upon him. He pants to smite down the enemies, and win back the spoil for his comrades.

Enough of this. I will only repeat my first point: fainting ones do occur even in the army of our King.

II. Secondly, THESE FAINTING ONES REJOICE TO SEE THEIR LEADER RETURN. Do you see, when David went back they went to meet him, and the people that were with him. I feel very much like this myself. That was one reason why I took this text. I felt, after my illness, most happy to come forth and meet my Lord in public. I hoped he would be here; and so he is. I am glad also to meet with you, my comrades. We are still spared for the wax. Though laid aside a while, we are again among our brethren. Thank God! It is a great joy to meet you. I am sorry to miss so many of our church-members who are laid aside by this sickness; but it is a choice blessing to meet so many of our kindred in Christ. We are never happier than when we are in fellowship with one another and with our Lord.

David saluted the stay-at-homes. Oh, that he might salute each one of us this morning, especially those who have been laid aside! Our King's salutations are wonderful for their heartiness. He uses no empty compliments nor vain words. Every syllable from his lips is a benediction. Every glance of his eye is an inspiration. When the King himself comes near, it is always a feast day to us! It is a high day and a holiday, even with the faintest of us, when we hear his voice. So they went to meet David, and he came to meet them, and there was great joy. Yes, I venture to mend that, and say there is great joy among us now. Glory be to his holy name, the Lord is here! We see him, and rejoice with joy unspeakable.

David's courtesy was as free as it was true. Possibly those who remained behind were half afraid that their leader might say, "See here, you idle fellows, what we have been doing for you!" No; he saluted them, but did not scold them. Perhaps they thought, "He will upbraid us that we did not manage to creep into the fray." But no; "he giveth liberally, and upbraideth not." He speaks not a word of upbraiding, for his heart pities them, and therefore he salutes them. "My brethren, God has been gracious to us. All hail!" David would have them rejoice together; and give praise unto the most High. He will not clash their cup with a drop of bitter. Oh, for a salutation from our Lord at this good hour! When

Christ comes into a company his presence makes a heavenly difference. Have you never seen an assembly listening to an orator, all unmoved and stolid? Suddenly the Holy Ghost has fallen on the speaker, and the King himself has been visibly set forth among them in the midst of the assembly, and all have felt as if they could leap to their feet and cry, "Hallelujah, hallelujah!" Then hearts beat fast, and souls leap high; for where Jesus is found his presence fills the place with delight. Now, then, you weary ones, if you be here, any of you, may you rejoice as you now meet your Leader, and your Leader reveals himself to you! If no one else has a sonnet, I have mine. He must, he shall be praised. "Thou art the King of glory, O Christ! All heaven and earth adores thee. Thou shalt reign for ever and ever."

III. Thirdly, FAINT ONES HAVE THEIR LEADER FOR THEIR ADVOCATE. Listen to those foul-mouthed men of Belial, these wicked men: how they rail against those whom God has accepted! They came up to David and began blustering—"These weaklings who were not in the fight, they shall not share the spoil. Let them take their wives and children and begone." These fellows spoke with loud, harsh voices, and greatly grieved the feebler ones. Who was to speak up for them? Their leader became their advocate.

First, do you notice, *he pleads their unity?* The followers of the son of Jesse are one and inseparable. David said, "Ye shall not do so, my brethren, with that which the Lord hath given us, who hath preserved us." "We are all one," says David. "God has given the spoil, not to you alone, but to us all. We are all one company of brothers." The unity of saints is the consolation of the feeble. Brethren, our Lord Jesus Christ would refresh his wearied ones by the reflection that we are all one in him. I may be the foot, all dusty and travel-stained; and you may be the hand, holding forth some precious gem; but we are still one body. Yonder friend is the brow of holy thought, and another is the lip of persuasion, and a third is the eye of watchfulness; but still we are one body in Christ. We cannot do, any one of us, without his fellow; each one ministers to the benefit of all. The eye cannot say to the hand, "I have no need of thee." We are all one in Christ Jesus. Surely this ought to comfort those of you who, by reason of feebleness, are made to feel as if you were very inferior members of the body: you are still living members of the mystical body of Jesus Christ your Lord, and let this suffice you. One life is ours, one love is ours, one heaven shall be ours in our one Saviour.

David further *pleaded free grace*, for he said to them, "Ye shall not do so, my brethren, with that which the Lord hath given us." He did not say, "With that which you have conquered, and fairly earned in battle," but "that which the Lord hath given us." Look upon every blessing as a gift, and you will not think anyone shut out from it, not even yourself. The gift of God is eternal life; why should you not have it? Deny not to anyone of your brethren any comfort of the Covenant of grace. Think not of any man, "He ought not to have so much joy." It is all of free grace; and if free grace rules the hour, the least may have it as well as the greatest. If it is all of free grace, then, my poor struggling brother, who can hardly feel assured that you are saved, yet if you are a believer, you may claim every blessing of the Lord's gracious covenant. God freely gives to you as well as to me the provisions of his love; therefore let us be glad, and not judge ourselves after the manner of the law of condemnation.

Then he pleaded *their needfulness.* He said, "These men abided by the stuff." No army fights well when its camp is unguarded. It is a great thing for a church to know that its stores are well guarded by a praying band. While some of us are teaching in the school or preaching in the street, we have great comfort; in knowing that a certain number of our friends are praying for us. To me it is a boundless solace that I live in the prayers of thousands. I will not say which does the better service—the man that preaches, or the man that prays; but I know this, that we can do better without the voice that preaches than without the heart that prays. The petitions of our bed-ridden sisters are the wealth of the church. The kind of service which seems most commonplace among men is often the most precious unto God. Therefore, as for those who cannot come into the front places of warfare, deny them not seats of honour, since, after all, they may be doing the greater good. Remember the statute, "They shall part alike."

Notice that David *adds to his pleading a statute.* I like to think of our great Commander, the Lord Jesus, making statutes. For whom does he legislate? For the first three? For the captains of thousands? No. He makes a statute for those who are forced to stay at home because they are faint. Blessed be the name of our Lord Jesus, he is always looking to the interests of those who have nobody else to care for them! If you can look after your own cause, you may do so; but if you are so happy as to be weak in yourself, you shall be strong in Christ. Those who have Christ to care for them are better off than if they took care of themselves. He that can leave his concerns with Christ has left them in good hands. Vain is the help of self, but all-sufficient is the aid of Jesus.

To sum up what I mean: I believe the Lord will give to the sick and the suffering an equal reward with the active and energetic, if they are equally concerned for his glory. The Lord will also make a fair division to the obscure and unknown as well as to the renowned and honoured, if they are equally earnest. Oh, tell me not that she who rears her boy for Christ shall miss her reward from him by whom an apostle is recompensed! Tell me not that the woman who so conducts her household that her servants come to fear God, shall be forgotten in the day when the "Well dones" are distributed to the faithful! Homely and unnoticed service shall have honour as surely as that with which the world is ringing.

Some of God's people are illiterate, and they have but little native talent. But if they serve the Lord as best they can, with all their heart, they shall take their part with those that are the most learned and accomplished. He that is faithful over a little shall have his full reward of grace. It is accepted according to what a man hath. We may possess no more than two mites, but if we cast them into the treasury, our Lord will think much of them.

Some dear servants of God seem always to be defeated. They seem sent to a people whose hearts are made gross and their ears dull of hearing. Still, if they have truthfully proclaimed the Word of the Lord their reward will not be according to their apparent success, but according to their fidelity.

Some saints are constitutionally depressed and sad; they are like certain lovely ferns, which grow best under a constant drip. Well, well, the Lord will gather these beautiful ferns of the shade as well as the roses of the sun; they shall share his notice as much as the blazing sunflowers and the saddest shall rejoice with the gladdest. You Little-Faiths, you Despondencies, you Much-Afraids, you Feeble-Minds, you that sigh more than you sing, you that would but cannot, you that have a great heart for holiness, but feel beaten back in your struggles, the Lord shall give you his love, his grace, his favour, as surely as he gives it to those who can do great things in his name. Certain of you have but a scant experience of the higher joys and deeper insights of the kingdom, and it may be that you are in part faulty because you are so backward; and yet, if true to your Lord, your infirmities shall not be reckoned as iniquities. If lawfully detained from the field of active labour this Statute stands fast for ever, for you as well as for others: "As his part is that goeth down to the battle, so shall his part be that tarrieth by the stuff: they shall part alike."

IV. Now, fourthly, FAINT ONES FIND JESUS TO BE THEIR GOOD LORD IN EVERY WAY. Was he not a good Lord when he first took us into his army of salvation? What a curious crew they were that enlisted under David! "Every one that was in debt, and every one that was discontented, gathered themselves unto him, and he became a captain over them." He was a captain of ragamuffins; but our Lord had not a better following. I was a poor wretch when I came to Christ; and I should not wonder if that word is near enough to the truth to describe you. I was a good-for-nothing, over head and ears in debt, and without a penny to pay. I came to Jesus so utterly down at the heel, that no one else would have owned me. He might well have said,—"No, I have not come to this—to march at the head of such vagrant beggars as these." Yet he received us graciously, according to his promise, "Him that cometh to me I will in no wise cast out." Since then, how graciously has he borne with us! We are not among those self-praising ones who have wrought such wonders of holiness; but we mourn our shortcomings and transgressions; and yet he hath not cast away the people whom he did foreknow. When we look back upon our character as soldiers of Christ, we feel ashamed of ourselves and amazed at his grace. If anybody had told us that we should have been such poor soldiers as we have been, we should not have believed them. We do not excuse ourselves: we are greatly grieved to have been such failures. Yet our gracious Lord has never turned us out of the ranks. He might have drummed us out of the regiment long ago; but here we are still enrolled, upheld, and smiled upon. What a captain we have! None can compare with him for gentleness. He still owns us, and he declares, "They shall be mine in that day when I make up my jewels."

Brethren, let us exalt the name of our Captain. There is none like him. We have been in distress since then: and he has been in distress with us. Ziklag smoked for him as well as for us. In all, their affliction he was afflicted. Have you not found it so? When we have come to a great difficulty like the brook Besor he has gently eased his commands, and has not required of us what we were unable to yield. He has not made some of you pastors and teachers, for you could not have borne the burden. He hath abounded towards us in all wisdom and prudence. He has suited the march to the foot, or the foot to the march. How sweetly he has smiled on what we have done! Have you not wondered to see how he has accepted your works and your prayers? You have been startled to find that he did answer your feeble petitions. When you have spoken a word for Jesus, and God has blessed it, why you have thought, "Surely there is a mistake about this! How could my feeble word have a blessing on it?" Beloved, we follow a noble Prince. Jesus is the chief among ten thousand for tenderness as well as for everything else. How tenderly considerate he is! How gentle and generous! He has never said a stinging word to us ever since we knew him. He is that riches which has no sorrow added to it. He has rebuked us; but his rebukes have been like an excellent oil, which has never broken our heads. When we have left him, he has turned and looked upon us, and so he has cut us to the quick; but he has never wounded us with any sword except that which cometh out of his mouth, whose edge is love. When he goes away from us, as David did from those two hundred who could not keep up with him, yet he always comes back again in mercy, and salutes us with favour. We wonder to ourselves that we did not hold him, and vow that we would never let him go; but we wonder still more that he should come back so speedily, so heartily, leaping over the mountains, hastening like a roe or a young hart over the hills of division. Lo! he has come to us. He has come to us, and he makes our hearts glad at his coming. Let us indulge our hearts this morning as we take our share in the precious spoil of his immeasurable love. He loves the great and the small with like love; let as be joyful all round.

There is one choice thing which he will do, that should make us love him beyond measure. David, after a while, went up to Hebron to be made king over Judah. Shall I read you in the second book of Samuel, the second chapter, and the third verse? "And his men that were with him" (and among the rest these weak ones who could not pass over the brook Besor), "and his men that were with him did David bring up, every man with his household; and they dwelt in the cities of Hebron." Yes, he will bring me up, even me! He will bring you up, you faintest and weakest of the band. There is a Hebron wherein Jesus reigns as anointed King, and he will not be there and leave one of us behind. There is no kingdom for Jesus without his brethren, no heaven for Jesus without his disciples. His poor people who have been with him in faintness and weariness shall be with him in glory, *and their households.* Hold on to that additional blessing. I pray you, hold on to it. Do not let slip that word—*"and their households."* I fear we often lose a blessing on our households through clipping the promise. When the jailer asked what he must do to be saved, what was the answer? "Believe on the Lord Jesus Christ, and thou shalt be saved." You have heard that answer hundreds of times, have you not? Did you ever hear the rest of it? Why do preachers and quoters snip off corners from gospel promises? It runs thus: "Thou shalt be saved, *and thy house.*" Lay hold of that blessed enlargement of grace, "and thy house." Why leave out the wives and the children? Will you let the Amalekites have them? Do not be satisfied without household salvation. Let us plead this word of the Lord this morning:—O thou blessed David, whom we have desired to follow, who has helped us so graciously even unto this day, when thou art in thy kingdom graciously remember us, and let it be said of us, "and David went up thither, and his men that were with him David brought up (they did not go up of themselves) every man with his household; and they dwelt in the cities of Hebron;" *"Every man with his household."* I commend that word to your careful notice. Fathers, have you yet seen your children saved? Mothers, are all those daughters brought in yet? Never cease to pray until it is so, for this is the crown of it all, "Every man with his household."

What I have to say lastly is this: how greatly I desire that you who are not yet enlisted in my Lord's band would come to him because you see what a kind and gracious Lord he is! Young men, if you could see our Captain, you would fall down on your knees and beg him to let you enter the ranks of those who follow him. It is heaven to serve Jesus. I am a recruiting sergeant, and I would fain find a few recruits at this moment. Every man must serve somebody: we have no choice as to that fact. Those who have no master are slaves to themselves. Depend upon it, you will either serve Satan or Christ, either self or the Saviour. You will find sin, self, Satan, and the world to be hard masters; but if you wear the livery of Christ, you will find him so meek and lowly of heart that you will find rest unto your souls. He is the most magnanimous of captains. There never was his like among the choicest of princes. He is always to be found in the thickest part of the battle. When the wind blows cold he always takes the bleak side of the hill. The heaviest end of the cross lies ever on his shoulders. If he bids us carry a burden, he carries it also. If there is anything that is gracious, generous, kind, and tender, yea lavish and superabundant in love, you always find it in him. These forty years and more have I served him, blessed be his name! and I have had nothing but love from him. I would be glad to continue yet another forty years in the same dear service here below if so it pleased him. His service is life, peace, joy. Oh, that you would enter on it at once! God help you to enlist under the banner of Jesus even this day! Amen.

PORTION OF SCRIPTURE READ BEFORE SERMON—1 Samuel 30.

HYMNS FROM "OUR OWN HYMN BOOK"

Hymn # 917— *Sweet Rest.*

My Lord, my Love, was crucified,
 He all the pains did bear;
But in the sweetness of His rest
 He makes His servants share.

How sweetly rest Thy saints above
 Which in Thy bosom lie!
The Church below doth rest in hope
 Of that felicity.

Welcome and dear unto my soul
 Are these sweet feasts of love;
But what a Sabbath shall I keep
 When I shall rest above!

I bless Thy wise and wondrous love,
 Which binds us to be free;
Which makes us leave our earthly snares,
 That we may come to Thee!

I come, I wait, I hear, I pray!
 Thy footsteps, Lord, I trace!
I sing to think this is the way
 Unto my Saviour's face!
   John Mason, 1683

Hymn # 731— *The Refiner sitting by the Fire.*

God's Furnace doth in Zion stand;
 But Zion's God sits by,
As the refiner views his gold
 With an observant eye.

His thoughts are high, His love is wise,
 His wounds a cure intend;
And though He does not always smile,
 He loves unto the end.

Thy love is constant to its line,
 Though clouds oft come between:
Oh could my faith but pierce these clouds,
 It might be always seen.

But I am weak, and forced to cry,
 Take up my soul to Thee:
Then, as Thou ever art the same,
 So shall I ever be.

Then shall I ever, ever sing,
Whilst Thou dost ever shine:
I have Thine own dear pledge for this;
Lord, Thou art ever mine.
John Mason, 1683

Hymn # 733— *I will never leave thee.*

O Zion, afflicted with wave upon wave,
Whom no man can comfort, whom no man can save;
With darkness surrounded, by terrors dismayed,
In toiling and rowing thy strength is decayed.

Loud roaring the billows now nigh overwhelm,
But skilful's the Pilot who sits at the helm,
His wisdom conducts thee, His power thee defends,
In safety and quiet thy warfare He ends.

"O fearful! O faithless!" in mercy He cries,
"My promise, My truth, are they light in thine eyes?
Still, still I am with Thee, My promise shall stand,
Through tempest and tossing I'll bring thee to land.

"Forget thee I will not, I cannot, thy name
Engraved on My heart doth forever remain:
The palms of My hands whilst I look on I see
The wounds I received when suffering for thee.

"I feel at My heart all Thy sighs and thy groans,
For thou art most near Me, My flesh and My bones,
In all thy distresses thy Head feels the pain,
Yet all are most needful, not one is in vain.

"Then trust Me, and fear not; thy life is secure;
My wisdom is perfect, supreme is My power;
In love I correct thee, thy soul to refine,
To make thee at length in My likeness to shine.

"The foolish, the fearful, the weak are My care,
The helpless, the hopeless, I hear their sad prayer:
From all their afflictions My glory shall spring,
And the deeper their sorrows, the louder they'll sing."
James Grant, 1784

Other Solid Ground Titles

THE COMMUNICANT'S COMPANION by *Matthew Henry*
THE SECRET OF COMMUNION WITH GOD by *Matthew Henry*
THE MOTHER AT HOME by *John S.C. Abbott*
LECTURES ON THE ACTS OF THE APOSTLES *by John Dick*
THE FORGOTTEN HEROES OF LIBERTY by *J.T. Headley*
LET THE CANNON BLAZE AWAY by *Joseph P. Thompson*
THE STILL HOUR: *Communion with God in Prayer* by *Austin Phelps*
COLLECTED WORKS of James Henley Thornwell (4 vols.)
CALVINISM IN HISTORY *by Nathaniel S. McFetridge*
OPENING SCRIPTURE: *Hermeneutical Manual by Patrick Fairbairn*
THE ASSURANCE OF FAITH *by Louis Berkhof*
THE PASTOR IN THE SICK ROOM *by John D. Wells*
THE BUNYAN OF BROOKLYN: *Life & Sermons of I.S. Spencer*
THE NATIONAL PREACHER: S*ermons from 2nd Great Awakening*
FIRST THINGS: F*irst Lessons God Taught Mankind Gardiner Spring*
BIBLICAL & THEOLOGICAL STUDIES *by 1912 Faculty of Princeton*
THE POWER OF GOD UNTO SALVATION *by B.B. Warfield*
THE LORD OF GLORY *by B.B. Warfield*
A GENTLEMAN & A SCHOLAR: *Memoir of J.P. Boyce by J. Broadus*
SERMONS TO THE NATURAL MAN *by W.G.T. Shedd*
SERMONS TO THE SPIRITUAL MAN *by W.G.T. Shedd*
HOMILETICS AND PASTORAL THEOLOGY *by W.G.T. Shedd*
A PASTOR'S SKETCHES 1 & 2 *by Ichabod S. Spencer*
THE PREACHER AND HIS MODELS *by James Stalker*
IMAGO CHRISTI: *The Example of Jesus Christ by James Stalker*
LECTURES ON THE HISTORY OF PREACHING *by J. A. Broadus*
THE SHORTER CATECHISM ILLUSTRATED *by John Whitecross*
THE CHURCH MEMBER'S GUIDE *by John Angell James*
THE SUNDAY SCHOOL TEACHER'S GUIDE *by John A. James*
CHRIST IN SONG: *Hymns of Immanuel from All Ages by Philip Schaff*
DEVOTIONAL LIFE OF THE S.S. TEACHER *by J.R. Miller*

Call us Toll Free at 1-877-666-9469
Send us an e-mail at sgcb@charter.net
Visit us on line at solid-ground-books.com
Uncovering Buried Treasure to the Glory of God

www.ingramcontent.com/pod-product-compliance
Lightning Source LLC
Chambersburg PA
CBHW021800220426
43662CB00006B/137